LIFE OF
JAY GOULD

HOW HE MADE HIS MILLIONS

THE MARVELLOUS CAREER OF THE MAN WHO, IN THIRTY YEARS, ACCUMULATED THE COLOSSAL FORTUNE OF $100,000,000; BY FAR EXCEEDING IN RAPIDITY AND VOLUME THAT OF ANY OTHER MAN IN THE HISTORY OF THE WORLD

BY

The noted Journalist and Litterateur,

MURAT HALSTEAD

AND

J. FRANK BEALE, JR.

TO WHICH ARE ADDED

SKETCHES OF THE GREAT MONEY KINGS OF THE PRESENT DAY MORE OR LESS ASSOCIATED WITH HIM.

BY

W. FLETCHER JOHNSON, ESQ.

ILLUSTRATED

**Books for Business
New York - Hong Kong**

Life of Jay Gould:
How He Made His Millions

by
Murat Halstead
J. Frank Beale, Jr.

ISBN: 0-89499-218-X

Copyright © 2003 by Books for Business

Reprinted from the 1892 edition

Books for Business
New York - Hong Kong
http://www.BusinessBooksInternational.com

All rights reserved, including the right to reproduce this book, or portions thereof, in any form.

In order to make original editions of historical works available to scholars at an economical price, this facsimile of the original edition of 1892 is reproduced from the best available copy and has been digitally enhanced to improve legibility, but the text remains unaltered to retain historical authenticity.

CONTENTS

TABLE OF CONTENTS.

CHAPTER I.
IN THE BEGINNING, ... **PAGE** 17

CHAPTER II.
THE DAYS OF YOUTH, ... 36

CHAPTER III.
MARRIAGE AND HOME LIFE, ... 58

CHAPTER IV.
CAREER IN NEW YORK, ... 71

CHAPTER V.
WALL STREET WARS, ... 89

CHAPTER VI.
LYNDHURST AND THE "ATALANTA," 123

CHAPTER VII.
ILLNESS AND DEATH, ... 141

CHAPTER VIII.
INCIDENTS AND ANECDOTES, ... 166

TABLE OF CONTENTS.

CHAPTER IX.

		PAGE
A Character Estimate,		190
Newspaper Characterizations,		202

CHAPTER X.

Last Will and Testament, ... 214

CHAPTER XI.

Mr. Gould's Colaborers, ... 254
Recollections of Surviving Friends, ... 284

CHAPTER XII.

Mr. Gould's Greatest Enterprise, ... 299

CONTEMPORARY FINANCIERS.

The Vanderbilts, ... 379
Leland Stanford, ... 397
Chauncey M. Depew, ... 409
Andrew Carnegie, ... 429
The Rothschilds, ... 439
The Astors, ... 453
John W. Mackay, ... 469

MR. GOULD'S GREAT OPPONENT.

Terence V. Powderly, ... 483

LIST OF ILLUSTRATIONS.

	PAGE
JAY GOULD,	33
JAY GOULD AND HAMILTON BURHAM,	51
GEORGE J. GOULD,	69
MRS. GEORGE J. GOULD,	87
MR. EDWARD GOULD,	137
MR. HOWARD GOULD,	155
WILLIAM H. VANDERBILT,	173
JIM FISK,	191
RUSSELL SAGE,	225
CORNELIUS VANDERBILT,	243
CYRUS W. FIELD,	261
LORD ROTHSCHILD,	279
INSIDE THE GREENHOUSES,	297
COMMODORE VANDERBILT,	315
LINDEN TREE AT LYNDHURST,	333
VIEW OF THE HUDSON FROM IRVINGTON,	351
MR. GOULD'S RESIDENCE AT IRVINGTON,	369
A VIEW OF THE CONSERVATORIES AT LYNDHURST,	387
NORTHEAST VIEW OF LYNDHURST,	405
ENTRANCE TO LYNDHURST,	423
DINING SALOON ON THE " ATALANTA,"	441
STERN OF THE " ATALANTA,"	459
MRS. GEORGE GOULD AND MISS ANNA GOULD,	477
A STATE-ROOM ON THE " ATALANTA,"	121

INTRODUCTION.

THE object of this volume is to give the public an intelligible and fair account of a remarkable man, whose greatest distinction was that of exceptional success in gaining wealth—making millions.

Of course, no man earns millions with the labor of his hands. One who gathers a vast fortune must do it by the appropriation in some form of the fruits of the productive industry of others, and yet it is a stupidity to say that large properties are criminal accretions.

The equitable distribution of wealth, the riches that arise from the soil, the climate, the intelligence, the toil, the skill, the thrift of the country at large is a most difficult problem, and has thus far been an impossible task. If there is a mass of value in the possession of one man equal to $100,000,000, can we be quite sure that in the long run and the largest way, it would be better to parcel it out into a hundred fortunes of a million each or a thousand of one hundred thousand each, or that any further subdivision would more completely answer the highest social requirements ?

It is said that the head of the house of Rothschild,

INTRODUCTION.

in Paris, when informed by a caller that he had no right to so enormous sum of money as he commanded so long as there were poor men, replied by asking whether, if his treasure was equally distributed among all the French people that would be satisfactory, and when told it would, said: "I have made a calculation, your share is five francs, and there it is. Allow me the use of my time."

As our country grows we more and more understand, from familiarity with the facts, the uses of capital and how its utilities expand and its importance increases as civilization advances. Now, this capital is the margin that is produced beyond the consumption. It is gain for labor, and it is of value to those whose personal possession it is not. Capital at rest does not profit the people, save by indirection. Capital in activity is profitable to all who are laborers, stimulates industry by providing enterprise, finds imployment, improves conditions.

Mr. Gould's millions were not inherited. He was the son of a farmer who was poor but not dependent, and had the capacity to make himself comfortable, and the courage to stand for his rights and maintain them. The story of Mr. Gould's youth is pathetic as well as instructive. The delicate boy, trudging away from home, seeking his fortune in the great world, with as humble and honorable beginnings as any farmer's son who ever turned his back on the old farm, ambitious to extend his horizon and enlarge his opportunities, should not be deprived of

INTRODUCTION. 13

his share of human sympathy, because his fortunes were so extraordinary, because he must rank in the history of his race as one of the conquerors whose achievements appeal to the imagination. It was not in military warfare that he won. He was a winner in the game of brains. The boy who fell on his knees and prayed for a chance to make his own living became the wizard of Wall Street and a power in the land. He had three palaces, one in the country, one in the city, and one afloat. His millions were not made by the increase of the value of lands. His investments were put to the front in the latest inventions and the most adventurous lines of business.

If we candidly study this man's career fairly, not setting down aught in malice, because he died many times a millionare, or striving to flatter, but simply as a record of things done, good and evil, striking the average, we shall find more that is attractive than we have been accustomed to comprehend as credible. There have been many men in Wall Street who partook of the peculiar wickedness proverbial across the continent and beyond the seas in as great or a greater degree than Mr. Gould, who did not attract attention to themselves by excess of accumulation. It is only reasonable that the magnitude of success should not be the measure of prejudice, and a man should not be a monster because a millionaire.

After his early railroad wars Mr. Gould abandoned strife for the mastery of the great Eastern lines of transportation, and the Gould system is west of the Mississippi and south of the Missouri Rivers, in the section of the Republic the most undeveloped in comparison with its natural advantages, and the most promising with perhaps the exception of the gigantic Northwest. The country in which he has operated exceeds in dimensions Germany, Italy, France, and Spain combined, and its steady growth is as certain as the progressive development of the continent. Mr. Gould has been engaged in laying cables under the Atlantic, and running steamlines over the Pacific, and building roads of steel and stringing miles of iron for transportation and telegraphing from shore to shore of our ocean-bounded Republic, an occupation as grand and genial as ever enlisted the energies of manhood. We find the bulk of this man's fortune invested, first, in the railroads of the huge Southwest; second, in the elevated roads of New York city, the most comfortable, safe, and crowded system of rapid transit in the service of any immense aggregation of humanity on the earth; the Western Union Telegraph Company, which is one of the wonders of the world, doing a work that is a daily marvel and benefaction—doing it in a style that is superior to that of any of the governments that abroad have taken in charge the communications of the people with themselves in part or wholly, with revenues and responsibilities that would match the resources and

INTRODUCTION. 15

augment the dignities of empires, and doing it in accordance with the best interests and the truest traditions of the Republic.

Not only is the estate left by Mr. Gould the largest ever gathered within the same length of time by one man ; it shows in the properties we have described the highest intelligence of investment, the broadest statesmanship in management, the most enlightened reliance upon the latest influences in affairs, the finest appreciation of the indestructibility of good will, and its material and money-making force in affairs. No great estate was ever before so thoroughly committed to, and identified with the progress of industry and the prosperity of the people ; and the boy who left the house of his father to school himself, and make his own way, has had the crowning success of his life in leaving as his representatives modest daughters and manly sons.

M. H.

CHAPTER I.

IN THE BEGINNING.

IN the little town of Roxbury, Delaware County, New York, about 150 miles from that great metropolis of the United States, New York City, on the 27th day of May, 1836, there was an unusual stir in a certain little farm cottage toward the outskirts of the town. There were hurrying footsteps, and muffled words of congratulation. A little boy was born that day—a rosy, plump little bit of humanity, not one iota different from the other tiny babes of the village, though it was destined to become the mightiest money king of the country.

Jason Gould this child was named by a happy mother, whose highest ambition for her darling offspring was that he might become a pillar in the church, a successful farmer and dairyman. Her prayers were that her boy might have at least a small share of this world's successes. As her fond eyes fell upon her baby boy, she wondered if their slender means would warrant the expenditure of enough money to give him an education.

Her husband was a small farmer and dairyman, and his earliest thought for the little child's welfare was scarcely beyond the hope that he would fast de-

LIFE OF JAY GOULD.

velop and become a useful helper in managing the few homestead acres and the small dairy. In any biography we must needs take into account the effect of hereditary traits, of associations, of climate, and of environments. These were, to say the least, unpromising to the future of the little child. There are, however, strange turning-points in history, and many real miracles beyond the hope of explanation. We shall see how this little man progressed from the humble farm cottage to the millionaire's manse. It is a thrilling tale, full of romance, and fraught with importance to generations.

It will be seen that through babyhood and boyhood Jason Gould was the personification of plain people. His parents were people of strong sense and sterling integrity, but it was with difficulty and stringent economy that they held their own. Roxbury was but an insignificant village in the Catskill County region. The Goulds had moved there not long after the Revolutionary War, and Jay's father, John B. Gould, was the first white male child born in the county. His birth occurred in 1792.

Jason grew rather rapidly, mentally as well as physically. His growing mind had not the exercise which was accorded to his growing body, for from the time he outgrew his toddling state, donned little blue jeans and round-about, he was given his duties on the farm, while his education was sadly neglected. His father was known as a " good provider," but in those days this meant one suit of clothes sufficiently

IN THE BEGINNING.

good to protect the wearer from the cold and storms of that mountain region, and enough food to maintain physical strength. It did not mean luxuries of education any more than it meant luxuries of diet or apparel. The young lad's mind, though untrained, was active, and he often thought he might, if he had an opportunity, study books and know something of the world of letters, which to him had an unaccountable fascination.

On many occasions while driving the cows from the meadow field through the wooded lane to the old thatched barn for his sisters to milk, he revolved in his mind various methods to help himself. There were schools not far from his home, but the unimproved public-school system made it impossible for him to attend any other than a private institution for that higher knowledge which he so earnestly desired. The youth of to-day with either wealthy parents or charity's outstretched arms to aid him in securing an education, cannot possibly understand or appreciate the struggle with which Jay Gould one morning as he came down from his little room in the attic, faced his father with the declaration that he would like to have his freedom, in order that he might seek an education at an academy in a neighboring town.

He knew that his father understood his lack of sympathy with any part of the work on the farm, and too well he knew that his pale slender physique was a subject of no little fear on the part of his father. He had disliked even the customary sports of the people around him ; he was different from any other boys in the village school in which he got the rudiments of his education. He was not what was generally termed a manly boy. He did not participate in the rough-natured games of his school-mates, and preferred to remain in-doors, and at recess time to cuddle up in some remote corner of the school-house, busy with his own thoughts and his own plans and hopes for the future. When approached by his school-mates to come and join a game he declined all invitations. If bantered or teased by the boys, he would break away in tearful anger and make a complaint to the schoolmaster, who would thrash his tormentors, much to the relief of little Jason.

He was but twelve years old on the eventful morning when he asked his father for his freedom. He was told he might go, as he was of little use on the farm. Much to the man's surprise, this delighted his son, for Jason had thoroughly made up his mind that he would either live or perish in the attempt to get an education. Perhaps he did not fully realize the immense importance of his determination ; perhaps the gratification of a desire to shirk the farm duties, which had become so irksome to him, was a potent factor in his determination. Be that as it may, Jason Gould's career began on that day.

To give the reader an idea of the principle with

IN THE BEGINNING. 21

which young Gould started out to make his fame and fortune, we present in full text the last "composition" he wrote in the little village school-house in Roxbury, before leaving it forever. It has been preserved through all these years in the original manuscript, by his old schoolmaster and his descendants.

It is as follows:

COMPOSITION.

JASON GOULD.

BEECHWOOD SEMINARY.

APRIL 9TH, 1850.

"Honesty is the Best Policy."

"By this proposition we mean that to be honest, to think honest, and to have all our actions honestly performed is the best way, and most accords with the precepts of reason. Honesty is of a self-denying nature; to become honest it requires self-denial; it requires that we should not acquaint ourselves too much with the world; that we should not associate with those of vulgar habits; also, that we should obey the warnings of conscience.

"If we are about to perform a dishonest act, the warnings of conscience exert their utmost influence to persuade us that it is wrong, and we should not do it, and after we have performed the act, this faithful agent upbraids us for it; this voice of conscience is not the voice of thunder, but a voice gentle and impressive; it does not force us to com-

LIFE OF JAY GOULD.

ply with its requests, while at the same time it reasons with us and brings forth arguments in favor of right.

"Since no theory of reasoning can be sustained without illustration, it will not be unbecoming for us to cite one of the many instances that have occurred, whose names stand high upon the scroll of fame, and whose names are recorded on the pages of history—George Washington, the man 'who never told a lie in all his life.'

"In youth he subdued his idle passions, cherished truth, obeyed the teachings of conscience, and 'never told a lie.' An anecdote which is much related, and which occurred when he was a boy, goes to show his sincerity. Alexander Pope, in his 'Essay on Man,' says 'an honest man is the noblest work of God.'

"And again, we find numerous passages in the Scriptures which have an immediate connection to this, and summing up the whole we cannot but say: 'Honesty is the best policy.'   JASON GOULD."

How interesting is this little composition. It was written hastily and from the heart.

During his vacations, which in those days were very long, generally from the 1st of May to the 1st or 15th of October, young Jason had worked steadily on his father's farm despite his disinclination to do so, for it must be said of him that he was a dutiful son. Though he disliked to work at such

IN THE BEGINNING. 23

uncongenial employment, it was never necessary to urge him to his task, his having to do it was sufficient. He was generally known throughout the district as a " queer " boy. He was not understood, and this added to the many other difficulties in the way of his getting an education at the Academy, into which no pupils were admitted who did not pay for their tuition. Nevertheless, on the day after he was given permission to leave home to seek his fortune, he started out with fifty cents in the pockets of his blue jeans, and one extra suit rolled up in a bundle under his arm.

How many great men have had their sincerity and perseverance tested at the beginning of their career by a long, fatiguing walk ! It was a long and tedious tramp that at last brought him to Hobart, the seat of the seminary to which he hoped to gain admission as a student. With no little trepidation he sought the principal—for the head-master was not known as a president in those days—and told him his story. To his surprise and unbounded joy the old man sympathized with the boy, whose face and manner, as well as his story, were pathetic. He obtained board in the house of a blacksmith, who agreed to keep his little guest, provided he would attend to his books and accounts, for young Jason was a beautiful penman.

Now all the inate energy of the boy was brought to the surface. He was grateful for the kind reception he had received at the hands of the principal

LIFE OF JAY GOULD.

and the blacksmith. He set to work to please his teachers as well as his host. By the end of six months he had gained the confidence of all his associates, as well as those who had trusted him and interested themselves in his welfare. To be sure, six months was not a very long time in which to gain that education for which he had such a longing, and yet so well did the youth employ his every opportunity that at the end of that time he was well grounded in the rudimentary branches.

The innate industry before referred to of which there had been little evidence at home, had asserted itself immediately upon his contact with men of broader and more liberal minds. On leaving the Acádemy at the end of six months he obtained a position as clerk in a tin-shop at Hobart, and three years after, at the age of 15, became a partner in the management of the business. His ambitions were developing rapidly. He was up at daybreak every day to pursue the study of his chosen profession—surveying—as he found books and instruments to help him. He often went home to spend Sunday with his father and sisters, for his mother had died since he left the parental roof.

His father had become unpopular in the village by opposing the ante-rent movement, and the elder Gould was at last forced to sell his farm. Young Jason took him into his tin shop on a salary, and leaving his father in charge there, he engaged with some surveyors who were making a map of Ulster

IN THE BEGINNING. 25

County, at a salary of twenty dollars a month. The young man had had but little experience with shrewd business men, and he did not know that this salary was far below what he should have had; but probably had he known it, the knowledge would not have deterred him from accepting the position, for his main idea and guiding plan was to become practiced in what he then believed would be his chosen profession.

Mr. Gould said of his trip through Ulster County: "When I came to start I questioned whether I should take any of my own scant supply of money with me or not. I could have had it, but I thought it was better to break down the bridge behind me; so I took only enough to pay my fare. I met a gentleman, and he started me out to make these surveys. The map he was making was one on which all the roads and the residences are located— a map showing the general topography of the country. They are useful for reference.

"When this man came to start me out he gave me a small pass-book and said, 'As you go along you will get trusted for your little bills, what you will eat, and so on, and I will come around afterward and pay the bills.' I thought that was all right. I think it was on my second or third day out that I met a man who took a different view.

"I had stayed at his house over-night. They charged in that part of the country at that time a shilling for supper, sixpence for lodging, and a shilling for breakfast, making two shillings and six-pence in all. I took out my little book and said, 'I will enter that.' The man turned on me with an oath and said (referring to my employer), 'Why, you don't know this man! He has failed three times. He owes everybody in the county, and you have got money and I know it, and I want the bill paid.' There I was. I hadn't a cent in my pocket, so I just pulled my pockets out and said to him, 'You can see that I tell the truth. There are my pockets.' So finally he said he would trust me. 'I'll trust you,' said he, 'but I won't trust that man.' This incident had such an effect on me that it seemed to me as though the world had come to an end. This was in the morning, and I could not have the heart that day to ask anybody to give me a dinner; so along about 3 o'clock in the afternoon I got faint and sat down for a few minutes.

"After this rebuff I was naturally timid. It had a great effect upon me, and I debated with myself whether I should give up and go home or whether I should go ahead. I came to a piece of woods where nobody could see me, and I had a good cry. Finally, I thought I would try my sister's remedy— a prayer. So I got down and prayed, and felt bet-ter after it, and I then made up my mind to go ahead. I set my lips close together, and made up my mind that I would go ahead and die in the last ditch.

"I went on, and the first house I came to I deter-

IN THE BEGINNING.

mined right then and there to go in and get something to eat. I went in, and the woman treated me kindly, gave me some bread and milk and cold meats, and one thing and another, and when I got ready to leave I said to her, 'I will enter it down.' She said all right. In the meantime her husband came in, and they both said it was all right. I started, and had got, I guess, about forty rods away from the house when I heard him hallooing to me. Well, after the morning scene, I thought he was going to finish me; but he came right on, and when he got up to me he said, 'I want you to take your compass and make me a noon-mark.'

"That, as you perhaps know, is a north and south line right through the window, marked in so that the farmers can regulate their clocks by it. When the sun strikes the line it is twelve o'clock. I took my compass back and made the noon-mark for him. When I had made it, and was about to go away, he said: 'How much is that?' 'Oh!' said I, 'nothing.' 'Oh! yes,' said he; 'I want to pay you for it.' I thought a moment, and he went on to say: 'Our surveyor always charges a dollar for these jobs.' Said I, 'Very well. Take out a shilling for my dinner.' So he paid me the seven shillings. Everything went by 'shillings' in those days—eight shillings to the dollar—and he kept one and paid me the other seven. That was the first money I made in that business, and it opened up a new field to me, so that I went on from that time and completed

LIFE OF JAY GOULD.

the surveys, and paid my expenses all that summer by making noon-marks at different places.

"When I got through with the summer's work my employer had failed, and was unable to pay me. There were two other young men, wealthy men's sons, who had been engaged on the same work, and we three together had the control of it. I proposed to them that we should go on and finish the map ourselves, and finally we decided to do so. Then, as they lived in the county and were pretty conspicuous, they wanted to put their names to the map, so I said to them, 'Very well; I will sell you out my interest,' and I sold my interest to them for $500.

"This was the result of my first summer's work. I went on and finished the work and got it ready for the engraver, so that what I sold was the perfected map. This was a map of Ulster County."

There was a stimulus for young Gould in this comparatively small success. He saw that he was capable of doing work that was marketable. He reasoned that if the people of Ulster County would buy a map of their county, the people of Albany County and of his native county would do the same.

His little capital of $500 was a great deal to him, and, in fact, it was just what he needed to aid him in the prosecution of his work. Had the funds at his command been larger, he would have been tempted to extravagance—a fault which was not

IN THE BEGINNING. 29

then his, and never could be attributed to him. Had the sum been smaller, he would have been forced to call upon some one for financial aid, who would naturally have expected to offer advice and to share the profits.

Young Gould said of this work, "I had made up my mind that I would go it alone, and I made those surveys alone and completed them, and they were very successful in sale, so that I made about $5,000 out of the maps."

Of his next venture Mr. Gould says : "About that time, while I was carrying on these surveys, I met a gentleman who seemed to take a fancy to me, Mr. Zadoc Pratt, of Prattville. He was at that time one of the largest tanners in the county. I had done some surveying for him. He had a very beautiful place at Prattville, and I fixed that up for him, and finally he proposed to me to go into the tanning business with him. He knew my whole history. I accepted this proposal and the next day I started for Pennsylvania.

"The Delaware & Lackawanna Railroad had just been completed. I went over that road, and found some very large lots of hemlock timber land, and I came back and reported to Mr. Pratt what I had found and we decided to go on. He sent me back and I made the purchase of the land—made all the contracts myself, and then came back and took about fifty or sixty men down there with me to start the work. It was right in the woods, fifteen miles

30 *LIFE OF JAY GOULD.*

from any place. I went in there and chopped down the first tree. We had a portable saw-mill, and we sawed the tree up, and that day we built a blacksmith's shop out of the timber. I slept in it that night, on a bed made of hemlock boughs. We went on and built the tannery. It was a very large one—the largest in the country at that time."

The tannery improved the district wonderfully. A plank road was built, extending out into the country some miles, and a stage route was organized. A church, school-house, and bank soon followed, and then young Gould sought to develop the postal facilities of the region by becoming postmaster himself. In this position his executive ability and his penchant for development were eminently successful.

After awhile Mr. Gould bought out his partner, obtaining the needed funds from Charles M. Leupp, a hide and leather merchant of New York City. They formed a partnership. All went quietly for awhile, and then the daring ventures and schemes of Mr. Gould, the resident partner, attracted universal attention. This alarmed the New York house, which traded under the name of Leupp & Lee, and they sent their book-keeper to investigate the affairs at the tannery.

This excellent man could only report undecipherable accounts. He told his employers that he thought the tannery was badly involved and that the New York house was probably in the same unfortunate plight.

IN THE BEGINNING. 31

Young Gould had gone into speculations in hides and other tanneries, which might and might not have turned out well, but the old-fashioned notions of Mr. Leupp were shocked, and when he found that his partner had bought not only all the hides then in the market, but all that were to arrive in the ensuing six months, he literally lost his reason and shot himself after a stormy interview with Gould, who remained imperturbably cool and simply turned on his heel and left the office. Mr. Leupp lived in what was then called the Barretta Mansion, corner of Twenty-fifth Street and Madison Avenue, New York City, which cost in low-price time $150,000 to build, and which was filled with costly furniture and rare products of pencil and chisel.

On the death of their common partner Gould and Lee made a dash for the property in Goldsboro. Prior to the fatal shot Gould had arranged with Congressman Alley, of Massachusetts, to take the works, and thus relieve Leupp & Lee; but the suicide of the senior partner stopped the consummation of this plan, and, Gould always insisted, stopped the way to a profitable continuance of the works. Both Gould and Lee were men of nerve, and both determined to get and hold the tannery. Lee reached it first and garrisoned it with the employees. Information was received that Gould intended to use force, and preparations were made to receive and repel him.

32

LIFE OF JAY GOULD.

The New York *Herald* of March 16th, 1860, thus describes the battle:

"TANNERY INSURRECTION IN PENNSYL-VANIA.

"Battle between the forces of the Swamp Leather Dealers—The Leupp & Lee Tannery, in Goldsboro, attacked and defended.—Sides of leather used for breastworks.—Insurgents two hundred strong.—The tannery taken.—Flight of the defenders.—Wounded, four.

"About half-past 10 o'clock on Tuesday morning the lock was wrenched from the stable, the men having been concentrated into the tannery and the stable being unguarded. A little past 12 the tannery itself was attacked by a mob variously estimated at from 180 to 250 men, armed with axes, muskets, rifles, and other weapons. Without a demand of possession or summons to surrender the doors were beaten in, and but a few blows had been struck by the assailants before they began to fire ball and buckshot through the building, raking it in every direction. As vigorous a defense was made by a force of 15 men in the story attacked with tannery sticks, stones, and four revolvers as was possible against such overwhelming odds. The tannery was finally carried on all sides, and those who did not escape were violently flung from the windows and doors, while the assailants rushed through the buildings, yelling like Indians, pursuing the fugitives

JAY GOULD.

IN THE BEGINNING. 35

with their guns in every direction. In the action many contusions were received and four gunshot wounds, and had it not been for the large number of sides of leather hung up the lofts, very few of the defending party would have escaped without wounds.

"Mr. Jay Gould, in his version of the affair, says :

"'I quietly selected 50 men, commanding the reserve to keep aloof. I divided them into two companies, one of which I dispatched to the upper end of the building, directing them to take off the boards, while I headed the other to open a large front door. I burst open the door and sprang in. I was immediately saluted with a shower of balls, forcing my men to retire, and I brought them up a second and third time and pressed them into the building, and by this time the company at the upper end of the tannery had succeeded in effecting an entrance, and the firing now became general on all sides and the bullets were whistling in every direction. After a hard contested struggle on both sides we became the victors, and our opponents went flying from the tannery, some of them making fearful leaps from the second story.'

CHAPTER II.

THE DAYS OF YOUTH.

THE morning of May 27th, 1836, had been a very memorable time in the Gould family. The daughters were informed by the father that they had a dear little brother. What an event was this in a household where there were already five little girls! One of Mr. Gould's eldest sisters has often said, "I remember but as though yesterday my great delight. The first opportunity, I stole into my mother's room to see if what had been told me was really true. Sure enough, in the cradle, with a wealth of brown hair and dark eyes, lay our little treasure. We all thought him very wonderful, and watched with great fondness from day to day his growth and development. The first tooth, as usual, was looked for with great interest, and when he was nine months old, the whole house was overjoyed at his feat of walking and climbing the stairs. It is not necessary to say that with five older sisters he was the pet and idol of the household. His many baby pranks and precocious sayings were repeated to all who would patiently listen. Our grand-mother's especial gratitude for a boy was that the name might go down to future generations. Father

THE DAYS OF YOUTH. 37

rejoiced in the prospect of one to help him bear his burdens, and become, as he had done, an inheritor of the paternal acres. Mother accepted the treasure as a new responsibility, fraught with much anxiety for the future."

His first four years were uneventful, save in the home circle; years not particularly calculated to bring out the strong points of his character. Being frail and delicate, he was all the more petted and generally had his own way. When he entered his fifth year, all were anxious for him to begin his education, and his mother consented to his name being registered as a pupil in the little country school. His first day was an eventful one, as described under the chapter devoted to " Incidents and Anedotes." The next day was a success at school. When fully initiated, he took great delight in his studies, always keeping in advance of his class. It was only by taking plenty of exercise out-of-doors; riding, driving and running over the hills and mountains that his physical nature was able to endure the strain of his intense study after he became older.

Before he was five years old the sweet, gentle mother left that household for the better land, the greatest loss a little, delicate child could possibly have. The only memory he had of her, as he has since said during the latter years of his life, was the messenger summoning him from school in order that she might give him her dying blessing, and he never forgot how cold her lips were when she gave

LIFE OF JAY GOULD.

him her last kiss of love, but he could not know how hard it was for a fond mother to leave her youngest born. He inherited from his mother his ambition, his sweet and gentle nature, that evenness of temper which enabled him to control himself even when a boy and still more when he became a man, and also his wonderful ability to turn everything to his financial profit. From his father he inherited his indomitable will, his persistent perseverance to accomplish whatever he undertook, no matter what obstacles came in his way, and from him also he had a most sympathetic nature ; he shrank from sufferings he could not alleviate.

His first three years in school were in a little old school-house, gray with age and tottering with its infirmities. But at that time the Anti-Rent War broke out in New York State, and for some time the Gould home was in the midst of civil strife. Jay's father represented law and order itself ; mobs of armed and disguised men could not drive him from his position, but they did drive his children from the public school. After a threat to drown his boy, then eight years old, which frightened him greatly, he declared he should never enter that school again ; the result was a new comfortable building called Beechwood Seminary, with graduates from the State Normal School at Albany as its professors.

They were men fitted for their calling, and knew just how to lure their young student onward in the

THE DAYS OF YOUTH.

paths that led up the hill of science. This opportunity he improved to its fullest extent. His progress was a continual delight to his instructors; he would never accept assistance in working out hard problems. He was known to have worked at times for three weeks on a difficult problem in logarithms. When he gained the victory the whole house was made aware of the fact by a succession of somersaults and kindred demonstrations.

He was so studious that he almost always spent his evenings with his sisters, yet sometimes he would join a party for coasting by moonlight and such other outdoor sports as belong to the country. One day he and one of his young companions decided on a rare treat; he had a young colt which was his own property, so he very naturally concluded he had a right to its services. The sleighing was good, and his father absent from home, so they thought it a most excellent time to try the speed of the young, untrained horse. They succeeded in arranging a single harness to their entire satisfaction; the colt was put before a new beautifully-painted coaster large enough for the two boys; they took their places with great anticipation; they gathered up the reins, and were soon gliding down the inclined driveway which led to the main road. The beautiful bay arched his neck and to the consternation of the boys refused to be governed by bit and reins. He sped onward with ever-increasing speed until finally he conceived the idea of lifting his hind feet in a very violent manner. The boys were thoroughly frightened and concluding that retreat at that juncture would be the better part of valor, slipped off, willing to leave the post of danger. The pet animal dashed furiously onward until he was stopped by a neighbor, who readily divined what had happened. He brought the colt to its stall, rubbed it down, gathered up the broken sled, and put everything in as good a condition as possible for Mr. Gould's home-coming. The time when he should know what had happened was very much dreaded, but when the fact did finally become known, he was so grateful for the miraculous escape of the boys that he did not even scold, but thought he had better consider the colt his own property. Thus ended the episode.

Young Jay's first visit to New York about this time was a very memorable event. His father having business which would detain him for some days, thought it a favorable opportunity to introduce his youthful son to some of the wonders of the great city. His trip down the Hudson was a surprise and a delight, but when the city opened up before him with its many streets, its huge blocks of brick, stone, and marble; its fountains and tall spires, its beautiful shops filled with so much to attract the eye of a child that had never seen beyond the mountains that encircled his native valley, he was simply bewildered. The story of Aladdin and his wonderful lamp was verified. His sister waited anxiously for

THE DAYS OF YOUTH.

his return, wondering what he would have to tell them; but to their disappointment he was more quiet than usual, until he had had time to think over and arrange in his own mind the incidents of his visit. He then told them many very wonderful things.

His unpleasant experience with an untamed colt did not detract from his love of driving horses that were subject to bit and bridle. Before he was 12 years of age he was allowed to drive a pair of fleet-footed, spirited grays, that often felt their oats, up and down the hills and over the mountains for the convenience of his sisters. He never boasted of any inventive ability, but it was always sufficient to meet any emergency. Once while driving through Grand Gorge, a narrow pass between two mountains, the horses for some reason sprang to one side, breaking the tongue of the carriage. What was to be done was the next question. After a moment's consideration, he left one of his sisters in charge of the reins while he went to the nearest house and borrowed an axe with which he cut a young sapling, and with the help of a rope he mended the break and journeyed on. All went well until he crossed the bridge at Stratton Falls and began to ascend the hills up to the old farm. All at once the carriage began to move in the wrong direction; it was just above a roaring cataract. Realizing the danger, he sprang from the carriage as quick as thought and blocked the wheels, then

42

LIFE OF JAY GOULD.

turning the horses at right angles with the road, with a command to them to stand still, he mended up a second time. After all the delays his sisters congratulated themselves that they had reached home before any scouts had been sent out to look for them.

One of **Mr. Gould's** sisters who was much with him in his youth, has said : "We frequently had what we considered hair-breadth escapes, of which the following was an example. We had decided to visit one of our maternal uncles who lived on the Delaware River near Deposit. We left home very early one beautiful June morning, our horse was fresh and our carriage light, and we almost flew over the beautiful country until we reached Delhi, 20 miles from home, thence down to Walton, and by way of a plank road over the mountain to Shehocton. After leaving there we learned that the very rain which had made the country so charming in its freshness and so fragrant with its flowers, had carried away an important bridge, and that we would have to ford the river; we hesitated, but were told if we kept the track there was no danger. Instead of a heavy freighted wagon we were in a light buggy; we followed the track as directed, but found the water much deeper than we anticipated ; it came up into the carriage, the horse seemed to be losing his footing, and as we gazed at the rushing waters it looked to us as if we were going down more than across the river. Girl like, we were

THE DAYS OF YOUTH. 43

alarmed and wanted to turn back; all our brother said was: 'Girls, do not say one word, keep perfectly quiet, and I will take you over safely.' The tone and manner were sufficient. He touched the horse lightly with his whip, she plunged forward until she reached the other shore. As soon as we were on dry ground our escort remarked, though he was very pale, his lips even colorless: 'I would not have been afraid if you girls had not been with me.'"

Young Gould never enjoyed working for small returns, even in the days of his boyhood. A pleasant task of one of his sisters was to go out in the summer mornings while the grass and bushes were still glistening with dew to gather the luscious wild berries that grew around the stumps and along the fences of the farm. Jay was usually her companion. He would whistle away in a merry mood as long as he found plenty of fruit to lure him on, skipping around from one clump of bushes to another, until he had been over the whole ground, then informing his sister that there were no more worth remaining for, away he would go, leaving her to do the gleaning. He was often surprised at the contents of her basket; he could not see where she found them, but greatly admired her patient perseverance.

He was born with an ability to turn things to good account financially. In all his little purchases when a boy he had a plan arranged for the disposition of a property before making the purchase,

LIFE OF JAY GOULD.

unless he wished to retain it, just as in after years, when an opportunity offered for the purchase of a railroad he considered well the necessity for such a road, and the value it would be to the public or to himself as an investment before making the venture. This characteristic was one great feature in his financial success. His reticence in regard to his own plans was the same among his school companions and at home as in after years with men of business.

The winter of 1848 was marked by a wide-spread religious movement, which was felt in many parts of our country. It reached young Jay's native mountain-bound village. The Methodist Church, of which his sisters were members, caught the enthusiasm, and held a series of meetings. Among those who were deeply impressed was Jay, who gave his name to the chnrch, but afterward felt his mother's church, the Presbyterian, was the church of his choice. Two years later, at the age of 14, he secured a pew in that church and placed himself under the gospel care of the Rev. W. E. Taylor; between whom and himself there was begun a lifelong friendship. He saw much in the boy which led him to prophesy great things in the future, and he felt as he has said, only a few years since, that he had not been disappointed in the greatness of his achievements. When age and infirmity crept over the old pastor, rendering him unfit for the care of an important charge, he was fortunately called to

THE DAYS OF YOUTH.

Elmsford, a little church near Lyndhurst, the county seat of his once young parishioner, who had in the meantime arisen to wealth and position. Mr. Gould did not forget the old pastor, for he was welcome at his home, and had the freedom of his conservatories, where he could enjoy the study of plants from every clime. It is safe to say his purse was not often empty nor his purse unsupplied; and when the time came that he could not even serve that church and had to vacate the parsonage he was furnished a home free of charge. The old pastor still lives to speak of his benefactor.

When Jay was 13 he became very tired of farm life; it was too slow, too monotonous, too hard for his slight physique; the returns were too uncertain. All these things stimulated him to greater effort for a more extended education; often when deep in the midst of some intricate problem he would see father coming in, as he knew, for him to do some errand or piece of work. He would slip into some hidden corner, book and slate in hand, and a "hush, girls," on his lips until his father, despairing of finding him, would make other arrangements; then with his conscience a little tender he would say, "It is too bad, but I must study, you know."

When he had completed the course of study at home he greatly desired to go elsewhere, and had decided on the Hobart Seminary, nine miles from home; a distance he thought he could easily walk on Saturday, returning Sunday evening to be ready to answer

46 *LIFE OF JAY GOULD.*

the roll-call on Monday morning; he realized that father, from the small returns from his farm, could not afford to pay his bills; he decided he could and would pay them himself. It has previously been related how he gained admittance to Hobart Seminary. His father was a positive man, and when he said "No" to one of his girls it was considered final; but not so with our youthful hero; he would, without seeming to be discomfited at all, make some stragetic move and, prepared with new arguments, would bring the matter before the house for reconsideration, and if this did not bring the desired result the bill would come up for a third reading, and so on until the victory was won. In this way he gained permission, his father saying to him, "I do not know but you might as well go, for it is certain you will never make a farmer." His sisters thought he might make a lawyer, and were sure if time was given him he would always gain his point. He made his weekly visits home, as he proposed, until he completed his course.

During this time his father was considering what he could do that would give his son more congenial employment; he decided he would have to leave the old farm; notwithstanding everything connected with it was very dear to him; it was the place where his father and mother had lived and where he was born; many of the fruit trees were from trees from his own planting; he had nursed and cared for them in his own boyhood; the shade trees with their broad

THE DAYS OF YOUTH.

spreading branches, scattered here and there to protect the flocks and herds from the scorching sun and the pelting storm, the trout brook, the maple grove, the spring of luscious water, all were dear with memories of the past; but as he had to choose between leaving them or letting his son go from the household the choice was soon made and the farm was exchanged for the hardware business of A. H. Burhans & Co.

When Jay came from his school he at once entered this store as a clerk until father took possession and put him in charge, as was related in the preceding chapter. Very soon after he made him general manager and a partner in the business; he did all the purchasing and kept the books for the firm. He did not drop his studies, but rose early and sat up late in order that he might have time to devote to them and to a self-directed course of reading. His reading was not so much for recreation as for improvement; consequently he read standard works, as far as his limited purse would allow their purchase. By this study and the use of instruments, obtained from Mr. E. I. Burhans, he became in the next few years a practical surveyor, not an inventor, as has often been said of him. Even the wonderful mouse-trap, which has so often been ascribed to him, was the invention of his maternal grandfather, who had seen nearly four-score years; and who, with his failing mental vision, looked upon it as something very wonderful.

LIFE OF JAY GOULD.

The hardware business did not occupy all of young Gould's time. He began to feel he could accomplish more by going out from home, for the resources of the village and surrounding country were too limited for his ambition. He entrusted for once his thoughts and plans to his sisters, and they sympathized with him, but plead with him to remain at home for their sakes and for his father's sake as well as his own. He argued he could make all the purchases for the firm and that his father was perfectly able to do the rest. He did not feel that his living should come out of father's purse, it was enough for him to take care of his girls, a boy should take care of himself. The question naturally arose, if he left home what did he propose to do; then he divulged to his sisters a surveying scheme for the purpose of making a map of Ulster County. He had received a proposition, he had looked the ground all over, in fact, had, in his own mind, decided to accept it, but did not want to go without his father's sanction; therefore he wanted to enlist his sisters in his favor, that they might help to plead his cause; as he had not yet entered his sixteenth year, and to the family he seemed a mere boy, although he had been doing the work of a man, making purchases for the business for two years of such firms as Phelps, Dodge & Co., in New York City, and Ransom, Rappon & Co., in Albany. He had just returned from one of his trips to Albany and crossed the Hudson River on cakes of floating ice which did not have the effect to assure

THE DAYS OF YOUTH.

49

his father and sisters that his venturesome spirit might not take him into some greater danger; his arguments, however, prevailed, and in a few days his arrangements were made. He could not at that time draw much from his small capital which was needed in the business so he left home with five dollars in his pocket expecting that the company would furnish him means for his support.

He entered immediately upon his duties, found them laborious, but congenial. The reason they were congenial was because he saw they looked to something higher. The young surveyor progressed satisfactorily until his employer became suddenly embarrassed and unable to pay; but with his intuitive foresightedness he had retained a copy of all his surveys, and he at once concluded to take matters in his own hands and publish the map himself. Of his little stock of money he had only ten cents left and that small piece he has never parted with; it was among his treasures till he died. How he was to meet the expense was a thing to be considered. He could not spare time to go to Roxbury; he was among strangers and consequently had no credit, but just when things were the darkest and failure of the project seemed inevitable a new way of increasing his supplies providentially opened before him—the making of a noon-mark, described in the preceding chapter, for which he received his dinner and fifty cents was the avenue which led to success. The value of his noon-marks preceded

LIFE OF JAY GOULD.

him, and out of this new supply he paid all the expenses of the remaining surveys and came out with six dollars in his pocket, and his labors were crowned with success. Gould's map of Ulster County was pronounced accurate in every detail, consequently he realized a very respectable sum from its sale.

Soon after this we find the young man in Albany. While prospecting there he became associated with the late John Delafield in an application to the State Legislature for aid in the completion of a topographical survey of the State of New York. Favorable progress was made, but before anything material was accomplished Mr. Delafield died. He at once abandoned the idea of legislative aid, but with characteristic pluck decided to prosecute the enterprise upon a more limited scale upon his own account ; accordingly during the summer of 1853, then in his seventeenth year, he completed his survey of Albany County, and during the ensuing winter he drafted out his surveys and produced a map which, on completion sold at a handsome profit.

During the same summer, 1853, he was employed by the Cohoes Mfg. Co. to survey and make a map of their village which netted him $600. In the same year he also surveyed and laid out the Albany and Muscayuna Plank Road. This was a task which presented great difficulties to our young surveyor. The practical calculation of grades, excavations, and embankments was an untried field.

JAY GOULD AND HAMILTON BURHAM.

THE DAYS OF YOUTH.

but he successfully mastered them all and completed his work to the entire satisfaction of the company, and was liberally rewarded.

The amount of hard work accomplished by Gould in 1853 was almost incredible, and it may well be believed that he invariably rose long before day-break and seldom retired to rest before midnight. In the spring of 1854 he returned to Albany, perfected his plans and business arrangements for the ensuing season. He did his drafting at home ; early in April he sent a surveyor into Delaware County, New York, for the purpose of taking surveys for a prospective map. He sent similar expeditions into Lake and Geauga Counties, Ohio, and Oakwood County, Michigan. His personal attention was given to the drafting department, but he kept himself familiar with all the details of the business ; nothing escaped his notice ; during the summer he usually traveled from point to point during the night and such were his powers of endurance that only a few hours of rest would fit him for the next day. He kept the most vigilant watch over his employees ; never giving them notice of his coming. Thanks to his iron constitution and his wonderful powers of endurance, he not only completed all the work he had mapped out for himself, but was able to devote sixty days during the summer to the survey of a proposed railroad from Newbury to Syracuse.

It must be remembered that by this time he had

LIFE OF JAY GOULD.

made himself a proficient practical engineer. The labors of the latter enterprise proved far more laborious than had been anticipated, but having undertaken the work he was determined to complete it; but he paid dearly for thus overtaxing himself; he completed the last profile of the proposed road, affixed his signature, and in one hour afterward was prostrated with typhoid fever. His illness was severe and his recovery slow; engagements were pressing; an effort to resume business too soon brought on a violent relapse, followed by inflammation of the lungs—his physician thinks he never fully recovered his lung power from that attack. Feeling compelled to curtail his operations he sold his interest in all surveys. While surveying Delaware County he had collected many facts of historical importance. He visited every old man and woman in the county. During his period of convalescence he felt the need of some employment for his active, restless mind. He set to work compiling his notes, and shortly afterward, at the age of 17, published the history of Delaware County, a well-written book of 450 pages, and far more valuable now if it could be obtained.

With returning health he laid down the pen and picked up the implement of the engineer. While thus engaged his mind was attracted to the subject of tanning as a business more profitable than engineering. After mature deliberation he concluded to try his future in that line, as outlined in the preced-

THE DAYS OF YOUTH.

ing chapter. Some idea may be formed of the energy and ability displayed in this new enterprise from the fact that in 100 days from the time the first tree was felled the tannery was in full operation. At this juncture came the terrible panic of 1856, and while so many firms were swept out of existence the foresight and financial ability of Gould, though scarcely 20 years of age, maintained the credit of Pratt & Gould, and they weathered the gale in safety. They employed at one time 250 men and manufactured one and a half million pounds of sole leather annually; yet Mr. Gould was not satisfied to remain in this narrow sphere. Tanning, like surveying, was only another step in the direction of his life's great work. He had had many opportunities of familiarizing himself with railroad maps which he had improved. He understood the geography of our country. He was possessed of valuable information regarding its agricultural and mineral resources, and took the deepest interest in all enterprises for facilitating communication between these different sections. He longed to connect himself with some kindred spirits who would aid in carrying out his great schemes.

About this time the opportunity he had so long desired presented itself. The celebrated Schuyler frauds had caused railroad securities to decline to a nominal figure. The far-seeing young man invested all his capital and every dollar he could borrow and secured for himself the control of the Rutland &

LIFE OF JAY GOULD.

Washington, and Troy & Rutland R. R. It was a daring venture, but proved profitable beyond his daring expectations. In less than two years he had succeeded in extricating the roads from their financial embarrassment and consolidating them with the Saratoga, White Hall & Renssalear R. R.

He closed his connection with that railroad to embark his operations in the Erie Railway—being the only man who believed in the advisability of saving the property from bankruptcy and ruin and make it the principal business thoroughfare through the State. He met with opposition from such men as Drew and Vanderbilt; while they could not see a way out of the difficulties themselves they were not willing to be guided by the vision of any other man, and especially one so youthful. He was financially prepared to accept the Presidency; but difficulties more perplexing arose; he could not carry out the only plan which to him promised success.

The narrow limits of his own loved State and where he has always chosen to dwell, were too contracted for his gigantic schemes. His mission has been to open up the great West and aid in developing its mining and agricultural interests which he dreamed of in his early years. For the last 20 years our youth, no longer young in experience, has planned and worked and used his capital to promote this object until he has seen three transcontinental lines of railroad and the great Missouri system extending north and south, with hamlets and towns

THE DAYS OF YOUTH. **57**

following in their wake where thousands and thousands of families, native born and from far shores, have found a place to call a home. The West and the East brought so near together by the railroads and throbbing electric wire are not strangers any more. The West bows in reverence to the culture of the East; and the East looks in breathless astonishment upon the progress of the West. Thus have the dreams of his boyhood become real. He might have retired to his beautiful home on the banks of the Hudson many years ago and lived at his ease regardless of the needs of our great country; but he would have lost his identity. Forces within and without have urged him on. To think and formulate plans have seemed a necessity with him. Labor was rest; idleness would have been stagnation.

CHAPTER III.

MARRIAGE AND HOME LIFE.

WHEN Mr. Gould was a prosperous business man and before he resided in New York city he stopped at the Everett House, and on the square at that time resided a wealthy and retired merchant, Daniel G. Miller, of the strong firm of Lee, Dater & Miller, dealers in produce and groceries. Passing the house frequently, Mr. Gould was attracted by the gentle face of the merchant's daughter Helen, and he succeeded in making her acquaintance, and they were married in January, 1862, and lived most happily. She was a noble woman in every sense of the word, and seemed by nature endowed with just those qualities necessary to make a happy home. She was a kindly, loving, and trustful wife and tender, affectionate mother; four sons and two daughters blessed their union. For more than a quarter of a century she was the light and joy of his home. January 13th, 1889, she left her earthly home for the better land, and a stricken household mourned her departure. Her daughter Helen has ever since lovingly and unselfishly tried to fill her mother's place.

Mr. Gould never recovered from the shock caused

by the death of his wife, to whom he was most devoted. After her death he began to show marked signs of age, grew gray, and, though he was never robust in appearance, he lost flesh.

The home life of the great millionaire was most peaceful and happy. He was a most secretive man in regard to his business affairs, and even more so with respect to his home. He did not care for the pleasures of society, but was thoroughly happy when in the bosom of his family, either at the Fifth Avenue residence or at Lyndhurst. It may readily be imagined what a loss to Mr. Gould was the death of his beloved wife.

Their first New York home was in Seventeenth Street, and they were most tenderly devoted to each other then as always. Even in his busiest years Mr. Gould had a great deal of time for home, for he did not care for clubs, and was seldom an attendant upon public amusements.

The late Mrs. Gould took great interest in charities, but, like her husband, so arranged her beneficence that her own right hand scarcely knew the actions of its mate, and the public was entirely unaware of her bounty bestowed.

Miss Helen Gould, her namesake, is much like her mother in this respect, and her father was wont to say to his more confidential friends, "Since my wife died I take great comfort in Helen, and it is a source of constant pleasure to observe those characteristics which are so plainly inherited from her dear mother." Mr. Gould's friends were seldom invited to his home, but when it was their privilege to enter those portals, they felt that an object lesson in home life in its noblest aspect had been given them. An open fire, a lounging chair, a pair of slippers, and a gown do not make home for a man like Mr. Gould. Mutual love and respect are the magnets that attract such a man from the office or the club to "home." Mr. Gould was rich in these as well as in stocks and bonds. He had two "worlds" in which he lived. The business world, in later years, claimed most of his time; but those who knew him best knew that his home was worth more to him than his enormous wealth.

The house at No. 579 Fifth Avenue where Mr. Gould died had been regarded as his home for several years, for, of course, his residence was there more than at Lyndhurst. Before that he lived across the Avenue, almost directly opposite his present house, which, before Mr. Gould bought it, was the home of George Opdyke, the banker, who enjoyed the distinction of being one of the few Republican Mayors which New York has had. The house stands at the northeast corner of Fifth Avenue and Forty-seventh Street. It is a square brownstone house, about double the width of the average house, with an extension in the rear. It is three stories in height, with a mansard roof, which gives another story. The main entrance is in the middle of the Fifth Avenue front, under a portico into a deep ves-

MARRIAGE AND HOME LIFE. 61

tibule with handsomely-carved oaken doors and mosaic floor. The hall is fifty feet long. On the left of the hall is a small reception-room, with one window facing Fifth Avenue. On the other side of the hall are the great drawing-rooms. The library and the dining-room are in the rear. Mr. Gould had a fine collection of standard books.

The whole house was entirely redecorated only a short time before Mr. Gould's death, and is everywhere a model of comfort, unostentatious elegance, and good taste. It is filled with most exquisite tapestries and the finest paintings. Mr. Gould had specimens of the work of Diaz, Rousseau, Daubigny, Henner, Vibert, Rosa Bonheur, Voley, Jacquet, Schreyer, Bouguereau, Dupre, and Meyer von Bremen.

Attached to the house is a conservatory, which is kept constantly filled with the finest plants from the hot-houses at the country house at Irvington.

Mrs. Gould, for several years before her death, had been in delicate health, could not attend church, and never took part in social pleasures. Her trouble was a nervous one, and she could not endure excitement. Thus the house was never given over to festivities to any extent. Sumptuous as it was, it did not compare in size or display with that of other men whose fortunes rivalled Mr. Gould's, or, in fact, with the homes of many whose wealth was not a tenth of his. All looked at the place with interest, however, when it was pointed

LIFE OF JAY GOULD.

out as the retreat of the remarkable man whose public life was so dramatic, and whose home life was so quiet and so peaceful.

There was a charity organization society that existed in Mr. Gould's own household which would serve as a model for many rich men. Its sessions were held each morning after breakfast. Like other rich men, he was assailed constantly with showers of begging letters. These were regularly sorted out every morning, and each member of the family chose as many from the pile as desired until none were left. If a letter appeared to describe a case of real need it was placed in the centre of the table. The others were burned. Then ensued quiet investigation, conducted as secretly as the operations of the closest detective bureau. People in want were given aid commensurate with the needs of the particular case but were never able to thank the donor, for the identity of the giver was never disclosed. In this way many hundreds of poor people were relieved.

At the time when what was known as the geometric craze prevailed, hundreds of begging letters urging Mr. Gould "not to break the chain" were destroyed without any reply being vouchsafed the sender, as to encourage such correspondence would soon have brought on the necessity of a force of clerks at the Gould mansion equal in number to that of the Gould offices, and would have proved a fruitful mode of operation for those who consider millionaires their legitimate prey.

MARRIAGE AND HOME LIFE.

As Mr. Gould became more and more prominent as a monarch of the stock market and a manager of gigantic enterprises his name naturally became more intimately associated with rises and falls in the prices of stocks. Reckless plungers who had large amounts of money "margining" stocks would often in the bitterness of their chagrin at loss on account of increase or decrease in the price of their stocks, attribute their financial ruin to Mr. Gould, especially if any operation of his had for a time unsettled values of certain stocks.

These men, insanely jealous of the great financier's success, or with a spirit of revenge for a supposed wrong, caused much anxiety and worriment on the part of the members of Mr. Gould's family by their threatening letters, though Mr. Gould himself seldom gave them a serious thought. It has been said that he employed a detective to watch and guard him constantly, but this is not true. He had, however, very pleasant and cordial business relations with that remarkable man, Thomas Byrnes, Inspector of the New York police; in fact, few men in New York city had closer confidential relations with Jay Gould in recent years than those sustained by Mr. Byrnes. When Mr. Byrnes was Chief Inspector, in charge of the Detective Bureau, he performed valuable services for the millionaire in the line of police duty and gained his lasting respect and friendship. The advice of the police official was sought on several occasions when

LIFE OF JAY GOULD.

Mr. Gould was beset by "cranks" and by other strangers who tried to blackmail him or impose upon him by means of threatening letters or appeals for financial aid. Mr. Byrnes was consulted also on other subjects of importance, and he became a frequent visitor at Mr. Gould's house. Superintendent Byrnes is said to have made many thousands of dollars in stock speculations in Wall Street by following the advice of Mr. Gould.

One important service which Mr. Byrnes, as Chief Inspector, gave to the millionaire was the capture of Colonel J. Howard Wells, eleven years ago. The affair created a great sensation at the time. Wells was a broken-down speculator, with good social relations, and he conceived a plan to frighten Mr. Gould into aiding him to recover the money which he had lost. He at first wrote anonymous threatening letters to Mrs. Gould, thinking that she would show them to her husband. On October 15th, 1881, he sent an anonymous letter to Mr. Gould, beginning thus: "Sir:—It is my painful duty to inform you that within six days from the date of this letter your body will have returned to the dust from whence it came. I therefore entreat you to make your peace with God and prepare for the fate which awaits you." The letter further declared that Mr. Gould's death would be painless, as he would be shot through the heart. "Victim" was the signature to the letter.

Mr. Byrnes was consulted by Washington E. Connor, Mr. Gould's broker, and plans were laid to

MARRIAGE AND HOME LIFE. **65**

capture the writer of the letter. With the consent of Mr. Gould personal notices were published, requesting " Victim" to write again and offering him assistance. Wells wrote other letters asking Mr. Gould to assist him by giving " tips" on stocks. He insisted that the correspondence on the part of Mr. Gould should be conducted through personal notices, and he sent a cipher code by which the directions about buying or selling stocks could be conveyed in the notices, without informing the public.

Later a number of notices giving the " tips" asked for were published, and Wells continued to write letters. It was ascertained that all of the letters were mailed at street letter boxes in the district of post-office Station E. With the aid of the post-master Mr. Byrnes set a watch upon each of the letter boxes in the district of Station E, on Sunday, November 13th, 1881. As soon as a letter was placed in a box a letter-carrier went to the box and looked at the address of the letter, while a detective kept watch of the person who had deposited the letter, until a signal was given by the carrier. At 3 P. M. Wells went to the box at Seventh Avenue and Thirty-fourth Street and dropped into it a letter addressed to Mr Gould. He was arrested by a detective-sergeant as he was walking away. Finding himself fairly caught, Wells confessed that his letters had been written to compel Mr. Gould to give the " tips" on stocks. He, however, expressed sorrow that he had not killed Mr. Gould and then

66   *LIFE OF JAY GOULD.*

committed suicide, and his conduct as a prisoner in the Tombs led to his commitment as an insane person.

The correspondence which led to the capture of Wells and the manipulation of the stock market which was necessary to keep the correspondence going, cost Mr. Gould a large sum of money, it was said. Mr. Byrnes's reputation as a detective was increased by the arrest of Wells. During the entire affair Mr. Gould's solicitude seemed to be entirely for his wife, whose weak nerves were under a terrible strain, and not for his personal safety.

Jay Gould left six children, four sons and two daughters. They are George J. Gould, Edwin Gould, Helen Miller Gould, Howard Gould, Anna Gould, and Frank Gould.

George J. Gould is about thirty years old. Instead of going to college he went into business with his father, and has himself amassed a considerable fortune. He lived with his father until his marriage to Miss Edith Kingdon. He has three children, two boys, Kingdon and Jay, and one little girl. After his marriage George bought the house No. 1 East Forty-seventh Street, adjoining the rear of his father's home. A passageway was built connecting the house with the Fifth Avenue mansion. George J. Gould lived there until a month before his father's death, when he moved to the house at Fifth Avenue and Sixty-seventh Street. Edwin Gould then moved into the Forty-seventh Street house.

MARRIAGE AND HOME LIFE. 67

As Mr. George Gould has been made by the provision of his father's will the head of the Gould family, the chief executor of the will, and successor to the management of the vast interests which are now in trust, it has been thought proper to give a more extended account of his life in the sixth chapter of this work. Edwin Gould is twenty-six years old, and a graduate of Columbia College in the class of '88. His marriage to Miss Shrady, on October 26th, by the Rev. Dr. Robert Collyer, followed a courtship of about one year, and an engagement which was announced in June, 1892. Edwin Gould is Inspector of Rifle Practice in the 71st New York Regiment, and was formerly a private in Troop A.

Miss Helen Miller Gould is twenty-five years old. She is an active Church worker and a member of Dr. Paxton's the Presbyterian Church. To her interest in missionary work has often been attributed the ministers' meeting at Mr. Gould's house, and the millionaire's gift of $10,000 for missions. Howard Gould is twenty-one years old, Anna is a school girl, and the youngest, Frank, is thirteen years old.

Mr. Gould was as punctual as he was methodical. He breakfasted regularly at eight o'clock, and immediately went down-town to his offices in the Western Union Building, at 195 Broadway. Usually he spent an hour before breakfast reading financial news and familiarizing himself with the main facts in the leading articles. He took a light lunch about one o'clock. and returned home at five. unless business of great importance detained him, when he would sometimes spend the time until twelve or one o'clock poring over figures and plans, and he never appeared to feel the loss of rest and sleep consequent upon such long hours devoted to business.

GEO. GOULD.

CHAPTER IV.

CAREER IN NEW YORK.

JAY GOULD was twenty-three years old when he went into Wall Street as a broker. That was in 1859. Gould had considerable money of his own at that time, and had the confidence of two or three large capitalists. He started on his Wall Street career in a small office, and frequently took his stand with the curbstone brokers. He made money right along. In 1860 he became intimately acquainted with Mr. Henry N. Smith, who was then one of the big men in Wall Street. Soon the firm of Smith, Gould & Martin was formed, and it was prosperous from the start. Gould made a careful study of the railroad situation, and became an expert in the manipulation of railroad securities in the speculative market. He paid the closest attention to business, allowing himself few of the social pleasures of which young men are usually fond. He had no small vices, and he was a teetotaler.

The remarkable story of Mr. Gould's early railroad investments and his striking successes is told in these words:

After retiring from the leather business under very dramatic circumstances, Mr. Gould turned his attention to speculating in railroad stocks. About the same time he married. Mr. Gould was wont to say that his love for civil engineering had got him into the railway business, to which he devoted himself thereafter exclusively, until he also found telegraph properties sources of profit. The first of Gould's railways was the Rutland & Washington Railroad, 62 miles long, running from Troy, N. Y., to Rutland, Vt. The panic of 1857 had left this road in a demoralized condition, and Mr. Gould found that he could buy a majority of the first mortgage bonds at 10 cents on the dollar. He had now found the true field for his special talents. He made himself President, Treasurer, and General Superintendent of the road, studied the business of railroading on the ground, developed the local traffic, and finally effected the Rensselaer and Saratoga consolidation. By this time both bonds and stock were good, and he sold the latter for 120. There has been no time when it was possible to estimate the wealth of Mr. Gould, and as he was as secretive in those days as in his later, there is no way of saying what he was worth when, in 1859, he came into Wall Street. One statement has it that when the firm of Smith, Gould & Martin was organized, Mr. Gould's possessions amounted to $30,000 in cash; another is that when he sold out his holdings in the Rensselaer and Saratoga consolidation he was worth $750,000. With a mind peculiarly alert to all the influences which affected the values of railway securities, with habits of great industry, with phenomenal tenacity of purpose, with a fair amount, at least, of capital to back him, it is not surprising that Mr. Gould profited largely by his speculation in railway stocks and gold during the war of the rebellion. The keen-sighted intelligent men in "the Street" at that time nearly all made money, and Mr. Gould was at least a millionaire when the Confederacy fell.

During the war of the rebellion Gould's firm did a large business in railway securities, and also made a great deal of money speculating in gold. Gould had private sources of information in the field, and he was able to turn almost every success or defeat of the Union army to profitable account. Daniel Drew was one of the heaviest customers of Smith, Gould & Martin, and through him the attention of Gould was drawn to the Erie Railway. That company was embarrassed for money, and its stock was selling cheaply. Gould bought as much of it as he could carry, and when the bitter fight came on between Daniel Drew and Commodore Vanderbilt for the possession of the Erie, Gould, being one of the largest stockholders, was taken into the directory by Mr. Drew. He was made a member of the executive committee, and he was Drew's chief lieutenant throughout the long struggle against Vanderbilt.

What his methods were at the time it is useless to speculate about. It was before the day when by absolute mastery of gigantic railway and telegraph systems he could at his will depress the value of almost any institution on which he fixed his eye by setting on foot a ruinous war in rates until he had made it to his own interest to restore a more normal and healthful condition of affairs by ceasing his antagonism and building up the property which he had acquired cheaply during the period of depression. But the details of his operations were always so subtle as to be shut out from the discovery of either friend or foe. He got into the management of Erie through association with Drew and Fisk, and shared the profits in some of the tremendous battles which were waged between the giants of those days, Vanderbilt and Drew. It was found soon after he took up Erie as a director, that the company owed him $4,000,000, and after the cataclysms which devastated that notorious concern were over, he got his money.

The character of some of the strokes of good fortune which came to him during this period of his career may be illustrated briefly. When he got his $4,000,000 from the Erie and left the management of the company, he operated in the market with the stock, as doubtless he had done while he was in office (following in this particular the notorious example of Daniel Drew, the " speculative director.") One of his first transactions was to sell 50,000 shares short. The purchaser was a broker who was trying to bull the market by loudly offering 65 gold, seller 12 months, for that amount of stock.

CAREER IN NEW YORK. 75

Mr. Gould sold him the lot at that price, and in a very short time quietly took it in again in the neighborhood of 40. So, too, it is said that he bought 25,000 shares of Cleveland & Pittsburgh stock at 65 or 70.

In explaining this investment Gould always insisted that he had merely taken the stock to oblige a friend who had overloaded himself with it and was on the point of failure. He reorganized the road, developed its earning capacity, so that from the beginning to the end of his management it never passed a dividend, and when its stock was worth 1 20 he leased it to the Pennsylvania company, realizing certainly between a million and a half and two millions on the transaction.

A transaction of twice the magnitude of this, and one which, like it, illustrates how Mr. Gould's abilities often worked with equal advantageousness to both himself and the property in which he took an interest, makes one of the interesting anecdotes touching his connection with the Union Pacific Railroad. Following is Mr. Gould's story of how he went into this road, as told in his testimony before the Senate Committee on Labor and Education:

" I met the late Horace F. Clark in Chicago. He and Mr. Schell had been over the road and they gave me a good account of it; spoke about the coal deposits, and one thing and another, and I concluded to buy a lot of it. I telegraphed to New York an order to buy in the neighborhood of 30, from 30

76 LIFE OF JAY GOULD.

down. I did not expect to get much. Mr. Clark came home and was taken sick, and as soon as his brokers found that his illness was to be a fatal one, they sold his stock. That broke the market down and filled up orders which I had never expected to get filled, so that when I got home I found myself a very large owner in that property, and I began to inquire into its condition. I found that there was a large floating debt to begin with, which I did not know about before. Then I found that there was $10,000,000 of bonds that came due in about a month or two—income bonds. It was rather a blue condition of things. In the meantime, some of the directors were consulting as to who should be the receiver of the road. I made up my mind that I would carry it through; so I told the directors that if they would furnish half the money I would furnish the other half, and we would carry it through, and finally I pressed them into it. The stock went down to 15. I bought it, and kept buying it, and finally I had a large loss staring me in the face if I had made it; but instead of that I kept on buying, so that when the turn came there didn't seem to be any top to it; it went right along up to 75. I immediately went to work to bring the road up. I didn't care anything about the price in the market; I wanted to give it a substantial foundation. I went out over the road and started coal mines to develop that interest, and very soon we began to pay dividends, to the surprise of every-

CAREER IN NEW YORK.

body, and the road came up. It never passed a dividend."

This statement of the rapid improvement of the Union Pacific is strictly correct. Mr. Gould made his purchases in 1873. How much he bought when the price of the stock ranged from 15 to 30 it is impossible to say. In February, 1879, however, he was reported to be the holder of no less than 190,000 shares, and on the 17th of that month he sold 100,000 shares at an average price of 70 per cent. cash to a syndicate composed of James R. Keene, Russell Sage, David P. Morgan, Frank Work, Charles J. Osborne, Addison Cammack, David Jones, and William L. Scott. It was estimated at the time that the 100,000 shares which Mr. Gould sold cost him $3,000,000, and this was probably a high estimate, as he himself says that he had to buy largely at 15, and that his orders were from 30 down. Unless he bought during the subsequent rise, therefore, he cannot have paid $3,000,000 for the stock which he sold to the syndicate. But if he did, the transaction represents a profit of $4,000,000. At the annual meeting of the stockholders of the Union Pacific, which took place on March 5th, three weeks after this tremendous transaction of stocks, Jay Gould voted in his own right on 123,700 shares and on 20,000 shares by proxy. To afford one an opportunity to indulge his imagination with guesses at what Mr. Gould may have gained by speculating in Union Pacific stock during the six years preced-

LIFE OF JAY GOULD.

ing the sale, it is only necessary to add that in 1873 the stock fluctuated between 14¾ and 39½ ; in 1874, between 23 and 38¾ ; in 1875, between 36 and 82¾ ; in 1876, between 57¾ and 74½ ; in 1877, between 59¾ and 73, and in 1878, between 61¼ and 73. On the day of the sale the stock was advanced nine per cent. before the terms were generally known.

As Jay Gould took the Cleveland & Pittsburgh Company just to oblige a friend and save him from ruin, so it would seem from the few public explanations which he has made of his actions, most of them after the " storm and stress " period of his speculative life was over, that he also went into most of his big enterprises. Thus, he said that he bought Texas Pacific of Thomas Scott because he met him in Switzerland in the summer of 1879 and felt sympathy for him. Scott being, as Gould expressed it, " very much depressed and broken up financially, physically, and mentally." He asked Mr. Gould to take the Texas Pacific off his hands, and Mr. Gould did so, consenting afterward to include also *The World* newspaper in the transaction. About four years later he disposed of *The World* to Joseph Pulitzer. Another version of the story is that Gould only bought a small interest in the road of Colonel Scott, and on the strength of it was made a director. In April, 1881, Mr. Gould and Colonel Scott, being both still in the directory, there was a meeting of the board in Philadelphia. Mr. Gould and

CAREER IN NEW YORK.   79

Mr. Sage went into the private office to have a preliminary talk with Colonel Scott touching a difference in policy. Gould adhered to his plans with such pertinacity that Scott finally ceased arguing and said that he would rather sell out his interest than follow Mr. Gould.

"What will you sell for?" was the response to this challenge.

Colonel Scott set his price and Jay Gould without a moment's hesitation, drew his check for $2,400,000, handed it to Scott, and entered the director's room the owner of the controlling interest in the Texas Pacific road. When the disputants joined their colleagues, Colonel Scott's resignation was tendered and accepted, and this was the first intimation that the directors had that a sale had been contemplated. In fact, it is said that before the conversation between Scott and Gould began, the former at least was as ignorant as the rest of the board on the same subject. Mr. Gould's readiness can safely be accepted as proof that he was not entirely surprised in the premises.

The Missouri Pacific he also bought in the same way. After some negotiations with Commodore Garrison, he named his price, which Mr. Gould accepted, sent his check, and took control of the road on the same day. The road thus purchased was 287 miles long, and ran from St. Louis to Kansas City. In a few years Mr. Gould made it the controlling factor in a system which contained 10,000

80   *LIFE OF JAY GOULD.*

miles of railway, running from St. Louis west to Omaha, southeast to El Paso, connecting there with the Texas Pacific, to Laredo, on the direct line to the City of Mexico, and to Galveston. The eastern termini, beside St. Louis, are Chicago, Detroit, and Toledo.

In his testimony before the famous Senate Committee on Labor and Education, before referred to, Mr. Gould testified: "The next great enterprise, if I may call it great, that I engaged in was the Missouri Pacific. I bought it one day of Commodore Garrison, or, rather, the control of it. I had a very short negotiation with him. He gave me his price, just as we are talking here, and I said, 'All right; I will take it;' and I gave him a check for it that day. All that time I did not care about the money made; it was a mere plaything to see what I could do. I had passed the point where I cared about the mere making of money. It was more to show that I could make a combination and make it a success. I took this road and began developing it, bringing in other lines which should be tributary to it. I developed new parts of the country, opened up coal mines, etc., and continued until, I think, we have now 10,000 miles of road.

"When I took the property it was earning $70,000 a week. I have just got the gross earnings for the last month, and they amount to $5,100,000, and we have accomplished that result by developing the country, and while we have been doing this we

CAREER IN NEW YORK. 81

have made the country rich, developing. coal mines and cattle raising, as well as the production of cotton. We have created this earning power by developing the system. All this 10,000 miles is fully built. The roads pass through the States of Ohio, Illinois, Michigan, Iowa, Missouri, Kansas, Nebraska, Arkansas, Texas, Louisiana, and the Indian Territory, and we go into Mexico."

One of the most memorable events connected with Gould's management of the Missouri Pacific was the great Knights of Labor strike in 1885, which disabled the road for a long time.

An interesting feature of the strike was a Sunday conference at Mr. Gould's house between him and General Master Workman Powderly, at which negotiations for a settlement were entered into. The foremost representatives of capital and labor thus met to settle vital questions at issue affecting the wealth of the capitalists and the livelihood of the workingmen. Mr. Gould said of this famous strike :

"I have been all my life a laborer or an employer of laborers. Strikes come from various causes, but are principally brought about by the poorest and therefore the dissatisfied element. The best workers generally look forward to advancement in the ranks or to save money enough to go into business on their own account. Though there may be few advanced positions to be filled, there is a large number of men trying to get them. They get better

LIFE OF JAY GOULD.

pay here than in any other country, and that is why they come here. My idea is that if capital and labor are let alone they will mutually regulate each other. People who think they can regulate all mankind and get wrong ideas which they believe to be panaceas for every ill, cause much trouble to both employers and employees by their interference."

To the Congressional Committee which investigated the Missouri Pacific strike, Mr. Gould made known his belief in efficacy of arbitration in settling difficulties between labor and capital by saying, "I am in favor of arbitration as an easy way of settling differences between corporations and their employees."

The idea of invariable success has attached itself to Mr. Gould's reputation, and there has been a feeling there was something uncanny in his luck. In truth, he lost often and heavily. Mr. Morosini, referring to the panic of 1873, said :

"He was not responsible for it. A man would hardly precipitate a panic and lose his own money, would he ? The panic of 1873 left Mr. Gould comparatively a poor man. He had more reason to regret the disaster than almost any one else concerned. I doubt if any man parted with more cash and securities than did Mr. Gould by reason of that catastrophe."

Mr. Thomas G. Shearman, for ten years Mr. Gould's counsel, says :

"He was a very hard worker in point of appli-

CAREER IN NEW YORK. 83

cation, and worked a good deal. In times of financial excitement or uneasiness he was at his desk by eight o'clock each morning, and often remained until 11 o'clock or midnight. I have frequently known him to go with no more than four or five hours' sleep. When intensely interested in any matter, he devoted his whole concentration of thought upon that one thing, and would seem to lose interest in things, often of greater pecuniary importance but of not so much commercial fascination. He loved the intricacies and perplexities of financial problems.

"While his success was owing, of course, to his shrewdness and sagacity, it was because those qualities were applied to different efforts than those which the world has generally credited as the source of his success. I am satisfied that he lost money by some of these speculations, pure and simple, which gave him the widest prominence. All his gold speculations, his stock speculations—I speak of those which were purely speculative as brokers use the term—generally resulted in losses. This is the most misunderstood fact in Mr. Gould's career.

The New York *Herald* very justly once said of Mr. Gould:

"One of the almost universal mistakes made in discussing Mr. Gould's career is that of considering him as distinctively a speculator. He never was a speculator except in the few instances in which he was forced by circumstances into that *rôle*, and at

LIFE OF JAY GOULD.

those times he was almost without exception unsuccessful.

"If Gould had died poor what would have been the general verdict on his career? And yet, startling as the statement may appear, only eight years ago he was on the verge of failure. This was after the panic of May, 1884, one of the few times when he was tempted into the stock market as a speculator in order to hold up the price of stocks with which he was burdened.

"The late Charles F. Woerishoffer, Henry N. Smith, and other operators were united in a combined effort to bear the securities which Gould was carrying. He had supported them for a time by obtaining sterling bills (giving his securities as collateral) and then converting the bills into cash. But sterling loans like all others come to maturity; the bears were unscrupulous as himself, bold and skillful and persistent. Gould's Western Union fell to 49 and his Missouri Pacific to 63. He was beaten. One morning he had his lawyers execute an assignment of his property, and on the following day—a beautiful Sunday morning—his yacht went down to Long Branch where the bear operators were summering. Gould's emissaries landed and held a conference with his foes. They bore his ultimatum—a copy of the assignment, and the statement that unless the bears made terms with him he would on the following morning file the assignment and give public notice that he was unable to meet his engagements."

CAREER IN NEW YORK. 85

At that time he was supposed to be borrowing some $20,000,000, and his failure would create a bigger panic than the one the Street had just passed through. Many of the firms with which the bear combine had "short" contracts outstanding would doubtless fail, and in the general crash the successful bears themselves might be very heavy losers. It was a bold coup. After protracted conference, the bears agreed to "let up" on Gould on condition that he should turn over to them 50,000 shares of Western Union at the current market price, $50 per share. This enabled them to make delivery of the shares they had sold at high prices, but, of course, left the rank and file of their followers in Wall Street still short of the stock. In speaking of this "deal" the following day, one of the bears expressed his confidence that Gould would have to fail anyhow— the help he had received would be transient in its effects as a glass of brandy given to a dying man.

He was wrong. He underestimated the fertility of resource in Gould and his associates. The bears were heavily short of Gould's Missouri Pacific. With the $2,500,000 of their own money obtained for the 50,000 shares of Western Union, he speedily rushed up Missouri Pacific to par ($100 per share, a rise of nearly $40), and forced them to step up to his office and settle on terms of his own dictation. If the bears had had enough grit on that Sunday Gould's career would have terminated very differently. His name would have gone on the long roll of "kings of the

Street," who ruled for a time only to fall with a crash—with the names of Jacob Little, A. W. Morse, W. S. Woodward, and a score of others. As it was, the shock resulted in Gould making preparations to consolidate and conserve the securities he owned, and he never again took any active part in manipulating the market.

MRS. GEO. GOULD.

CHAPTER V.

WALL STREET WARS.

ONE of the accusations that has been influential in forming public opinion against Mr. Gould has been that he oppressed and betrayed Mr. Cyrus W. Field, and succeeded in getting from him his Manhattan Railway stock at a low figure, after which he placed much of it at a higher price with his own friends, thus enriching himself both ways. The full history covering this subject would be tedious, but the outlines should be clearly stated, and do not lack general interest. Mr. Field was a man of remarkable enthusiasm. His memorable work in uniting Europe and America by cable telegraph is the most conspicuous example. His wonderful success was as highly estimated, and in a personal sense, better appreciated in England than in the United States. He received the most distinguished consideration, and the capitalists of London, more than of New York, had confidence in his judgment, and would place money according to his recommendation. So certain were they of his understanding that their willingness to trust him, without seeking

LIFE OF JAY GOULD.

collateral testimony, was at times embarrassing, and it is due him to say that he was most chary in the use of this peculiar and powerful public favor. His caution in making recommendations was very great. He did, however, tell his English and Scotch friends his opinion during the depressed times in the war of the inevitable increase in the value of Government securities. Some of them made large purchases, and consequently profits, and Mr. Field's reputation as a safe adviser was extended. He saw earlier than others the enormous requirements of rapid transit systems in our great cities, and the adaptation of the elevated roads to the needs of New York, and believed the intuition of discovery in this enterprise was greater as a matter of business than the Atlantic Cable leadership. He had no shadow of doubt in his mind that the achievement of rapid transit by elevated roads would be of enormous public value and personal emolument. He saw, too, that the system that increased the values on the upper end of Manhattan Island would have the same influence down-town. The influence of the roads would be to expand the city and augment the demand for property at both ends of the line. The Field building, No. 1 Broadway, may be noted as proof of his foresight and his executive force.

The vast elevated railway systems of New York and Brooklyn—the most extensive and most comfortable rapid transit roads with which great com-

WALL STREET WARS. 91

munities are provided anywhere in the world—and with a wonderful record for reliability and safety, are the realization of his dreams. But more years and more money than he thought were required to make them what they are. The growth of the elevated roads has been steady, as he was assured, but not so swift as his anticipations. His intelligence did not fail him, but his characteristic impetuosity led to his losses. Mr. Gould and Mr. Field were closely associated in the elevated road enterprise, and highly estimated each other.

They were so unlike that they formed a rare combination. The placid coolness of Mr. Gould was in fine contrast with the fiery ardor of Mr. Field. It was the weakness of Mr. Field that it was misery to him to wait. In accordance with his temperament, zeal, anxiety, and temperature a stalk of corn should reach its full height in a few days instead of months. He knew Manhattan was one of the best things in the world. He actually knew—was perfectly right about it—but there was one of many calculations wrong. He did not make a sufficient allowance for the time nesessary for the great city to adapt itself to the roads. He had a handsome fortune and had been so close to failure and ruin that he had gained what he believed were conservative habits of thought and circumspection in action. He insisted upon popularizing the roads, and carried his point of making the fares uniform and all the time five cents. Once—the fact is almost forgotten—there

92 *LIFE OF JAY GOULD.*

were five-cent and ten-cent hours. When the popular price was established the people accepted it as their right, and did not feel grateful to anybody about it, and there were always many ready to assume that the Manhattan system was a horrid monopoly owned by improperly rich men. The spirit of Mr. Field was as aggressive as it was intense, and if he had things at all he had them his way. He invested all the capital that he could command in Manhattan and when it was for sale bought great blocks of it, raising money by putting up the stock as collateral. This was not according to the judgment of Mr. Gould, who could see that the five-cent fares were not yielding the dividends to sustain the property at the height of the figures of Mr. Field's purchases. He wisely held that carrying such masses of stock on margins growing narrow through the time needed for development was dangerous.

Mr. Field held the opinion that the Manhattan stock could eventually be very largely disposed of on the London market at rates far above any that had been reached. The property was so famous, so much in evidence, so easily inspected, so under the eye, and obviously of enormous earning capacity; it was the best thing in the world for England. What Mr. Field could not permanently hold, he might easily and at an advance part with, and British gold would have been far better bestowed in Manhattan than in South America.

WALL STREET WARS.

93

where such a flood of it was poured out to evaporate. While Mr. Field was hopefully waiting and witnessing the gradual increase that was so absolute a matter to him that he had few misgivings, there came a financial flurry. The usual excitement—contraction, loud calls and sharp strain—and Mr. Field finally, with all his resources, found himself embarrassed. Mr. Gould has been accused of producing this state of things, but it was not his interest, not his game, his policy to do anything of the kind, and he had nothing more to do with it than with the tides or the procession of the seasons. Mr. Field was carrying 88,000 shares of the stock ($100 shares) par value of $8,800,000, and it had been boomed until it stood in the market at about $15,000,000. Several banks were overloaded with it. There was imminent danger of the failure of Mr. Field, and if that event should occur there would be widespread disaster.

There was one man with the nerve and other abilities equal to the emergency, and Mr. Field saw him and made a frank statement, and he took 78,000 shares of the stock at 120 or $9,360,000. This was the old figure of Mr. Gould's valuation of the property. He alone could or would make the purchase, and retained 50,000 of the shares that had been in Mr. Field's possession, and distributed 28,000 shares at the price he paid, several of his friends declining the stock because they did not want it, and it fell to 77 before the advance set

LIFE OF JAY GOULD.

in, and it is not even yet quite up to the point where Mr. Field had it. Of course Mr. Gould did not lose any money by this transaction, but he had to wait. He could afford to wait, and so saved himself and won at last. If he had not met the crisis with courage and had not been equipped for the emergency, there would have been a great public calamity.

Mr. Field was relieved, but his losses impaired his fortune, and after a time other troubles came for which he was not accountable. Mr. Gould cannot justly be charged with his misfortunes, and the incident we relate is a display of his capacity to grasp great affairs, and the unerring integrity of his judgment.

Following is the full text of the correspondence between Mr. Gould and Mr. T. V. Powderly, Grand Master Workman of the Knights of Labor, at the time when Mr. Gould was President of the Missouri Pacific Railroad, which was plunged in a terrible strife with the Knights of Labor. Those strikes have gone down into our history as among the most disastrous conflicts between Capital and Labor that have ever taken place.

No better idea of the principles involved in the strike or of the animus of the leaders on both sides can be obtained than through this official correspondence. The following letters are a history in themselves.

WALL STREET WARS. 95

NOBLE ORDER OF THE KNIGHTS OF LABOR OF
AMERICA,
OFFICE OF GENERAL SECRETARY,
PHILADELPHIA, March 27th.

Mr. Jay Gould:

SIR.—The General Executive Board would be pleased to have an interview with you at your convenience to-day for the purpose of submitting the Southwest difficulties to a committee of seven (7) for arbitration, three of the committee to be appointed by yourself and three by the General Executive Board, the six to select the seventh member of the committee, their decision in the matter to be final. Should this proposition be acceptable, we will at once issue an order for the men to return to work.

By order of the General Executive Board,

FREDERICK TURNER,
Secretary of Board.

THE MISSOURI PACIFIC RAILWAY COMPANY.
NEW YORK, March 27th.

Frederick Turner, Esq., Secretary, etc., Philadelphia, Pa.:

DEAR SIR.—I have your note of this date proposing an interview between your Executive Committee and the officers of this company, for the purpose of submitting to arbitration by a committee of seven what you term the ' Southwestern difficulties.' You are doubtless aware, that, in the negotiations which took place here last August between Mr. T. V.

LIFE OF JAY GOULD.

Powderly, Grand Master Workman, and associates, and the officers of this company, it was agreed, that, in future, no strikes would be ordered on the Missouri Pacific Road until after a conference with the officers of the company and an opportunity to adjust any alleged grievances. In view of this fact, attention is drawn to the following correspondence between Mr. A. Hopkins, vice-president, acting for this company in my absence, and Mr. Powderly:

NEW YORK, March 6th, 1886.

T. V. Powderly, Scranton, Pa.:

Mr. Hoxie telegraphs that Knights of Labor on our road have struck and refuse to allow any freight trains to run on our road, saying they have no grievance, but are only striking because they are ordered to do so. If there is any grievance we would like to talk it over with you. We understood you to promise that no strike should be ordered without consultation.

A. L. HOPKINS.

PHILADELPHIA, PA., March 8th, 1886.

A. L. Hopkins, Secretary Missouri Pacific Railroad, 195 Broadway, New York:

Have telegraphed West for particulars. Papers say strike caused by discharge of man named Hall. Can he be reinstated pending investigation?

T. V. POWDERLY.

WALL STREET WARS. 97

NEW YORK, March 8th, 1886.

T. V. Powderly:

Thanks for your message and suggestion. Hall was employed by the Texas & Pacific and not by us. That property is in the hands of the United States Court, and we have no control whatever over the receivers or over the employees. We have carried out the agreements made last spring in every respect, and the present strike is unjust to us and unwise for you. It is reported here that this movement is the result of Wall Street influence on the part of those short of the securities likely to be affected.

A. L. HOPKINS.

No reply to this message was received, but this company's request for a conference was ignored and its premises at once invaded and its property destroyed by the men of your Order in great numbers, who also seized and disabled its trains, as they have since continued to do, whenever attempting to run. The Board of Directors of this company thereupon had a copy of the correspondence above given made and transmitted to Mr. H. N. Hoxie, the First Vice-President and General Manager at St. Louis, with instructions to use every endeavor to continue the operation of the road, and committed the whole matter to his hands.

Mr. Hoxie's overtures, made through the Governors of Missouri and Kansas, who stated that they

LIFE OF JAY GOULD.

found no cause for the strike, were rejected by your Order. These and the subsequent correspondence between him and Mr. Powderly are well known to you, and Mr. Hoxie's course has been confirmed by the Board and the matter is still in his hands. I am therefore instructed by the Board to refer you to him as its continuing representative in the premises.

I am directed to add in behalf of the Board, that in its judgment so long as this company is forcibly kept from the control of its property and from performing its charter duties, its business is done, if at all, not under the conditions of law, which are common to all citizens, but only at the will of a law-breaking force. Any negotiations with such a force would be unwise and useless. Terms made with it would not be a settlement of difficulties, but a triumph of force over the law of the land. It would mean nothing in their judgment but new troubles and worse. This is the result of their experience.

In the meantime, the Governor's proclamation enjoins upon your men to return to duty, and this company's continued advertisement offers them employment on the same terms as heretofore. The Board further suggests that inasmuch as your order assuming in your communication responsibility for these men, and power and control over them, the following, from the proclamation of the Governor of Missouri, is expressive of their duty and of your own:

"I warn all persons, whether they be employees or not, against interposing any obstacle, whether in

WALL STREET WARS. 99

the way of said resumption, and with a firm reliance upon the courage, good sense, and law-abiding spirit of the public, I hereby call upon all good citizens to assist in carrying out the purposes of this proclamation; and I also hereby pledge the whole power of the State, so far as it may be lawfully wielded by its chief executive officer, to sustain the company and its servants in said resumption, and to restrain and punish all that may oppose it."

When this proclamation shall be obeyed, and when the company's late employees shall desist from violence and interference with its trains, the Board hereby assures them that they will find themselves met by Mr. Hoxie in the spirit in which he has heretofore so successfully avoided rupture and cause for just complaint, and in that just and liberal spirit which should always exist between the employer and the employed. By order of the Board,

Very respectfully yours,

JAY GOULD,

President Missouri Pacific Railway Company.

" Personal."

MISSOURI PACIFIC RAILROAD COMPANY,

NEW YORK, March 29th, 1886.

T. V. Powderly, Esq., New York City :

DEAR SIR.—The papers this morning publish the following message:

" President J. Gould has consented to our proposition for arbitration, and so telegraphs Vice-President Hoxie. Order the men to resume at once. Signed, T. V. Powderly, G. M. W."

100 *LIFE OF JAY GOULD.*

They also publish an interview with you, which leads me to think that the officers of your Order in St. Louis may misconstrue your message into a consent on the part of this company to conform to the request contained in the letter from the Secretary of your Order, dated Philadelphia, March 27th, which in my letter to you of the same date I declined to consider. You will remember that in our conference of yesterday, I said to you that the position of this company was unchanged in this respect, and that the whole matter was left in the hands of the First Vice-President and General Manager, with the instructions contained in my telegram to him, which was written before my interview with you and read to you at the time. This telegram stated, "We see no objection to arbitrating any difference between the employees and the company, past or future." While I feel confident that your understanding of this matter is the same as my own, I write you this in order that there may be no grounds for misunderstanding hereafter.

Very respectfully yours,

JAY GOULD,
President Missouri Pacific R. R. Co

MR. POWDERLY TO MR. GOULD.

SCRANTON, PA., April 11th, 1886.
Jay Gould, Esq., President Missouri Pacific Railroad:

DEAR SIR.—The events of the past 48 hours must have demonstrated to you the absolute necessity of bringing this terrible struggle in the South-

WALL STREET WARS.

west to a speedy termination. You have the power, the authority, and the means to bring the strike to an end. I have done everything in my power to end the strife. The gentlemen associated with me on the General Executive Board of the Knights of Labor have done the same. Everything consistent with honor and manhood has been done in the interest of peace. No false notions of pride or dignity have swayed us in our dealings with you or the gentlemen associated with you.

In that conference with you on Sunday, March 28th, I understood you to mean that arbitration would be agreed to. The only method of arbitration that was discussed was in line with that suggested in the letter which I sent to you in the name of our Board the day previous. There was nothing particular agreed upon, as you well know. You said that in arbitrating the matter the damages sustained by the company during the strike ought to receive consideration. I said to you that it would not be the part of wisdom to bring that question up in the settlement of the strike. When I called upon you again that evening you had prepared, as the result of your understanding of the morning's interview, a letter which you intended to give me. That letter included a telegram to be sent to Mr. Hoxie, and in that telegram you said that the damages sustained by the company would be a proper subject for the arbitration board to discuss. This latter part of the letter or telegram you agreed to strike off after we had talked the matter over for some time, and I left you as you were about to go to your room to rewrite the letter, which you afterward placed in the hands of Mr. McDowell to be given to me, for I had to leave at that time in order to keep an appointment at the hotel where I stopped. The statement which you have since made, to the effect that you had prepared that letter before I called, is not quite correct, or if you did have it prepared you changed it after we talked the matter over for some time. This I believe you will admit to be true. In the conference held between the members of our Executive Board and the directors of the Missouri Pacific Company, at No. 195 Broadway, on March 30th, you said to me that you understood me to say that the men along your lines would be ordered back to work at once, they having violated the rules of our organization.

I then reiterated the statement which I have made to you, and now repeat it: " The men out along the lines of your railways can be ordered back to work, but if they are given to understand that they are deserted, that we do not take any interest in them, it will not in any way mend matters; on the contrary, it will make things worse. There are, all along the roads out there, a great many men who have no regard for organization or law, men of hardy spirit, energy, and daring. Such men as have left the East and have taken up their homes out in a wild country such as that is will not submit as

WALL STREET WARS.

103

quietly as the men they left behind in the East; they are apt to do rasher things than they would do elsewhere, and I have no doubt we have some in our Order, in fact, my experience with the men of that vast section leads me to think that the men on both sides out there are more dare-devilish than they are in the East. Even the business men of that country are of that stamp of character."

Both you and Mr. Hopkins heard me make that statement, and I believe the latter agreed that that was his experience also. The danger of the strike spreading was also discussed, and I said to you that it would not spread, that an effort had been made to have the men of the Union Pacific take a part in it, but that the Knights of Labor on that road had a standing agreement with the management of the road that there was to be no trouble or strike until the last effort to effect a settlement had failed; and not then until the court of last resort had been reached. When I made that statement Mr. Hopkins remarked that they had better strike then, for if they did not, the Union Pacific would not much longer have sufficient money to pay their employees. The impression made on me was that you would be pleased to see a strike take place on the Union Pacific.

This, I believe, covers the chief points of discussion. I did not hear either you or Mr. Hopkins say that the present trouble out along your road would not be arbitrated with the men who were not at

LIFE OF JAY GOULD.

work. It was my firm belief when I left you that night that you meant to have the entire affair submitted to arbitration at the first possible moment. That belief is shared by Mr. McDowell, who was present during the entire interview.

When you sent the telegram to Mr. Hoxie you sent it as President of the Missouri Pacific Railroad Company. You sent it as the chief sends his message to an inferior officer, and it meant as much to a sensible man as the most imperative order could possibly mean. When I, as the chief officer of the Knights of Labor, send a message such as that, it is understood to be my wishes, and those wishes are respected by the subordinate officer to whom they are sent. It is not his place to put a different construction on them and give them his own interpretation. His duty is to obey the spirit of the instruction. The man in power need not be an autocrat in order to have his wishes respected. "I would like to see it done," comes with as great a force from the man in authority as "I must have it done." That was the idea that I entertained when I left your house that night. I also explained to you at your house that night that the men who had entered upon the strike had not violated any law of the Order in so doing; that, while I thought it would have been better if they had laid their grievances before the General Executive Board before striking, yet there was nothing in our laws to command them to do so. I said that a District Assembly of the Knights of

WALL STREET WARS.

Labor bore the same relation to the General Assembly, of which I am the chief officer, that one of the States of the American Union had to the General Government of the United States, and that, while I could interfere, it was under the law which gave me jurisdiction over the entire Order, and not under any particular law. I furthermore explained to you that the spirit of our organization, its genius, was opposed to strikes, and that was the reason why our General Convention never enacted any particular legislation for the government of them. I also said that the occasion had never before called for any interference from the general officers, but that this strike would show the necessity for the passage, at our next convention, of laws that would place the subject of strikes under the control of the General Executive Board of the general Order.

When, on Monday, March 29th, you sent me the letter marked "Personal," you, at the same time, told a newspaper correspondent that you had done so. What your motive was in marking your letter "Personal" and at the same time informing a representative of the press that you so addressed me, I do not know, nor do I question your motive. I felt it to be my duty to let the public see the letter, which contained nothing of a personal nature whatever. There are people who might be uncharitable enough to say that your intention was to give out the impression that there was something between you and me which would not bear the light of public

LIFE OF JAY GOULD.

scrutiny. I have had no such dealings with any man since this trouble began, nor previous to that time. I am quite willing to allow the fullest light possible to shine upon my every transaction. I have nothing to conceal.

You can settle this strike. Its longer continuance rests with you, and you alone. Every act of violence, every drop of blood that may be shed from this time forth, must be laid at your door. The Knights of Labor were not founded to promote or shield wrong-doing, and to-day the Order of the Knights of Labor stands between your property and ruin. We are willing to absolve the men along your railways from their allegiance to our Order. We leave that to themselves. We will not allow any claims which the Order may have on them to stand between them and their restoration to their former positions. The Order of the Knights of Labor asks of no man to remain a member if it is not to his interest to do so. You may deal with them as citizens if you will. We will surrender our right to claim these men as members if they wish, but we will not surrender our right to see this affair thoroughly investigated.

You have said that the Order of the Knights of Labor was a conspiracy, a secret menace, etc. I am willing, as the chief officer, to lay everything connected with our Order bare to the world, if you will, on the other hand, lay open to the public the means and methods whereby you have piled up wealth which you control, and allow the tribunal of

WALL STREET WARS. 107

public opinion to pass in judgment on the two and say which is the conspiracy. Do you accept the challenge?

You have instructed your legal adviser to proceed against every man connected with the Knights of Labor for the damages sustained since the strike began. Two weeks ago I said: "Do not do this." To-day I say begin at once, lay claims for damages in every court within whose jurisdiction a Knight exists. Proceed at once, and in every State where you can recover damages do so if the law will sustain you in it. Let the majesty of the law be vindicated; it is just and right that it should be so. We are willing to face you before the law. We will fight you with no other weapon. For every violation of the law of State or Nation we will enter suit against you, and in this crusade against you do not understand that we mean to prosecute. On the contrary, we wish to see the law vindicated. If you have at all times obeyed the law in your dealings, in the methods by which you have acquired your immense fortune, then it is time that the many offenses with which you are charged should be refuted. You have remained silent under many a damaging charge of injuring the State. We will be your avengers. If you have been wronged we will let it be known to the world through the medium of the courts of justice. And let me say right here that no money will buy a verdict at the hands of these courts.

LIFE OF JAY GOULD.

There are people who say that this struggle is the beginning of the war between capital and labor. That statement is false. This certainly means war; but it is a war between legitimate capital, honest enterprise, and honest labor on the one hand, and illegitimate wealth on the other hand. This is a war in which we court the fullest investigation of our acts. Do you dare to do the same? This war means no further strike, no shedding of blood; it is a war in which every business man, every commercial man, every professional man, every workingman will be invited to enlist. It will not be a war upon the innocent and the battle-field upon which it will be fought out will be before the two courts—of law and that which makes law, public opinion. There will be no mobs in this supreme hour to silence any man's opinion. No converts will be made by physical force. "That flag which floats over press or mansion at the bidding of a mob, disgraces both victor and victim," and under such a flag as that we will not wage the battle; but this battle of the people against monopoly may as well be fought now as ten years from now, and what field so eminently proper in which to fight it out as before the courts? Let us know whether laws were made to be obeyed or not; and if they were not so framed then the people must make laws that will be obeyed. No man, whether he be rich or whether he be the poorest of the poor, shall in future shirk the responsibility of his acts and shield himself behind the

WALL STREET WARS.

109

courts. It was to see that the laws were obeyed that the Order of the Knights of Labor was founded and if the day has come to make the trial, so let it be.

I do not write this letter to you either in the spirit of anger or revenge. For you personally I have no dislike. I believe that, if allowed to follow your own impulses in this matter, you would have had the strike ended ere this. Those who advise you do not mingle with the people, they do not care for the people. You have been warned that your life is in danger. Pay no attention to such talk ; no man who has the interest of his country at heart would harm a hair of your head. But the system which reaches out on all sides, gathering in the millions of dollars of treasure and keeping them out of the legitimate channels of trade and commerce, must die, and the men whose money is invested in the enterprises which stock-gambling has throttled must make common cause with those who have been denied the right to earn enough to provide the merest necessaries of life for home and family. When I say to you that we will meet you in the courts I do not speak rashly or ill-advisedly. I have taken counsel from the best legal minds of the United States. We are prepared to face you before the courts, and now await your action in the matter. This is no threat. I play no game of bluff or chance. I speak for 500,000 organized men, who are ready to pay out the last farthing in order that justice may prevail You have it in your power to

LIFE OF JAY GOULD.

make friends of these men by acting the part of the man, by taking this matter in your own hands. Will you do so, and end this strife in the interest of humanity and our common country? It is your duty to brush aside every obstacle, assert your authority and take this matter in your hands, settle every grievance, restore every man to his place, except those who have been engaged in the destruction of property or who have broken the laws. Will you do this? You can then make rules and agreements with your men which will forever preclude the possibility of another such disastrous conflict as this one has proved itself to be. I remain

Yours very truly,
T. V. POWDERLY, G. M. W. K. of L.

THE REPLY OF MR. GOULD.

The reply of Mr. Gould includes copies of previous correspondence. It is as follows:

NEW YORK, April 14th, 1886.

T. V. Powderly, Esq., G. M. W. K. of L :

DEAR SIR.—At 12 o'clock to-day I received from Mr. William O. McDowell, whom you brought with you to our recent conferences, a letter in which he says:

"By yesterday's mail I received a letter written by Mr. Powderly addressed to you, inclosed in a letter addressed to me. With this, I hand to you the letter addressed to you by Mr. Powderly, and a copy of Mr. Powderly's letter to me inclosing the same."

WALL STREET WARS. 111

The following is a copy of the letter Mr. McDowell sent me as coming from you:

"GENERAL ASSEMBLY ORDER OF KNIGHTS OF LABOR OF AMERICA.

" OFFICE OF GENERAL MASTER WORKMAN,
" SCRANTON, PENN., April 13th, 1886.

" MY DEAR MR. McDOWELL.—I inclose you a letter which you are to read and deliver to the man for whom it is intended. I do not care whether you deliver it in person or through the medium of another, only ask that it be placed in his hands. If you have succeeded in effecting a settlement with him, do not give it to him. If you think there is a prospect of an immediate settlement do not give it to him ; but if such is not the case, then I want it placed in his hands, Allow him to either consent or to make a reply. If he consents to an honorable settlement, then the letter will never see the light of day, but if he does not so act, then it will be published to the world, and from the time he opens up the ball in a legal way, we will continue to wage the battle with him. His wealth cannot save him if this fight is begun. Let no one know of the existence of this letter until after five o'clock of the day you deliver it ; then if he makes no reply, let it go to the world. Let him know the limit of time allowed. I sincerely hope that there will be no necessity for its publication. Hoping for the best, I remain, " Very truly yours,

" T. V. POWDERLY.

LIFE OF JAY GOULD.

I have received your letter to me dated "Scranton, Penn., April 11th, 1886," at the same time and by the same agency that I received your foregoing letter of instructions to Mr. McDowell. The animus and purpose of your letter to me cannot be fully understood without knowing the contents of that one. I was peremptorily notified at the same time that I must answer your letter by five o'clock to-day, and I was graciously given until that hour to respond. Your letter to me embraces two subjects, one relating to me personally, and the other to the relation of the Knights of Labor to a railroad company of which I am the President, and, in some degree, the representative of its public and private duties. I shall refer to the first subject very briefly. The circumstances above given, under which your letter was delivered, as well as its tenor and spirit, place the purpose in writing it beyond any fair doubt. It would seem to be an official declaration that the Knights of Labor had determined to pursue me personally unless the Missouri Pacific Company should yield to its demands in what you call the strike on that road.

In answer to these personal threats, I beg to say that I am yet a free American citizen. I am past forty-nine years of age, was born at Roxbury, Delaware County, in this State. I began life in a lowly way, and by industry, temperance, and attention to my own business have been successful, perhaps beyond the measure of my deserts. If, as you say, I am

WALL STREET WARS.

now to be destroyed by the Knights of Labor unless I will sink my manhood, so be it. Fortunately, I have retained my early habits of industry. My friends, neighbors, and business associates know me well, and I am quite content to leave my personal record in their hands. If any of them have aught to complain of, I will be only too glad to submit to any arbitration. If such parties or any of them wish to appoint the Knights of Labor or you as their attorney, such appointment is quite agreeable to me, but until such an election is made it will naturally occur to you that any interference on your part in my personal affairs, is to say the least, quite gratuitous. Since I was nineteen years of age I have been in the habit of employing in my various enterprises large numbers of persons, probably at times as high as 50,000, distributing $3,000,000 or $4,000.000 per month to different pay rolls. It would seem a little strange that during all these years the difficulty with the Knights of Labor should be my first. Any attempt to connect me personally with the late strike on the Southwestern roads, or any responsibility therefor, is equally gratuitous, as you well know. It is true I am President of the Missouri Pacific, but when this strike occurred I was far away on the ocean and beyond the reach of telegrams. I went away relying on your promise made to me last August that there should be no strike on that road, and that if any difficulties should arise you would come frankly to me with them. Mr. Hop-

LIFE OF JAY GOULD.

kins, the Vice-President of this company, who was present and cognizant of this arrangement with you, in my absence sent you promptly, when the present strike broke out, the following telegrams:

NEW YORK, March 6th, 1886.

T. V. Powderly, Scranton, Penna.:

Mr. Hoxie telegraphs that Knights of Labor on our road have struck and refuse to allow any freight trains to run, saying they have no grievances, but are only striking because ordered to do so. If there is any grievance we would like to talk it over with you. We understood you to promise that no strike would be ordered without consultation.

A. L. HOPKINS.

PHILADELPHIA, PENNA., March 8th, 1886.

A. L. Hopkins, Secretary Missouri Pacific Railroad, New York :

Have telegraphed West for particulars. Papers say strike caused by discharge of man named Hall. Can he be reinstated pending investigation?

T. V. POWDERLY.

NEW YORK, March 8th, 1886.

T. V. Powderly:

Thanks for your messages and suggestion. Hall was employed by the Texas & Pacific, and not by us. That property is in the hands of the United States Court, and we have no control whatever over the receivers or other employees. We have car-

WALL STREET WARS. 115

ried out the agreements made last spring in every respect, and the present strike is unjust to us, and unwise for you. It is reported here that this movement is the result of Wall Street influence on the part of those short of the securities likely to be affected.   A. L. HOPKINS.

This dispatch you never answered. This correspondence places the continuance of this strike on your shoulders. You sat still and were silent after Mr. Hopkins' appeal, and allowed the strike to go on—allowed the company's property to be forcibly seized and the citizens of four States and one Territory to be deprived of their rightful railway facilities. Thus forced. the Board of Directors, prior to my return, placed the matter in Mr. Hoxie's hands by a formal resolution, and that disposition of it has never been changed. You knew this well, because you had a correspondence with him on this subject. Hence it was that when Mr. Turner, Secretary of your Order, wrote to me on the subject, I fully advised him, in my letter of March 27th, that the matter had been placed by the Board in the hands of Mr. Hoxie, and that I must refer you to him as its continuing representative. At the same time I reminded you that a standing advertisement of this company was at that moment inviting its former employees to return to their accustomed posts ; and that regardless of their being or not being members of your Order, and regardless also of their indi-

LIFE OF JAY GOULD.

vidual participation in the strike which your Order had recently inaugurated. When, in spite of all this, you desired to see me personally, I cordially met you, and, having put myself in communication with Mr. Hoxie, arranged with him for you the following, which was widely published by you at the time :

NEW YORK, March 30th, 1869.

Martin Irons, St. Louis.

Have been in conference all day, with the result that Vice-President Hoxie agrees to the following: Willing to meet a committee of our employees without discrimination, *who are actually at work in the service of the company at the time such committee is appointed, to adjudicate with them any grievance that they may have.* Have your Executive Committee order the men to return to work, and also *select a special committee from the employees* of the Missouri Pacific to wait on Mr. Hoxie to adjust any difference. Do this as quickly as possible. Board will leave for St. Louis to-morrow.

FREDERICK TURNER, *Secretary.*

Ever since then Mr. Hoxie has stood ready to receive any and all persons in the actual employ of this company as a committee or otherwise, and confer upon or arbitrate any matter of difference or complaint either between the company and themselves or between the company and its late employees, and, for that matter, between the company

WALL STREET WARS. 117

and anybody else. No such committee or individual employee has, so far as known to me, ever made any such application. In this connection it will be remembered that they left not because of any complaint whatever of this company's treatment of themselves, but only because of this company's refusal to comply with their demand that this company refuse to do what the law requires in the way of interchange of business with another company, with which some of your Order had a quarrel.

In the meantime this company has of necessity gone on to extend employment to such of those persons who recently, and without even alleged provocation, left its service, as saw fit to return. These returning employees have been very many, and in this way its rolls are already nearly, if not quite, as full as its shops and equipment, crippled by acts of violence attendant upon recent action of your Order, can employ. Mr. Hoxie advises that every such person applying to be received back has been employed, unless believed to have taken part in recent acts of violence. This company still stands ready to make good in the fullest sense its agreement as expressly set forth.

In the face of all this you notify me that unless by five o'clock I personally consent to something, precisely what I do not see, then personal consequences of a sort vaguely expressed, but not hard to understand, will at the hand of your Order be visited upon me. Let me again remind you that it

LIFE OF JAY GOULD.

is an American citizen whom you and your Order thus propose to destroy. The contest is not between your Order and me, but between your Order and the laws of the land. Your Order has already defied those laws in preventing by violence this company from operating its road. You held then that this company should not operate its road under conditions prescribed by law, but only under conditions prescribed by you. You now declare in effect that I hold my individual property and rights, not as other men hold theirs, but only at the peril of your letting loose irrevocably after five o'clock your Order upon me. If this is true of this company and of me, it is true of all other men and companies. If so, you and your secret Order are the law, and an American citizen is such only in name.

Already for weeks your Order, in your attack upon this company, has not hesitated to disable it by violence from rendering its duty to the public and from giving work and paying wages to men at least three times your own number, who, working as they were by your side, were at least deserving of your sympathy. Having pushed this violence beyond even the greatest forbearance of the public, and found in this direction cause to hesitate, you now turn upon me and propose that the wrongs you have hitherto inflicted on the public shall now culminate in an attack upon an individual.

In this, as I have said, the real issue is between you and the law of the land. It may be, before you

WALL STREET WARS. 119

are through, those laws will efficiently advise you that even I, as an individual citizen, am not beyond their care. Very respectfully,

JAY GOULD.

The following condensed report, embracing the operations of the Missouri Pacific Railway Company, and its leased, operated, and independent lines, for the year ending December 31st, 1891, is here given. It will give the reader an excellent idea of the vast scope of the system for which Mr. Gould fought so valiantly :

The average mileage of all lines operated during the year was 5,282.61 miles, an increase of 173.61 miles over the previous year. The mileage of all lines on December 31st, 1891, was 5,288.85 miles, an increase of 163.85 miles, compared with same date of previous year.

The above increase in mileage consists of the Fort Scott & Southern Railway, Fort Scott to Cornell, Kan., 27.20 miles, opened January 26th, 1891 ; the Fort Scott Belt Terminal Railway, comprising terminal and connecting tracks at Fort Scott, Kan., 3.91 miles, opened January 26th, 1891 ; Omaha Southern Railway, Union to Plattsmouth, Neb., 14.71 miles, opened September 9th, 1891 ; Houston, Central Arkansas & Northern Line, McGehee, Ark., to Riverton, La. (Ouachita River), 118.68 miles, included in system mileage January 1st, 1891 ; a net deduction of .65 miles from the system mileage of

LIFE OF JAY GOULD.

1890 was effected by correction of distances, making the aggregate increase in mileage during the year 163.85 miles.

The relations of the several properties remained practically unchanged during the year. By indenture, dated January 1st, 1891, the Kansas City & Southwestern Line, Paola, Kan., to Cecil, Mo., 48.23 miles, was leased to the Missouri Pacific Railway Company for a term of ninety-nine years, making the aggregate main line mileage of the Missouri Pacific Company 1,542.45.

The Kansas & Colorado Pacific Railway comprises 1,057.13 miles of lines in Kansas, to which has been added, since the close of the year, the Fort Scott, Wichita & Western Railway (by purchase), 309.85 miles, and the Pueblo & State Line Railroad (by lease), 151.89 miles. Additional independent lines, agregating 130.21 miles, complete the mileage of 1,649.08 miles, treated in operating accounts as branch lines of the Missouri Pacific Railway.

The St. Louis, Iron Mountain & Southern Railway, including the Little Rock and Fort Smith, Little Rock Junction, and Kansas & Arkansas Valley divisions, comprises an aggregate mileage of 1,547.22 miles.

The Houston, Central Arkansas & Northern Line, McGehee, Ark., to Riverton, La., 118.68 miles, was operated during the year as an independent property, in connection with the Iron Mountain System.

A STATEROOM ON THE ATALANTA.

WALL STREET WARS. 121

The Central Branch, Union Pacific Railroad, embraces 388.19 miles of leased railway, the net earnings of which are paid to the Union Pacific Railway Company as lessor.

The Sedalia, Warsaw & Southwestern Railway (successor to the Sedalia, Warsaw & Southern Railway), a narrow-gauge line, 43.23 miles in length, was operated as an independent line in connection with the Missouri Pacific Railway.

The aggregate gross earnings of the Missouri Pacific System for the year were $25,918,106.24, an increase of $444,522.38 over previous year. The earnings from freight traffic were $18,224,486,30, an increase of $323,209.05 ; the earnings from passenger traffic were $5,070,047.60, a decrease of $49,734.82 ; the earnings from mail, express, and miscellaneous sources were $2,623,572.25, an increase of $171,048.15.

The gross earnings, operating expenses, and net earnings of the several properties, separately, were :

	Gross Earnings.	Operating Expenses.	Net Earnings	Increase Net Earnings
The Missouri Pacific Ry and branches	$13,221,097 52	$9,920,148 19	$3,300,949 33	$19,126 24
St. Louis, Iron Mountain & So. Ry.,	11,581,930 72	7,704,897 38	3,877,033 34	*12,453 84
Houston, Central Arkansas and Northern Line,	183,629 32	186,085 49	*2,456 17	*11,473 27
Central Branch Union Pacific R R	894,160 28	648,086 92	246,073 36	47,230 52
Sedalia, Warsaw & Southwestern Ry.,	37,288 40	36,138 64	1,149 76	3,687 68
Total	$25,918,106 24	18,495,356 62	$7,422,749 62	$46,117 33

The officers and directors of The Missouri Pacific

* Deficit or Decrease,

8

LIFE OF JAY GOULD.

Railway Company, at the time of the above report, were:

GENERAL OFFICERS.—Jay Gould, President, New York; S. H. H. Clark, First Vice-President and General Manager, St. Louis; George J. Gould, Second Vice-President, New York; George C. Smith, Assistant General Manager, St. Louis; A. H. Calef, Secretary and Treasurer, New York; Guy Phillips, Second Assistant Secretary, New York; D. S. H. Smith, Local Treasurer, St. Louis; C. G. Warner, General Auditor, St. Louis; Alexander G. Cochran, General Solicitor, St. Louis; C. A. Parker, Freight Traffic Manager, St. Louis; H. C. Townsend, General Passenger and Ticket Agent, St. Louis; James W. Way, Chief Engineer, St. Louis; A. W. Dickinson and R. E. Ricker, General Superintendents, St. Louis.

DIRECTORS.—Jay Gould, New York; Sidney Dillon, New York; Samuel Sloan, New York; Russell Sage, New York; John P. Munn, New York; Thomas T. Eckert, New York; A. L. Hopkins, New York; George J. Gould, New York; John G. Moore, New York; D. D. Parmly, New York; Edwin Gould, New York; C. S. Greeley, St. Louis; S. H. H. Clark, St. Louis.

EXECUTIVE COMMITTEE.—Jay Gould, Sidney Dillon, Russell Sage, Thomas T. Eckert, George J. Gould, Samuel Sloan, D. D. Parmly, A. L. Hopkins.

EXPENSE COMMITTEE.—Jay Gould, *ex-officio;* Russell Sage, George J. Gould, A. L. Hopkins, Edwin Gould.

CHAPTER VI.

LYNDHURST AND THE "ATALANTA."

MR. GOULD'S house on the Hudson above Irvington is called "Lyndhurst." It was named so on account of the enormous linden trees which adorn the place, the largest of which is shown in one of the illustrations of this book. It is a stone structure of Elizabethan architecture, situated on a high green bluff overlooking the river and surrounded with a well-kept park. The entrance to the park is about a mile from Irvington, and is marked by two tall granite posts. A stone porter's lodge is by the gate. Passing into the grounds one sees on every side the marks of the gardener's care and the skill of the landscape gardener. A large force of men work under the head-keeper of Lyndhurst, who is an intelligent German of great ability in his profession. These employees are remarkably well acquainted with the routine of work, for Mr. Gould paid them so well it became almost a labor of love for them to follow out his wishes to the letter. Every employee at Lyndhurst rejoices in a salary far above the compensation usually given in similar positions. There are not too many trees, only enough, and they are so grouped that while

LIFE OF JAY GOULD.

they make the house at the end of the driveway seem retired, they yet afford vistas through which glimpses can be caught of the stone towers and gables of the mansion.

Beyond the limits of the park lie fruitful and well-cultivated farm lands and orchards, belonging to the Gould estate. One opening among the trees shows a gray tower and slender minarets. These mark the dog kennels. The driveway is broad and smooth, and winds over the undulating surface of the park toward the house. Some of the trees through which it runs are old oaks, which have not been interfered with in the general plan of the grounds, but have been brought into stronger effect by the arrangement of the newer trees and the shrubbery. The road descends a little before it reaches the house and passes through a grove of evergreens. As one comes in out of the dark grove, the beautiful house bursts at once on the sight of the visitor. Trim lawns surround it, and beyond it the view is closed by the broad Hudson and the Palisades beyond. This beautiful view is given in one of the illustrations.

The central tower of the house rises high, bearing turrets at each of its four corners. The house is built of graystone, which is shot with bluish tints. It covers a large area, and its many parts are grouped together so as to give an appearance which is at once beautiful and imposing. There are multitudes of graceful angles, mullioned windows,

LYNDHURST AND THE "ATALANTA." 125

turrets, and spires all in harmony, and forming a picture delightful to look upon. Here and there are verandas with great windows opening upon them, and now and then a stone balcony high up. The great double doors of the main entrance are of stone even up to the sashes of the diamond-paned windows at their top.

Inside the house there is a great hall in the centre. On the right from the main entrance in the dining-room and on the left a large drawing-room. Everywhere are works of art, statuary, and paintings. The house has a multitude of rooms in it and is built on a generous plan throughout. It is an ideal country home. Every window commands a beautiful view, but those on the west front have the finest. The Hudson can be seen for miles to the south and north. The Palisades are seen in a magnificent sweep across the river, and the town of Nyack looks like a toy city on the further shore of the river. To the north are the mountains of the Highlands. The lawn at the west of the house slopes down to the edge of the bluff. Then there is a steep descent to the railroad track, which is hidden from view by thickly-planted trees and shrubs growing on the declivity. A path leads down to a bridge over the track, and a short distance on the other side brings one to the little wharf and boat-house. It was off this wharf that the "Atalanta" used to lie when Mr. Gould was at Lyndhurst.

126 *LIFE OF JAY GOULD.*

The library in the house contains a splendid collection of books, which Mr. Gould bought from a man who had spent many years and much money in collecting them in all the markets of the world. Mr. Gould's stables, which are at some distance from the house, contain some good carriage and saddle horses. On the farm are herds of cattle of excellent breeds, in which Mr. Gould took great interest. He was always interested in the farm, and was well informed regarding the breeding of fancy cattle. Not far from the house are the extensive greenhouses, including a large grapery. The larger portion of the greenhouses is filled with the rarest ferns, palms, and flowering plants. Mr. Gould was a botanist of unusual attainments, and liked nothing better than to walk through his greenhouses with a friend, and talk on that subject. He was especially fond of orchids, of which he had probably the largest and finest collection in the country, embracing as it did over 400 varieties. He made a special study of this peculiar plant, and spent large sums of money in obtaining rare specimens.

The greenhouses cover about three acres. One building is an eighth of a mile long. In short, the country seat at Irvington was perfectly equipped in every way. He bought it from the widow of a prosperous New York merchant, from whom he had rented the place for several summers, and at once began most extensive alterations in the grounds. The actual assessed value of Lyndhurst was greatly

LYNDHURST AND THE "ATALANTA." 127

below its actual worth to its owner. It is doubtful if any offer of money would have bought this charming place from Mr. Gould.

In 1883 Mr. Gould had built at Cramps' shipyards in Philadelphia, the big steam yacht " Atalanta," and for several years he was well known in yachting circles. He was elected a member of the Eastern and Larchmont Yacht clubs, and applied for membership in the New York Yacht Club. The opposition to his name which was developed in the club was so strong, however, that his friends withdrew his name. This furnished a sensation at the time. George J. Gould, who had for some time taken an active interest in yachting, and was a member of the club, at once resigned. Mr. Gould at one time had an idea of making a cruise around the world in the " Atalanta," but abandoned it.

Soon after the launching of the " Atalanta," Mr. Gould and others formed the American Steam Yacht Club. The " Atalanta " developed remarkable speed, and is to-day the fastest large steam yacht afloat. Mr. Gould had her built because he felt his health to be failing, and thought yachting would be beneficial to him. He would often feel that he must have absolute rest for a few days. This he could not have as long as he was on dry land, although he tried many ingenious schemes to outwit the business men and reporters, who were always after him. Until within the last two years he spent much time on board of her. She was used princi-

128 *LIFE OF JAY GOULD.*

pally as a means of transportation between Lynd-hurst, his home on the Hudson, and the city, though he made several extended cruises in her. It was not often that Mr. Gould would allow the " Atalanta " to be raced, but on the occasions when he did per-mit this she made records.

Mr. Gould presented to the Larchmont Club a cup called the Gould Cup, which is raced for every year. He also contributed largely to the Interna-tional Challenge Cup, offered by the American Yacht Club for competition by steam yachts of different nations. He was always anxious to see a challenge for this cup, but so far no nation has challenged, owing to the great superiority in point of speed of the American steam yachts.

Mr. Gould seldom entertained people on board the " Atalanta," but when he did entertain, his hos-pitality was perfect. He had the happy faculty of making his guests feel that the yacht was theirs and he himself was a guest on board. There was an excellently well-selected library on the yacht, and the craft was fitted throughout with quiet and sub-stantial elegance.

The " Atalanta " is 243 feet long, $26\frac{1}{2}$ feet beam, and $15\frac{1}{2}$ feet deep. She is built of iron. In June of 1886 she ran over the 85-knot course of the American Yacht Club, from Milton Point to New London, in 4 hours 34 minutes and 57 seconds.

The views of the stern and interior of this re-markable steam yacht, which are elsewhere in this

LYNDHURST AND THE "ATALANTA." 129

book, give an excellent idea of the substantial elegance of the craft and its comfortable fittings.

At the present writing the "Atalanta" is out of commission and is entirely dismantled. Mr. George Gould, who is fond of yachting, will probably re-commission and appoint her.

As the recognized head of the Gould family since Jay Gould's death, Mr. George Gould's history is a matter of great interest to the public. He distinctly resembles his father and yet is very unlike him. Before he was twenty years old he was intrusted with his father's business, and was notably a quiet youth with a dark, bright eye, who was a close observer.

When he reached his twenty-first birthday his father called him into his private office, gave him a power of attorney which would have enabled him to control Mr. Gould's entire property, and also furnished him with the combinations for his private safes and deposit vaults. When Edwin Gould was twenty-one years of age Mr. Gould made the same birthday present, excepting that the power of attorney was a joint one, the survivor in the case of the death of either one retaining it, and he also gave this second son the combinations to his safe. It was his intention to go through that impressive formality upon the twenty-first birthday of each one of his sons, and this ceremony of itself awakened a sense of responsibility in the young men which has **been valuable and which was precisely what Mr.**

130   *LIFE OF JAY GOULD.*

Gould desired to develop.   Moreover, he knew that
these instruments would make it impossible for any
disaster to come to his property in case he became
disabled or suddenly died.   " My sons are good
business men," **Mr. Gould** frequently said.

For a good while George Gould was only his
father's son, and there were advantages and dis-
advantages in that.   After awhile he began to be
known as himself.   Evidently he knew what was
going on.   The boy insensibly became a man, and
a man of affairs.   His father took him into his deepest confidence, and rejoiced in his ability, industry,
faithfulness, and constant attention to duty.   The
responsibilities that rest upon him are very great,
and he is made grave beyond his years.   He is incessantly consulted, not as a matter of form, but of
fact.   He must pass upon a thousand things every
day, but he likes it.   The joy of work that all strong
men have felt is upon him.   He has no thought of
rest until he has earned it.   He inherits his father's
domestic tranquillity, and home with wife and children gives him repose and delight.   He is early,
not late, at his office, and lunches often on a glass
of milk and piece of pumpkin pie.   He does not
rush eagerly into conversation, but waits, and when
the point comes, discusses it if it is business.   He
says " Yes " cordially and " No " softly, but it is final.
He shakes his head very slightly, but it is enough.
He extends his hand heartily, and his " I am glad to
see you " has a winning tone of sincerity.   When

LYNDHURST AND THE "ATALANTA" 131

he says "Take a seat," it is an invitation; his "Not to-day" or "In a few minutes" mean exactly one thing or another. A slip of paper is handed him with initials and figures—meaning millions, perhaps—and with a glance and then a few short words that affair is settled.

There is a card—and "show him in"—or a negative gesture, or "not now," and the caller comes or goes. There is a letter to write; he goes to the desk or table most convenient, and is absorbed until the letter is written and directed. He has not taken the room and desk that were his father's, but remains where he has for years been accustomed to pass his working hours. He cannot, of course, be seen by all comers, for all his time would be taken if he consented to general conversation. The rooms where the business of the Gould properties is transacted are reached by those known to have something to say, while strangers are not regarded with favor. The value of time is seen in every face.

There are maps of the Gould system of railways, and the Manhattan Elevated Road system on the walls, but the Western Union Telegraph system is rather extensive to be mapped, showing all the lines, so it is represented in book diagrams. It is in the Western Union Telegraph building, at 195 Broadway, that the Gould offices are located, and Mr. George Gould's room has not an article of furniture in it or anything visible meant for display or adornment. When examined, it is found

LIFE OF JAY GOULD.

to be furnished with a view to its utilities, not as a curiosity-shop and a wonder. Evidently, not more than two or three persons are expected at one time. If the visitors to be accommodated are more, there are other apartments. Mr. Gould sits with his back to a south window, his rolling desk before him. At his right is a door opening into the other offices where bookkeeping is attended to, and the roar of Broadway becomes more distinct. In front is another door leading into a narrow corridor, where there are two young men, one on either side of the door, the private secretary and his stenographer, ever ready for service. There is a young man who attends to the telephone near by and takes down in short-hand the interview for Mr. Gould's examination later, that the precise words may be brought to his attention. At Mr. Gould's left is a "ticker" constantly picking and clicking, telling of important happenings about as fast as they occur. There are ivory buttons on a key-board that summon with a touch the man who is wanted. There is a room of swinging speaking tubes. Such detail would not be of the least interest, except in the extreme suggestiveness of such an array of appliances.

Mrs. George Gould is one of the most lovely and lovable members of the family. She became acquainted with her husband in a somewhat unusual and romantic manner.

Brooklyn, which is generally termed the City of

LYNDHURST AND THE "ATALANTA." 133

Churches, deserves also to be called the home of amateur actors. Every young lady in that city thinks she can act; every young man knows he can. The events of the year in that remarkable town are not only the regularly ordained legal holidays—the Thanksgiving, Christmas, or Fourth of July celebrations that are looked forward to in other quarters of the country. The performances of the Amaranth, Kemble, and Gilbert amateur societies are important social events in the city. To be elected to these organizations means social recognition ; to perform in them, promises local fame.

Among the most frequent patrons of the performances of these dramatic societies a few years ago was a young and very beautiful girl, who always came with her mother, sat near the stage, and enjoyed the acting in a keen, thorough, undemonstrative way. The chief players of the club were Robert Hilliard, who was considered very promising in sentiment, and Frank David, who was regarded with great esteem in comedy.

"Here," said Hilliard, one day when they were meditating over a play for the regular monthly performance, "we want some pretty girls to dress up the stage. It's all very well for you and me to do the acting, but we want some pretty girls."

"All right," said the comedian, "I know one, and I'll ask her."

"Who's that?" asked the romantic amateur.

"Why, it's Miss Edith Kingdon. She generally sits in front."

134   *LIFE OF JAY GOULD.*

"What!" cried Hilliard; "that glorious, dark-eyed young lady?"

"The very one."

The comedian's errand was rewarded with success only after some difficulty. Miss Kingdon protested that she did not know anything about the stage, that she was entirely ignorant of acting, and that she would be dreadfully frightened to stand up before an audience. But Mr. David finally persuaded her to make the attempt, and after much hesitation she became an active member of the Sclitery Union. Joining the club merely in a capacity similar to that of the supernumerary of the professional stage, she speedily proved her ability to be trusted with a speaking part.

Before the winter was over her talent was so manifest that she was elected by unanimous request to the aristocratic Amaranth. In this new and more advantageous field her talents quickly developed, and she was chosen for leading parts in almost all the performances. Her fame was widespread. It presently reached the ears of a professional manager. There was a tremendous sensation in Brooklyn when it was known that the beautiful and brilliant Edith Kingdon had decided to quit the amateur stage and join the ranks of the profession.

Miss Kingdon's first appearance on the stage was really her first step toward Hymen's altar. It was on Thursday night, October 16th, 1884. The play was "A Wooden Spoon," in which she performed

LYNDHURST AND THE "ATALANTA." 135

the character of Mysia Jessamy. The audience
examined the new-comer critically, but beyond com-
plimenting her extraordinary beauty, made no comment on her accession to the company. That piece
had a short run, unmarked by any particular event.
It was followed on November 26th by the production of one of the greatest successes of Daly's
Theatre. "Love on Crutches" was not only delightful in itself, but, in the character of Mrs. Mar-
gery Gwynn, it afforded a chance for the talent as
well as the beauty of Miss Edith Kingdon.

As the charming young widow of this comedy,
the new actress made a phenomenal hit. Always a
modest, unassuming young woman, she was quite
unconscious of the success she had achieved, and
after the close of the second act she hurried down-
stairs to her dressing-room to prepare for the next
scene. The applause of the audience was tumultu-
ous and long continued. In response to its bidding
Miss Ada Rehan and Mr. John Drew came out and
bowed. They were followed at a later interval by
Mrs. Gilbert, Mr. Lewis, Mr. Skinner, and the other
prominent members of the company. The applause
still continuing undiminished, the entire company,
with the exception of one member came out. Then
Mr. Daly, the manager, made his appearance before
the curtain, and after him Miss Rehan and Mr.
Drew once more emerged. Then the audience,
believing that the young widow was deliberately
kept in the background, broke out into a small riot,

136 *LIFE OF JAY GOULD.*

and cries of "Kingdon! Kingdon!" rang through the house. The young actress was hastily sent for, but in response to the entreaties of the stage manager she declared her inability to come out, inasmuch as she was at that moment in a state of transition between one gown and another.

"Never mind that," he whispered anxiously through the keyhole. "You can throw a shawl over your shoulders. You must go out or there will be a riot."

Thus adjured, Miss Kingdon seized a lace wrap, drew it over her shoulders, and ran up-stairs. In her dishabille it was out of the question for her to appear before the audience. So she pulled an edge of the curtain aside, peeped out smilingly at the audience, and blushingly nodded her thanks. Jay Gould and his son George sat in the proscenium box, which they always occupied at Daly's on first nights. George Gould caught the twinkle of the pretty actress's eye, and fell hopelessly in love. Next day the critics and public alike raved over the talent and beauty of Edith Kingdon in the new comedy. But the sentiment she had aroused in the bosom of the young man was worth much more to her than the applause of a nation. It meant a life of happiness and the union with a noble young man of fortune and position.

The business manager of Daly's was an old gentleman who had more enemies and good qualities than almost any other man in the profession. John

EDDIE GOULD.

LYNDHURST AND THE "ATALANTA." 139

Duff was the stern guardian of a theatre from which everybody wanted, and few obtained, privileges. A very honest and kindly old gentleman at heart, Mr. Duff preserved an exterior of continual menace to dudes, young men who annoy actresses at the stage door, and the army of people who wished to pass the gate-keeper without a preliminary interview at the box office.

George Gould was on friendly terms with the old business manager, and he made the request for an introduction without hesitation.

"Look here," said John Duff, slowly, "Miss Kingdon is a lady, and so long as I have anything to say in the matter she must be treated with respect. If you want to meet her under those conditions I guess it can be managed."

Mr. Gould hastened to reassure the manager, and an introduction was effected. The courtship was swift and silent. One morning the matchmaking mammas of America were horrified to learn that the wealthiest young man in the country was married to an actress. The Ward McAllister legions shook their heads ruefully and declared that the youthful millionaire should have secured his social position by marrying into one of the old families. But George Gould married the girl he loved, and nobody has ever been able to say that Edith Kingdon did not make a wife as good as she is beautiful, and few homes in the great metropolis or elsewhere will be found to be as happy as that of Mr. George J. Gould, with a young woman, beautiful in character and spirit, as well as feature, enshrined as wife and mother. It is where George Gould loves to be, and who will dare to say that a multi-millionaire may not be happy.

CHAPTER VII:

ILLNESS AND DEATH.

AS we have seen, Mr. Gould was never robust. He was slender and physically frail. He did not lack courage, for he confronted enemies often without flinching, and his father refused to surrender or consent to be humiliated by an armed mob. Mr. Gould was several times assailed, but not seriously harmed or subjected to intimidation. He did not dissipate his vitality with any sort of extravagance, but reserved his energies for his occupation. He was a man of intense mental activity. As an observer he was unrivalled in discovering and developing capacities for business. This was remarkable all along the lines of his railroads. His activity in the promotion of the coal trade, when he was on the Erie road, was an incident of his habit of realizing upon the natural resources. When in the mountains of Colorado, in his last years, wan and feeble, he was still making discoveries of the riches of that mountainous region, and pointing out casually where and how there were fortunes to be gained. His long-headed calculations, so obscure to others and so clear to himself, were exacting. His perceptions were singularly acute, and he had very

LIFE OF JAY GOULD.

strongly the gift of intuition, but as his interests grew his cares increased, so that at last it was revealed to him that he had forgotten to give himself consideration. Then he made the seeking of health a part of his business. He indulged his taste for books and flowers. His library and his conservatory became favorite objects. His home on the Hudson he "developed," to use his favorite word, as he did all his properties, and it became a comfort to him. So did his yacht, which was staunch and swift. He enjoyed his trips on the "Atalanta," from Lyndhurst to the great city, and going to and fro became a recreation and delight instead of a weariness. He gave himself all the chances he could to recuperate, but the strain had been too long and costly, and he could not rebuild himself. He gave more and more attention to the education of his sons to assume great responsibilities. He alone could be the teacher. How grateful he was for the response his sons gave to his affection and confidence, he has abundantly testified. The eldest son naturally was first in the training, and for years has been the master of his affairs. The young Goulds are not mere office men. They have traveled extensively. They are learned in their knowledge of men. Mr. George Gould is very fond of out-door life, rejoices in wholesome exercise and is sturdy and tenacious. With those nigh him he is gracious and winning with a manner hearty and kind, but his conscious responsibility and necessary reserve soften

ILLNESS AND DEATH. 143

the expression of his healthy humor. He has treasured up from his father serious lessons that he guards more sacredly that the many millions of his inheritance. There is no pomp about him. He goes right to the mark. Mr. Edwin Gould is a public-spirited citizen and at once strong and genial, something of an athlete, though not a devotee of athletics quiet and exceedingly well-informed. Mr. Howard Gould has had for several years the pleasure of his father's society in journeys, and in this companionship had rare advantages. He is a studious young man, who takes long walks and thinks and has grave purposes in life.

The devotion of the sons to the memory of their father, their absolute faith in him, and confiding love for him can be exceeded only by the like sensibilities of the daughters. As his strength failed him Mr. Jay Gould cared for himself with the same perseverance and particularity that he had employed in affairs of vast importance. Moved by the violation of the grave of Alexander Stewart, he built a beautiful tomb that would stand a siege of dynamiters. Long after he had retired from the street, there were stories associating him with every movement. The accusations that he is influencing public business for his own purposes have not been stayed even since his death; and there has even been published a cartoon of his " skeleton hand," in an association so absurd that the dismal assault becomes ghastly, and the blow that was meant is of no force

144   *LIFE OF JAY GOULD.*

save as it strikes backward and reaches those who would deliver it.   Mr. Gould was accustomed to the vicissitudes of Wall Street life and romance, and was reticent as to the state of his health and the use that could be made in the market of his bodily infirmities.   In this he was strictly on the defensive. The stories that he was dying were so often circulated that they were worn out.   At last when Mr. Gould really was ill there were few who believed the report had foundation.   The weakness that declared itself incurable and progressed steadily was first in the throat and then on the lungs.   Mr. Gould has been accused of an elaborate game of deception as to his fatal illness long after he was perfectly familiar with the speedy coming of the inevitable end; but he was like others with lung disease.   However hopeless the case of the consumptive he hopes on.   Mr. Gould had that ordinary weakness of humanity.   He was at his office in the Western Union Telegraph building repeatedly in the month before his death, and his last visit, when he was hopeful and alert, was but a week before his death.   Taking a ride in Central Park he was chilled and caught a cold, had hemorrhages, and died with his children by his bedside. Soon after midnight the day of his death it became certain the end was approaching.   The callers were told Mr. Gould was dying.   Dr. Munn held his hand.   The Rev. John R. Paxton, whose church the family attended, gave the following touching account of his last moments:

ILLNESS AND DEATH. 145

"Mr. Gould had been unconscious for a number of hours, but as the end approached consciousness returned. He opened his eyes and glanced around the room in which his family were gathered, a look of recognition lighting up his face as his eyes fell upon each of them. They came close to his bedside, and then in a perfectly distinct voice he spoke to each of his children in turn a word of love and farewell. Vitality enough for this was vouchsafed him, but when he had spoken the last word to his last child, he relapsed at once into unconsciousness, and in a few minutes entered into eternal rest."

An old friend of the family said of Mr. Gould's decline in health and death:

"My impression is that Mr. Gould's death was due mainly to exhaustion of his vitality, the sapping of which has been going on slowly for several years. This was complicated no doubt with his old stomach trouble and by an affection of the throat with which he has suffered for several years. Probably the latter trouble gave rise to the report that his disease was pulmonary consumption.

"The depletion of Mr. Gould's vitality dates back to a time previous to his wife's death in January, 1888. She then used to say that her husband suffered greatly from neuralgic headaches and profound fatigues, and on one occasion I found that she had spent a sleepless night in consequence of one of his attacks. The summer before his wife's death he took her to Europe on his yacht. Upon their return

146 *LIFE OF JAY GOULD.*

he put the yacht out of commission and said that what both he and his wife needed was not travel but rest. Neither looked the better for the voyage.

"After his wife's death, Mr. Gould's loss of strength was more rapid. His attacks of headache and nervous prostration were more frequent than before, and he rallied with greater difficulty and less completeness. He had a powerful will, and concealed his sufferings from his family to a great extent, so that to them these attacks were only tired spells. Although I could see that he was not strong there was nothing particular in his condition to note, except that he was pale and ate little.

"On the evening before Thanksgiving I was at his house and found that he had what his oldest daughter described as a return of his old fatigue. No one was alarmed. As late as yesterday morning one of his physicians said there was nothing to warrant a belief that Mr. Gould would not recover. His last three days were entirely free from suffering, and his conversation with his family in his conscious period before his death was most touching and beautiful."

His last appearance in public was at the wedding of his second son, Edwin, to Miss Sarah Cantine Shrady, daughter of Dr. George F. Shrady. This was on October 26th. Mr. Gould then appeared in good health, and none of the guests suspected that he was suffering from anything worse than nervous dyspepsia.

ILLNESS AND DEATH.

No others than the sons and daughters of Mr. Gould were present when he died except Dr. Munn and two old servants. In the street it was evident to all passers-by that something was happening within the big brownstone house on the corner. The curtains, which had been raised all over the house about 7 o'clock, were suddenly lowered shortly after 9.

People stopped in small groups on the opposite side of the street and watched the front door. About half-past 9 o'clock a messenger came out with a handful of telegrams. His appearance was the first announcement of Mr. Gould's death.

There had been many callers during the morning. They included bankers and railroad officials. A number of ladies were admitted to the house. These visitors stayed only a few moments. At half-past 9 the curiosity of the crowd reached such a point that several ascended the steps and rang the bell.

"Mr. Gould is dead," said the attendant.

It was at first the purpose of Mr. Gould's family that his funeral should be public, but they had hardly realized the universal interest in him, and it soon became evident that the number of those who would attend out of curiosity would be overwhelming and unmanageable. The cranks appeared on the scene, and the services were held privately as possible. Of this the *Sun* says : "Mr. Gould's face was rather waxy in color, but full in the cheeks. His beard had been trimmed with great care, and the snowy shirt bosom and black broadcloth coat contrasted

148   *LIFE OF JAY GOULD.*

with the pallor of the face. The fullness of the coat disguised the extreme slightness of the body. The arms were crossed on the chest, the right hand resting over the heart.

"The flowers were also placed in this room. The most beautiful was a floral cross which Miss Helen Gould had ordered. It was composed of pink orchids tied with a silk ribbon, and was placed on top of the coffin. Next to it was a bunch of bride roses from Howard Gould. A five-foot broken column of white roses, crowned by violets, with the word 'Father' in violets at the base, stood at the head of the coffin on a table. It was from George Gould. Miss Annie Gould sent a bunch of white orchids; Edwin Gould a wreath of lilies of the valley, bride roses, and orchids; Frank Gould a bunch of lilies of the valley and orchids, and George Gould's children an enormous pillow of orchids, roses, lilies of the valley, and violets, with the word 'Grandpa' in the centre. This rested on the floor beneath the coffin.

"A handsome wreath of lilies of the valley, orchids, and bride roses was received from Mrs. Hall. Mrs. Herbert sent a bunch of lilies of the valley and roses. Gen. Thomas Eckert sent a wreath of orchids and roses. Mrs. Dillon Brown sent a bunch of lilies of the valley and orchids. J. B. Hueston sent a full-rigged ship made of lilies of the valley, roses and violets, with two flags flying and this inscription in violets, 'The Voyage Ended —Safe in Port.' The ship was placed on a gilt

ILLNESS AND DEATH.

cabinet in the northeast corner, and the other pieces were disposed about the room. A large number of persons had been expected, and arrangements had been made accordingly. Many camp chairs had been piled up in the hall, the second drawing-room, and the dining-room.

"Although the services were not to begin until 4 o'clock, the friends began to come before 3. After passing the policemen at the entrance and Dr. Munn, four detectives from Police Headquarters were encountered. Detectives stood in the vestibule, in the inner hall, and near the dining-room. As the guests were admitted they were shown through the hall to the drawing-room. There they formed in line and passed by the coffin slowly, so that each could get a view of the body, and then passed into the second drawing-room or through the latter to the hall or dining-room. Three ushers found seats for them. None of the family was visible. George Gould had been down earlier in the day and had received some callers, but he retired before the first of the funeral guests arrived. He and the other members of the immediate family, Abraham Gould, Mrs. Northrup, and Mrs. Palen, and their children, were gathered in the hall of the second story, where they could hear the music and prayers without being seen by those below. Some remoter relatives and their friends sat in the rear of the second drawing-room. The dining-room was filled first, and here the directors of the Union Pacific, the Manhattan Elevated,

LIFE OF JAY GOULD.

and the Missouri Pacific railroads, and the Western Union Telegraph Company were seated.

"The shades were drawn in all the rooms and the electric lights were turned on. At half-past 3 o'clock the second drawing-room, the dining-room, and the hall were filled. Everybody sat silent during the half-hour that elapsed before the services began. The only man who spoke at all, and he confined himself to whispers, was Russell Sage. Except the coffin, the object that attracted the most attention was the oil portrait of Jay Gould which hung against the rear wall of the dining-room. All in that room and many in the hall could see it, and their eyes were turned toward it a large part of the time. It had been painted before Mr. Gould's illness, and looked utterly unlike the face in the coffin. Instead of the expression of peace and indifference which marked the latter there shone out from the countenance of the portrait a look of triumph. The face of the dead man was commonplace beside that in the gilt frame, and the attraction of the latter was felt by all.

"It was five minutes after 4 when the Rev. Dr. Paxton, Chancellor McCracken, and the Rev. Dr. Roderick Terry appeared at the entrance to the second drawing-room and sat down in the hall. The choir of Dr. Paxton's church began the services with the anthem, 'There is a Band Immortal.' Dr. Paxton followed with this prayer:

"Oh! eloquent, just, and mighty Death, whom none can outwit, thou takest all in thy toils. Thee

ILLNESS AND DEATH. 151

none can convince. Thou persuadest. Thee none can overthrow. Thou subduest. Mighty Death! We bless God for our Christian faith, in which Jesus Christ hath abolished death. We bless Thee that He plucked the stain from sin, that He robbed the grave of its victory. We bless our Heavenly Father for His Son, our Lord Jesus Christ; for our knowledge that the grave is not a dungeon, but a door opening into another world and a new and higher life. We bless Thee that the grave is not a terminus, the final resting place, the be-all and end-all of man, but that it is only the stopping place, an inn, where we humble travelers sleep the long, sweet sleep, on the way to our New Jerusalem. May the Divine Spirit be present with us in these sad, solemn services, and may the light of the resurrection morn shine into this darkened and bereaved house; and may comfort, that with which God comforteth His own, touch with heavenly and hopeful grace the hearts of our friends here, wounded, sore, and bleeding still for the loss of him they loved so well. Amen."

Dr. Paxton then read the lessons of the Presbyterian burial service, beginning, "I am the resurrection and the life." When he had finished the choir sang, "Lead, Kindly Light." Dr. Terry read the second lesson, and was followed by Chancellor Mc-Cracken in an extemporaneous prayer, in which he invoked the Divine care for the children who had early in life been deprived of both father and mother. The Chancellor ended with the Lord's Prayer. The choir then sang, "Nearer, my God, to Thee."

152   *LIFE OF JAY GOULD.*

Dr. Paxton announced that the funeral services would be concluded next day at the grave, where Chancellor McCracken read the burial service. He said that the body would be taken to Woodlawn at noon, and that the interment would be at the convenience of the family. He delivered the benediction, and announced that all who wished could take a look at the face of the dead man before leaving.

At 10.30 the following morning the funeral cortége left the Gould mansion.

As the hearse moved away Mr. and Mrs. George Gould emerged from the house. With them were Miss Helen Gould and Harold Gould. These four entered the first carriage. They were followed by Edwin Gould and his wife, Howard and Annie Gould, who took seats in the second carriage. The third carriage was occupied by Abram Gould, the dead financier's brother, and Frank Gould.

Mrs. Northrop, of Camden, and her daughter entered the next carriage, followed by Mrs. Palen, of Germantown, and Mrs. Northrop's two sons, who occupied the fifth conveyance. The remaining carriages—there were nine in all—were occupied by near friends of the family and a few of Mr. Gould's business associates. After all the carriages had been filled Chancellor McCracken and Rev. Dr. Terry drove up to the head of the line and took a place in front of the hearse. In this order the procession left the house and proceeded up Fifth Avenue.

ILLNESS AND DEATH. 153

As early as 9 o'clock a few stragglers entered Woodlawn Cemetery and made their way toward the Gould mausoleum. A half-dozen workmen were at the tomb. They had erected small open front tents on either side of the entrance of the tomb. Within, there was three dozen camp chairs. The floral tributes, which had been sent up from the city on an early train, were arranged about the open door.

At the right of the entrance, resting on supports, was the polished oak box in which the coffin was to be placed. This box was lined with zinc. Near by stood a little stove, such as plumbers carry, on which was simmering the metal which was to seal the lid of the box after the coffin had been placed in it.

A solitary mounted policeman arrived at 10.30 o'clock. Two cemetery policemen kept the people at a distance of 50 feet.

At 12.10 o'clock the solemn toll of the bell at the chapel at the Jerome Avenue entrance was heard and the hearse, followed by a line of carriages, entered the cemetery. Ten minutes later the hearse stopped in front of the pathway that led to the tomb. Four men lifted the coffin out, and carrying it to the tents, placed it in the box.

Out of the first carriages stepped George J. Gould, and on his arm rested Miss Helen Gould. He was very pale, but walked with a firm step. Miss Gould wore a heavy black veil that concealed her features.

154 LIFE OF JAY GOULD.

They were followed by Edwin Gould and his young wife, Frank Gould escorting Miss Anna Gould, Howard Gould with Mrs. George Gould, Mr. Abraham Gould, Mrs. Taylor, Mrs. Northrop, and the two Misses Northrop and Chancellor MacCracken and others.

As soon as the casket reached the entrance of the tomb it was placed in the oak case with the lead lining, and then as soon as the family and immediate relatives had grouped themselves within the tent, Chancellor MacCracken stepped to the head of the casket and, all heads being bared, he read the committal service of the Episcopal Church.

The service was concluded with a simple invocation for " Divine strength for the afflicted ones."

The case was rolled into a crypt opposite that of Mr. Gould's wife, and then the family entered. As they grouped themselves around the mouth of the crypt no word was uttered, and the workmen quickly placed the slab in position.

There was the keenest interest all over the country, and in all the money centres of the world, in the question what the effect of Mr. Gould's death would be upon his properties. This curiosity was the more intelligent and interesting, because the nature of the circumstances was so unusual. It was not so much on the earth as in the air. It reminded one of the words of Dr. Johnson, in describing the value of Mrs. Thrall's Brewery. " We are not," said he, " here to sell a few tubs and barrels, but the

MR. HOWARD GOULD.

ILLNESS AND DEATH. 157

potentiality of wealth beyond the means of avarice." The wisdom with which Mr. Gould had disposed of his estate was popularly recognized. There was the railroad system in the corner of the country where there is to be the greatest growth. The rapid transit system in New York, already over-tasked, and the stock possessing solid value, almost up to the mark that Mr. Cyrus W. Field laid out for it prematurely, as it proved unfortunately for him and the enormous Western Union Telegraph Company.

Mr. Gould has been charged with trying to un-load his Western Union stock upon the Government, but his policy and his pride was to hold it. He preferred the Western Union to all other invest-ments.

There is the vindication since his death of his financial genius and the wisdom of his use for capital and provision for its preservation in the increased market value of all his important stocks, the aggre-gate advance amounting to several millions of dollars.

Mr. Gould's physician "the Doctor of Million-aires," had for some years a great deal of celebrity in that character, and was advertised extensively when the story was published everywhere that Mr. Gould was very ill at a business meeting of the Board of the Missouri Pacific, and was nervously agitated over a proposition made by Mr. Russell Sage. January 3d, 1892, the New York *Tribune* satisfied the public curiosity in a sketch of "the

158   *LIFE OF JAY GOULD.*

Man who Cares for Jay Gould's Health," and
"how Dr. Munn reached Russell Sage after
the recent dynamite explosion." The colors are
not spared and the likeness is vividly drawn.

When Jay Gould recently went into hysterics
over the opposition of Russell Sage to the passing
of the Missouri Pacific dividend, one of the members of the Board who was present was instant in
attendance on Mr. Gould, and quickly doctored him
until his nerves were quieted and he was restored
to his normal condition of iciness. When a lunatic
note-broker recently attempted to take the life of
Mr. Sage by blowing him up in his offices in the
Arcade Building, Mr. Gould was not present. He
was quickly advised, however, of the attempted as-
sassination and summoned by private telephone the
same physician to Mr. Sage's aid. He was at his
office in West Fifty-eighth Street, five miles away
from the scene of the slaughter; but he reached
Mr. Sage in 38 minutes. His face and his coach
are known to the police, and his wild drive
through the streets was as uninterrupted by them
as was the rush of the numerous ambulances called
to the scene of the disaster.

Inspector Byrnes was in hearing of the explosion
half a mile away, but thinking it another of the
steam-heating pipe explosions frequent in Broadway he started in a leisurely way up Broadway in
the opposite direction. The rush of ambulances to
the scene only confirmed the idea of bursting pipes

ILLNESS AND DEATH. 159

in the veteran detective's mind. But when he saw the coach and recognized the face of the doctor as both were speeded down Broadway he recognized that somebody of importance had been injured, and he turned and was soon on the spot. When the doctor's coach reached the crowded scene a pathway opened for it, and he was driven directly to the police-guarded door of the drug store into which Mr. Sage had been carried. And as he alighted and pressed through the opening on the sidewalk make by the police to permit him to enter on his mission of mercy, the crowd whispered: "There's Jay Gould."

But it was not Mr. Gould at all, nor any of his kin nor kind, but the doctor of the millionaires who had been in attendance on Gould when he was in danger a week or two before. It was thus that, summoned by the "Little Wizard," as Mr. Gould was called, Dr. John P. Munn was one of the first to attend the wounded Knight of Puts, Calls, and Straddles. It is only when something unsual happens to disturb the quiet and apparently somewhat monotonous lives of his few patients that the public discovers how very closely the doctor of the millionaires watches over their bodily and more particularly their mental ailments. Especially was he in attendance on Jay Gould; at his office, if Mr. Gould came down-town, at his home on the Hudson, at his Fifth Avenue home, on his yacht when Mr. Gould sought relaxation, in his spe-

LIFE OF JAY GOULD.

cial car when Mr. Gould went on tours to inspect his roads ; everywhere that Mr. Gould went his attending physician was found at hand, and even closer in his observation and study of his important patient, for a very important matter was Mr. Gould's health, more important to more grave interests than that of any other man in the country.

Mr. Gould did not discover Dr. John P. Munn. He has counted among his patients during the last fifteen years several other millionaires. It was James Buell, the president of the Importers' and Traders' Bank, who first employed him as his special physician. The writer would have said family physician but for the fact that Dr. Munn has never had more than a limited family practice which did not include that of Mr. Gould, and that Mr. Buell had no family except a wife, and a niece who was joint heiress to all his millions. He married the lady shortly after Mr. Buell's death. Buell, while president of the bank, which, by the way, carried the heaviest line of deposits of any of the institutions in New York, with possibly one exception, was a heavy stockholder in a big insurance company which he thought was mismanaged. He had himself elected to the presidency, and began to look into the causes of its lack of business compared to that of some of the other big companies. He ran against one of the obstacles, as he imagined, in Dr. Munn, the chief assistant examiner of applicants for insurance policies.

ILLNESS AND DEATH. 161

Dr. Munn rejected a great many who were regarded as desirable clients for any insurance company, but Dr. Munn was positive in rejecting them for reasons which he did not explain. Mr. Buell was not satisfied with this system of his subordinate and yet could not fairly, either to the examiner or the company, overrule his frequent rejections of applicants, who appeared to be in splendid bodily condition. At length, Dr. Munn confided a professional secret to Mr. Buell, which half satisfied the President. The young examiner was in possession of a means of detecting the existence of Bright's disease of the kidneys in its incipiency. But Mr. Buell was fully satisfied with the explanation when the young doctor applied his test to Mr. Buell himself, and informed that surprised gentleman that if he were an applicant for a policy in his own company, Dr. Munn, as examiner, would have to report against him for the reason that he had Bright's disease in an incurable form. Mr. Buell made the candid physician the chief examiner of the insurance company, which position he still retains; and also his own personal medical attendant, and, finally, indirectly his heir. Mr. Buell died from Bright's disease.

Dr. Munn, as chief of the company's examiners, had to impart his secret to assistants; some of these naturally went to the other companies in time; and to-day no insurance company accepts an applicant who has not passed examination according to

LIFE OF JAY GOULD.

"Munn's method." Dr. Munn was so fascinated with his study of this subject that after his marriage he continued to devote himself to his researches and left his wife to manage her dead uncle's estate.

When the embezzlement of millions of dollars of the Second National Bank of New York by its President startled the Street in 1884, its effect on stocks was disastrous. It was immediately followed by a heavy drop in stocks of every kind dealt in on the Exchange. Russell Sage was then extensively engaged in selling "puts" and "calls," and there was a rush of those holding his privileges to have him cash his "puts" at prices far above the suddenly-depressed quotations in Wall Street. For several days his office was a veritable Bedlam; mischief seemed to have broken loose, and every avenue to Sage's office was filled with a crowd of excited, angry, and dangerous brokers and their clerks.

Mr. Sage was paying his losses reluctantly; his purse-strings and his nerves were equally tightened; he seemed about to "suspend," when Jay Gould gave him a verbal shaking up and induced him to meet a loss not far from five millions in dollars, not to speak of shattered nerves and almost tottering brain. It is a singular coincidence that while Mr. Gould was helping Mr. Sage through this crisis, to avert a more serious one which threatened to paralyze business in Wall Street, William Walter Phelps, now Minister to Germany, was exerting himself jointly with the father of John C. Eno, to

ILLNESS AND DEATH. 163

save the imperiled Second National Bank, to avert the ruin of many hundreds of women of Fifth Avenue who were the principal depositors of the "gilt edged" bank. And it cost Mr. Eno and Mr. Phelps $3,700,000 to do this, at the additional cost of life-long exile to the criminal President who had brought about the disaster.

Mr. Sage went into exile, too. It was at a quiet place on Long Island, and it was this same Dr. Munn who sent him there. Mr. Sage had been Vice-President of Buell's bank. It was in this way that Dr. Munn got his second millionaire patient. He was just as positive with him as he had been with Buell. Mr. Sage was for months prisoner in Dr. Munn's hands. Dr. Munn was eminently successful in the treatment of his distinguished patient.

From Buell to Sage was a long stride; it was a short step which brought Dr. Munn into his relationship to Jay Gould. The latter had seen his treatment of Sage, and he had heard of "Munn's method," and of the doctor's positiveness of character as a medical adviser. Jay Gould was too wise and cynical to want flatterers, especially about his health and his properties. He had absolute faith in Dr. Munn, especially because Dr. Munn had nothing of the instinct of the speculator about him. Mr. Gould put him on several boards of directors of his creation and control, but he took no control of him on financial affairs, nor did he confide his secrets of speculation to Dr. Munn. He had a social side for Dr.

10

164   *LIFE OF JAY GOULD.*

Munn, and probably displayed his geniality more to him than to any other person outside of his own family.

Numerous instances might be cited of Dr. Munn having impersonated Mr. Gould to crowds clamorous for a sight of the great financier, when from sheer exhaustion he was unable to appear. Their personal appearance was remarkably similar.

If Mr. Gould's physician saw the genial side of the great money monarch's life, his pastor, Dr. John R. Paxton, was equally privileged. Mr. Gould had a much stronger affection for his church, which was of the Presbyterian denomination, than he was credited with, and his unostentatious though extensive beneficences were not infrequently bestowed through the agency of his pastor. Rev. Dr. John R. Paxton is of Scotch-Irish descent, and was born in southwestern Pennsylvania about 50 years ago. Some say that he is bigoted in that he is orthodox, others that he is opinionated because he is firm in his beliefs. In the pulpit the doctor looks more of the soldier than the minister. He is essentially abrupt, and yet the spontaneity and simplicity of his utterances softens the rough edges of his orthodoxy. Dr. Paxton speaks with the frankness of a soldier who believes absolutely in what he is saying. He is a man who is imaginative and yet able to curb his fancies when they diverge from the doctrine. Dr. Paxton is a man brilliant in the warmth of his conceptions, filled with the romance of a soldier, and yet

ILLNESS AND DEATH. 165

disciplined in orthodoxy. He looks like a man with a history.

His career is interesting. After graduating from Jefferson College he entered the war of the Rebellion at the beginning of the second year and served in most of the critical battles that were fought in Virginia and in the northwestern department. He was throughout distinguished as a reckless fighter and has yet a hankering for his old companions in arms and the reminiscences of the field. He was ordained in 1871, and has ministered successfully in Harford County, Md.; in Harrisburg, Penna.; in New York Avenue Church, Washington, and has filled his present position since 1882. His church is one of the most wealthy in the city. Among those who have been among his flock are Jay Gould, General Horace Porter, H. R. Bishop, Russell Sage, J. C. Livezey, and Seth Lowe. Dr. Paxton was appointed chaplain of the Seventh New York Regiment November 17th, 1887. He is distinguished for his liking of and fairness to negroes, having frequently asked their ministers to assist him in his services. He was opposed to Dr. Briggs in the recent controversy.

CHAPTER VIII.

INCIDENTS AND ANECDOTES.

UNDER this chapter head it is the purpose to group such incidents in the life of Mr. Gould as have in them a point for the reader's consideration, and which bring out characteristics of the man, as well as some anecdotes told by intimate associates, and by himself, that it is thought will be pleasing as well as instructive.

Mr. Gould's indomitable will and intent perseverance were the strongest and most prominent features of his character. The following incident will show that these were innate and not acquired qualities. It also illustrates that love for flowers which went with him through life.

One morning, as young Jason Gould was on his way to the village school-house with his sisters, he noticed at the top of a high tree some very beautiful blossoms. He was but seven years of age, and could not climb the tree to get the treasures. He asked his eldest sister to get them for him, but she could not climb, and beside there was a storm coming on, which promised to be furious. The school-house was just at the foot of the hill on which stood the tree, and the sisters tried to

INCIDENTS AND ANECDOTES. 167

persuade their brother to leave the spot and go to school.

"No," said Jason, "I will not go to school till I have those blossoms."

Just then the first few pattering drops that so often precede a dashing rain, began to drop, and the girls scampered down the hill to the school-house, reaching it in safety. Young Jason was so occupied in his efforts to solve the difficulty of getting the blooms that were just beyond his reach that the rain was upon him before he was aware that a storm had brewed.

Still there was time to get to the school-house before he was showered, but he must act quickly. It would be unpleasant, indeed, to be thoroughly drenched on a day that was none too warm, and it would be even more unpleasant to receive severe punishment from his angry father when he arrived home with his new suit of clothes spoiled. But he had said he would not go to school till he had those blossoms, and as he had not got them, he could not escape to the school-house without breaking his word and discounting his boast. There was no further hesitancy; he marched home, a distance of a mile, and took the punishment for spoiling his clothes like a little man.

This same determination was evinced in everything Mr. Gould undertook, and his love of flowers was especially noted by those whose relations with him were at all familiar. The first costly luxuries

168   LIFE OF JAY GOULD.

he allowed himself after becoming possessed of sufficient means to warrant them were his magnificent
conservatories, and his rare plants, shrubbery, and
trees at Lyndhurst.   While he did not wear a bou-
tonniere as a personal adornment, and did not
have potted plants or cut flowers in his office, it was
only because they appealed too strongly to those
external senses which he knew he must control in
order to concentrate all his mental powers upon
those gigantic manipulations which earned for him
the sobriquet, "Wizard of Wall Street."

The "mouse-trap incident" has been referred to
by newspapers all over the country.   Without exception they have credited Mr. Gould with having
invented the famous trap, with having harbored
hopes that it would prove a profitable and fame-
making invention.   The facts of the case have
been carefully sifted and investigated, and it is
established that Mr. Gould was not the inventor
of the trap, though there is something in the story
about "the little man *with* the mouse-trap."

When Mr. Gould was fourteen years old he was
spending a winter evening by the side of the large
open fire in the living room in the home of his maternal grandfather who was of a mechanical bent,
and possessed of no small genius for making toys.
The old gentleman had been studying for some
time over a trap for animals, but as his house was
rapidly becoming over-run with mice he concentrated his powers on inventing a method of catch-

INCIDENTS AND ANECDOTES. 169

ing the little rodents that would have none of the inconveniences and faults of the ones exposed for sale in the stores.

He worked earnestly and long until one day he was enabled to give that sigh of relief so different from the sigh of endeavor, for he had combined the principles he desired in a very ornate model.

Then there came to the old man visions of fame and possibly of wealth. He inclosed the neat and really meritorious little toy in a small cherry box and began the round of his sons to show them the invention and secure their co-operation in securing a patent and a market for the trap after it was patented.

Strange to say, not one of them would volunteer to take the model to the Crystal Palace, which had just opened in New York city, and have it registered as an American invention, nor would they accept the task when pressed by their father.

As a last resort Jay was asked to aid the old man. Glowing pictures of the wonders of New York and of the Crystal Palace were painted for him, and he was told that business with the directors of the Palace would admit him free.

This decided Jay to take up the task, and with characteristic energy he immediately prepared to start the next morning for New York.

To a friend Mr. Gould once said of this visit to the great metropolis, "You will smile when I tell you that I got into a Sixth Avenue car, and every now

170 *LIFE OF JAY GOULD.*

and then ran out on the rear platform to see the buildings, leaving the case containing the mouse-trap on the seat. When I got to the street where I was to get off the mouse-trap had disappeared. I turned to the conductor and said :

"'What has become of my box?'

"'That box that was on the seat?'

"'Yes.'

"'Was it yours? Why,' replied the conductor, 'a man who got out and turned down the last street carried it off. If you run you will probably catch him.'

"I ran and caught him. He was a great, strong fellow, but I collared him. I really regretted that I had done so, and I tried to let him go, but the fact is, one of my figers caught in a buttonhole of his coat, and before I could get off there was a crowd around us, and a policeman, who took us both off to a near-by court. The statements of the policeman and of myself and of the thief were all heard. The magistrate drew some nice legal and technical distinctions, which came near costing me my liberty. While the thief who stole my mouse-trap was committed to trial, I was given to understand that, owing to my inability to furnish bail—for I knew no one in New York then—I should be detained as a witness until the trial. It was not a pleasant introduction to New York, but I have never forgotten it, and its recollection has often afforded me a good deal of amusement. Fortunately for me, there was a

INCIDENTS AND ANECDOTES. 171

detective in the place who had been hunting my mouse-trap thief for years, and who had a requisition from, I think, the Governor of Pennsylvania or New Jersey. He saved me."

The mouse-trap was registered as an American invention, but failed of great success, possibly, because it was never brought to the notice of the people in any concerted way.

*   *   *   *   *   *

Ezra Cornell's son has said of Mr. Gould: "He was the most misunderstood man in this country. My acquaintance with him began about 25 years ago, upon his ascension to the Presidency of the Erie Railway, and has continued until his death. For the last dozen years it has been my privilege to meet him two or three days in each week in the council chamber of the Western Union Telegraph Company, when we were both in the city.

"I have had little opportunity or inclination to follow the newspaper expressions since Mr. Gould's death. It has, however, been my opinion for many years that there was probably no man in the country more misunderstood. Beginning with the time when Mr. Gould became President of the Erie Railway, circumstances associated him with James Fisk, Jr. In every way Mr. Gould was the opposite of the late Mr. Fisk—socially, morally, religiously, in business affairs and in every possible respect. Knowing both men in business and knowing much of Mr. Fisk's career, I have never regretted his

LIFE OF JAY GOULD.

murder. If Mr. Fisk had been murdered three
times he would not have got what he deserved.

"I regarded Mr. Gould as one of the most remarkable men America has produced. As a business man he was the most far-sighted man I have
ever known. He was the soul of honor in his
personal integrity. His word passed in honor was
as good as any bond he could make. He was
never a stock gambler. He had no more to do
with Black Friday than you had. In all his transactions he meant always to be strictly just, and took
care to get what belonged to him. He never pre-
tended to be a philanthropist. Indeed, he never
made any pretensions of any kind. He knew what
he wanted, and if he could accomplish his purpose
by honorable means he seldom failed. Fisk undertook to steal the Albany & Susquehanna Railroad,
but Mr. Gould had no connection with that matter
except so far as legitimate means justified, in en-
deavoring to control that important new connection
between the Erie Railway at Binghamton and the
capital of the State.

" The Erie Railway has been owned in England
during most if not all of the last 40 years. It has
been controlled from time to time by proxies sent
out by London bankers, in charge of Englishmen,
sent here as their agents, or sent to New York
bankers for representation.

"The newspaper reputation of Fisk and Gould,
as they were always inseparably named, 20 years
and more ago, shook the confidence of the European

WM. H. VANDERBILT.

INCIDENTS AND ANECDOTES. 175

constituency, and the London bankers turned their proxies over to the control of General Dix, then the Minister of the United States at Paris. He came home with power to dethrone Mr. Gould from the presidency of the Erie road. Gould, then only thirty-six years old, in the prime of life, proud of his official position, and ambitious to make a reputation as a railway manager, naturally resisted the onslaught, and attempted to hold his place by means of the opposing interests which he might control. He was already a rich man for one of his age, and was a large creditor of the Erie Railway Company, and, under the advice of counsel to protect his own interests put in a safe place the available securities of what was then a pauper company, attempting to compete with the powerful administration of the elder Vanderbilt, who had just then succeeded to the ownership of the New York Central.

"Any prudent business man accustomed to deal with great values will understand the necessity of President Gould's position when assaulted by a clientelle ignorant of the interior affairs of the company, and whose interests had been placed in charge of the illustrious soldier, who desired to succeed Mr. Gould in the presidency of that company."

Concerning Mr. Gould, as a controlling power in the Western Union Telegraph Company, Mr. Cornell has said:

"I succeeded my father, Ezra Cornell, in the Board of Directors of the Western Union Telegraph Company in 1868, and have been a director

LIFE OF JAY GOULD.

continually until now. Mr. Gould was elected a director in 1881, to succeed the late William H. Vanderbilt, and has since that time been the controlling factor in the company's administration. He had long before appreciated the value and importance of the Western Union Company, and for several years had an ambition to become influential in telegraph affairs. You will remember that he forced an issue between his rival company, the American Union and the old Western Union, which resulted in the consolidation of the two companies at the period named.

"As to his policy, and looking back over the time during which he has been in control, I have no hesitation in saying that his influence has been the most conservative and far-sighted of any ten successive years in the company's history. He has desired to make the Western Union the great and only telegraph company in America. He has succeeded in covering the continent with its wires and offices, numbering of the latter now more than 20,000, in the cables connecting with the European continent and with Mexico and the West Indies and thence to South America. His policy, which has been a cordial and earnest support of the recommendations of the experienced officials who have had charge of the details of management, has resulted in adding more to the value of the company during the time than was ever added in any 20 years of its preceding life."

INCIDENTS AND ANECDOTES. 177

Mr. Gould's own version of the story of the Western Union is given in his testimony to the Senate Committee on Labor and Education.

"I am interested in the telegraph," he told the committee, " for the railroad and telegraph systems go hand in hand, as it were, integral parts of a great civilization. I naturally became acquainted with the telegraph business and gradually became interested in it. I thought well of it as an investment and I kept increasing my interests. When the Union Pacific was built I had an interest in a company called the Atlantic and Pacific, and I endeavored to make that a rival to the Western Union. We extended it considerably, but found it rather up-hill work. We saw that our interest lay more with the Western Union. Through that we could reach every part of the country and through a small company we could not; so we made an offer to sell to Western Union the control of the Atlantic and Pacific. At that time a very dear friend of mine was the manager, and I supposed that he would be made the manager of the Western Union, but after the consolidation was perfected it was not done, and I made up my mind that he should be at the head of as good a company as I had taken him from. The friend was General Eckert, and for him I started another company—the American Union—and we carried it forward until a proposition was made to merge it also into the Western Union. As the stock of the latter went down I bought a large interest in it, and found that

178   *LIFE OF JAY GOULD.*

the only way out was to put the two companies together. General Eckert became general manager
of the whole system. Meantime I bought so much
of its property and its earning power that I have
kept increasing my interest. I thought it better to
let my income go into the things that I was in myself,
and I have never sold any of my interests, but have
devoted my income to increasing them. This is the
whole history of it."

This is the testimony he gave to the Committee
on Labor and Education on the story of the Western
Union :

" I think the control by the Government is contrary
to our institutions. The telegraph system, of all
other business, wants to be managed by skilled ex-
perts, while the Government is founded on the idea
that the party in power shall control the patronage.
If the Government controlled it the general managers' heads would come off every four years and
you would not have any such efficiency as at present.
The very dividend of the Western Union is based
upon doing business well, keeping her customers
and developing her business. If the Democrats were
in power there would be a Democratic telegraph, if
the Republicans came into power there would a Republican telegraph, and if the Reformers came in I
don't know what there would be. (Laughter.) I
think it would be a mere political machine. I
would be perfectly willing, so far as I am concerned, to allow the Government to try it, to sell

out our property of our own citizens and make it valueless."

"Have you any idea what the Government ought to pay?"

"I think that it ought to pay what it is worth and no more. I think that the method that was provided in the law is a very just one, and I would be perfectly willing to let the Government take it on those terms."

"What, in your opinion, is the Western Union property worth?"

"Well, I judge of property myself by its net earning power, that is the only rule I have been able to get. If you show me a property that is paying no more than the taxes, I don't want it. I want property that earns money. You might say there is water in the Western Union, and so there is. There is water in all this property along Broadway. This whole island was once bought for a few strings of beads. But now you will find this property valued by its earning power, by its rent power, and that is the way to value a railroad or a telegraph. So it is worth what it earns now, a capital that pays seven per cent."

"That would be $100,000,000?"

"Yes, and it is worth much more than that, because there are a great many assets."

Mr. Gould was not a believer in cheap men. In the employment of help he regarded economy as poor policy. In the various branches of his extended

LIFE OF JAY GOULD.

business he aimed to secure the best men possible, and he was never known to dicker over the amount of pay. His conspicuous success in avoiding the legal shoals through which he was obliged to thread his way during his eventful career was due mainly to the fact that he always had in his employ the very best legal talent that money could procure.

The story about Mr. Sage and his office boy has been frequently told in Wall Street, but it has not appeared in print. Mr. Sage had an office boy who had been with him for several years, was familiar with his methods and moods, and understood perfectly well the status of each of Mr. Sage's customers. The boy was alert, tactful, and faithful, and in due course of time received tempting offers to leave Mr. Sage's employ. He, however, stuck to Mr. Sage for a long while, imbued with the false hope of advancement.

The boy's salary was fifteen dollars a week, and when he told Mr. Sage one day that he had been offered twenty-five dollars a week to go elsewhere, Mr. Sage coldly told him that he had better go—and he went. Jay Gould happened in Mr. Sage's office a few days afterward and casually remarked: "Why, where is John?"

"Oh! he has left me," said Mr. Sage. "He got extravagant notions in his head and I had to let him go. But I've got a new boy, and I save three dollars a week on his salary."

"You do, eh!" remarked Mr. Gould, with undis-

INCIDENTS AND ANECDOTES. 181

guised disgust. "Well, have you figured how much you will lose on his blunders?"

When Colonel F. K. Hain was made general manager of the elevated railroads in New York city, he was unknown to Mr. Gould. It was not long, however, before the quiet little millionaire began to take a lively interest in him. Colonel Hain possesses qualities which excited admiration in Mr. Gould's breast. One day, not many years ago, Mr. Gould, as President of the Manhattan Railway Company, received Colonel Hain's written resignation. In great surprise he sent for Mr. Hain and asked him to explain the reason for his resignation.

"Mr. Gould," said the Colonel, "I have received from the Reading Railroad Company an offer of the position of General Manager at a salary of $12,000 a year, and, in justice to myself and my family, I do not think that I ought to refuse it."

"How much are you getting here?" asked Mr. Gould.

"Six thousand five hundred dollars a year," replied Colonel Hain.

"Is the increase in salary your only reason for your resignation?"

"Yes, sir."

"Will you stay with us for $15,000 a year?" asked Mr. Gould.

"Certainly," responded Colonel Hain.

"Very well, let it be so," said Mr. Gould, "and,

182 LIFE OF JAY GOULD.

Colonel, I am perfectly satisfied with your work. Never let a question of money come between us."

The loyalty of S. S. H. Clark, General Manager of the Missouri Pacific and President of the Union Pacific, to Mr. Gould has been the object of frequent comment. Mr. Clark is by no means a low-priced man, and the fact that he has long been one of Mr. Gould's trusted lieutenants means that he has not worked for low pay.

It is related that the Atchison people once tried to get Mr. Clark to enter their employ by offering him an advance of $10,000 on the salary the Missouri Pacific Company was giving him. Mr. Clark promptly refused the offer and said nothing. Mr. Gould, however, heard of the matter from other sources, and on the Christmas day following Mr. Clark received a check for $50,000 with a short note which read: "A merry Christmas to my loyal friend.—JAY GOULD."

Mr. E. Ellery Anderson was the man appointed by President Cleveland to investigate the affairs of the Union Pacific Railroad. Mr. Anderson said at the time, " The developments before the convention were dramatic sometimes and always intensely interesting. It gave me an insight into the characteristics of Mr. Gould. Many intimate business connections with him have, as they continued, intensified interest in the man. One thing always impressed me, and it is interesting in connection with current statements and some popular impressions of the man. It is this: I have always found, even to

INCIDENTS AND ANECDOTES. 183

the most trivial detail, that Mr. Gould lived up to the whole nature of his obligations.

"Of course, he was always reticent and careful about what he promised, but that promise was invariably fulfilled.

"Contrary to the popular impression, I do not think that the basis of Mr. Gould's fortune was made as a constructor or operator of railroads, or as a speculator, as we generally understand the terms. In that sort of speculation I think he lost as often as he won. But his successes were in an art which makes his genius rank higher than those which are generally recognized as his successes could do.

"Jay Gould was the absolute master of the art of creating co-ordinate boards of directors that had comple control of adverse interests. He persuaded himself that it was just—to put it mildly—to allow his representatives in both to vote upon both sides of transactions in which interests were adverse. This characteristic was the kernel of the genius of his successes and his manipulations, first in the Erie; then in the Wabash securities; in the consolidation of the Kansas and Denver Pacific with the Union Pacific; in the deal between the Missouri Pacific and the Missouri, Kansas and Texas; in the International and Great Northern, and also, but perhaps not so directly, in the transactions with Manhattan Railway stocks and bonds in this city proved it. These great business movements created no excitement in the outside world. The climaxes were

LIFE OF JAY GOULD.

not dramatic outside of stock circles. Yet in these he made fortunes. In some of them his profits aggregated from $10,000,000 to $15,000,000.

"This financial art, of which he was such a master, was best illustrated by the subsequent disclosures of the proceedings by which the consolidation of the Kansas Pacific and Union Pacific was accomplished. While Gould was a director in the Union Pacific he acquired the Kansas Pacific securities at ten cents. With this line and its adjuncts in his complete control he moved at a meeting of the Union Pacific directors the consolidation upon equal terms of dollar for dollar. Boston men were in control of the directory, among them Gordon Dexter. They objected to the proceeding and Gould's motion failed to carry. Gould had probably expected this refusal, and his foresight had some useful plans. He came back to New York, and within three weeks he had bought, at low prices, securities of the Missouri Pacific, Kansas Central and minor roads with Western extensions. Then he announced his intention of immediately building to the Pacific by way of Salt Lake City.

"The Union Pacific people were startled at this prospect of a parallel road and hurried to New York. A meeting was held at Jay Gould's house. On half a sheet of note paper, which I saw, were written the terms of consolidation of the Kansas Pacific and Union Pacific. By these terms not only, as was first proposed by Gould, was Kansas Pacific and Denver

INCIDENTS AND ANECDOTES.

Pacific stock exchanged, dollar for dollar, for Union Pacific stock, but the Union Pacific agreed to take from Gould's hands, at the price he paid for them, the Kansas Central and other securities he had secured as his weapons. With this in mind Mr. Gould was asked during the investigation, if it was in conformity with the ethics of Wall Street for the director of one road to build a rival to the one in which he, with others, was interested.

"Mr. Gould hesitated perhaps twenty seconds, and then replied: 'No, that would have been wrong. I gave up that plan and made other arrangements.'

"By those other arrangements, which I have explained, he made a profit of $10,000,000.

"This illustrated, too, Gould's capacity for managing men, and playing them on the financial chessboard. He was always so far-sighted and adroit that, generally unconsciously to those with whom he was associated, he made a combination of arrangements so that it was to their interest to work with him. With such conditions, cleverly planned, it was easy for Gould in a meeting to point out real advantages to be gained by his propositions, with roseate prospects of success.

"Mr. Gould knew every detail of the management of his railroads and minute facts about obscure localities which they traversed. I happened by chance to call upon him once regarding the traffic of a little way station. Mr. Gould just leaned for-

186   *LIFE OF JAY GOULD.*

ward in his chair, extended the middle fingers toward some neatly folded papers in a pigeon-hole, and from the midst in a second drew out one which related to the subject then of interest.

"He was always courteous in personal relationships, but not talkative."

In 1878 Mr. Gould was rated at from $10,000,000 to $40,000,000, but a careful and conservative estimate placed the value of his holdings at $15,000,000. Four years later there arose an occasion for him to show his hand. His credit had been attacked. A more than usually strong bear movement in March, 1882, started many rumors in Wall Street calculated to weaken the credit of many men. Over the wires went the story that Jay Gould was financially embarrassed. It was denied, but only to be reiterated.

It was declared on the floor of nearly every stock exchange in the country that he was throwing his large holdings overboard and realizing at a loss in order to keep his head above water. Telegrams poured into New York asking for inside information. Doubt as to the standing of no other man could have so concerned the business world.

Mr. Gould and his friends realized that something must be done to put an end to all this talk. The great pulse of Wall Street was beating feverishly and fast. Men were becoming afraid to buy stocks in which Mr. Gould was heavily interested.

Even Mr. Gould's friends began to feel nervous,

INCIDENTS AND ANECDOTES. 187

when he sent for a number of those who were most closely identified with him. They met in his office. Turning to his secretary, Mr. Gould gave him directions in a few words, and in a very short time that man entered the office bearing in his arms a huge load of stock certificates. Again he departed and again returned similarly burdened.

" Now, gentlemen," said Mr. Gould, "I am prepared to show you that these stories are not true."

Then he had the certificates shown and their total value footed up. Of Western Union there lay on the table $23,000,000 worth, of Missouri Pacific $12,000,000, and of Manhattan Elevated and Southwesterns $18,000,000. There was a total of $53,000,000 in securities on the table. The men who saw this were Cyrus W. Field, Russell Sage, and Frank Work

In 1890 Mr. Gould held from one-quarter to one-half of all the stock in all the corporations which he made any effort to control. There was not a man in the whole of America, or in the world at large, who absolutely owned and controlled and had registered in his own name as many stocks. It is no exaggeration to say that he drew more revenue from his invested capital than did any other man living.

What was that income? From three of his stocks—Western Union, Manhattan Elevated, and Missouri Pacific—he for some years past had been drawing $2,000,000 annually. His income from

LIFE OF JAY GOULD.

other sources was four or five times as much, to say nothing of the vast profits which became his at nearly every turn of the market when he endeavored to guide its course.

Russell Sage in September, 1890, spoke of Mr. Gould thus:

" Mr. Gould cannot begin to use even a small portion for his own personal use—even a small part of the interest which his dividend money alone would yield. He must re-invest it, and he does re-invest it. It is safe to say that he takes this money as the dividend period comes around and buys other securities."

His holdings of Western Union stock are all bound in a book, which it may be believed is an interesting volume.

To financiers, railroad men, and business men Mr. Gould's life was a marvellous study. Mr. Gould had one life for his family and another in his dealings with men. It is not believed that any man in New York had a happier home circle than had he, and it is assuredly the fact that no man who has been so conspicuous before the people of this country for the last thirty years could count up more enemies.

He did not appear to care for commendation outside of his own family circle. With the assured regard of his wife, who died several years ago, and the esteem and affection of his children he seemed to be quite content. Once he was told by some one who was curious to see what effect the declaration would have upon him, that he was the most un-popular man in the United States. He replied, characteristically:

"I never notice what is said about me. I am credited with things I have never done and abused for them. It would be idle to attempt to contradict newspaper talk and street rumors."

CHAPTER IX.

A CHARACTER ESTIMATE.

THE personal prominence of Mr. Jay Gould was not exceeded by that of any living American, and there are senses in which, to the public intelligence and information and imagination, he was as mysterious as he was conspicuous. He a farmer's boy, without capital or the favor of influential friends, became a great power in the nation, and amassed a fortune that placed him among the foremost of the rich men of the world. He had little inheritance, but his singular allotment of genius, and his vast accumulations were not the accretions of values in lands from the labors and improvements of others, but resulted from his daring and skill in speculation and manipulation, guided by his marvelous understanding of the opportunities that the uncertain condition of transportation opened to the highest and keenest capabilities of men. His fortunes were the fruit of his foreknowledge of the wealth of the country and the development of the intercourse of peoples and nations. The secret of his success is that he always bet on the United States, and we may call the faculty behind it, at our pleasure, and according to our instruction or convictions, that of sporting or of

JIM FISK.

statesmanship. The country boy became the Wizard of Wall Street. In the games that are played there the great consume the small, and the principle prevails that Napoleon had in mind when he said, in walking over a battlefield, "One cannot make an omelette without breaking eggs."

Mr. Gould had the reputation of a man of iron nerve, and possessed the quiet courage of remarkable intelligence. Physically he was delicate and sensitive, and his tastes and habits were those of simplicity and refinement. In domestic life he was exemplary—a most loving husband and tender father. His sons are men of trained capacity in affairs, who have been educated for the management of the vast interests now committed to their hands. Practically, they have been managers of responsibility for years, with the general judgment of their father to guide them. They are thoroughly familiar with the principles and details of the business, chiefly that of railways and telegraphy, and there is no serious change anticipated. Of course the death of the most famous man in the history of Wall Street is an immense sensation in that world, but it was, in the language of the street, discounted long ago. Mr. Gould was the keenest and shrewdest and most daring of operators, and yet had the conservatism of large enlightenment. He was not an original force for good or evil of extraordinary volume, but a type of and the most striking representative of one who was an opportunist in Americanism, and his was an

194 *LIFE OF JAY GOULD.*

individuality that was the growth of circumstances. There is this to be said of the money he accumulated: It was never so invested as to be put away to rest, but it was placed so as to be active. His wealth was alive and associated with intense industry. The income from it has been very large, and the sagacity that animated the policy of government of the vast property was extraordinarily clear and tenacious.

Mr. Gould was the foremost man of his time in accuracy of estimation of the value of good-will, and his appreciation and realization of the invisible increments of wealth were the beginning of his success. When he had, as Dr. Johnson said, "riches beyond the dreams of avarice," Mr. Gould became sensible that he was an overtasked man; that peace, after all, was the first blessing; that his health was frail; and he turned more than ever for comfort to his home— his wife and children, his conservatory and books. In his grounds at Tarrytown he had under glass a little tropical farm, and could furnish green corn from his own field for a Christmas dinner. He had a singular, one might say a plaintive regard for beauty, that appeared in the love of flowers and ferns, the bloom and verdure of plants and perfumes of warm and distant regions. There was something dainty in his ways, and while at a feast he ate but a bird and drank no more of wine than a spoonful of good sauterne; he was large-eyed for the charm of a landscape; knew the joy of broad sunny fields, and the restless sparkle of the sea. Robust delights

A CHARACTER ESTIMATE. 195

were not for him. His early dreams were of a lit
erary life, and his later luxuries were in his library.
His fondness for his books often consoled him when
tortured with nervous dyspepsia and insomnia.

There must have been vivid feelings under the
undisturbed surface of his face, and yet the only
positive evidence of it he gave strangers was the
beguiling placidity of his remarks, as he attached
the deepest significance to his deftly-chosen words.
When he meant war he made a suggestion, and if
it was presented with special gentleness there was
in it the greater scope of warfare. His enemies
knew the importance of an inference, and there was
acumen in accepting a hint as influential. He understood conditions of society as elements of life.
The fine threads of which he was spun were strained
and fretted away before he had learned the limita-
tions of his strength, and he sought often the restoration of change of air and scene; but no climate or
scenery within reach of yacht or car revived his
drooping energies. He was told to amuse himself,
and his pale face was seen for a time in festive entertainments; but theatrical noise and glitter were
not congenial, and help could not be found in the
glare and fan-fare of professional merriment. The
sincerity of his interest in the religious work of the
Church, to whose funds for good works he contributed, was, no doubt, absolute, but there was not
generosity or even meagre justice permitted him in
the public comment relating to the incidents, of his

196

LIFE OF JAY GOULD.

A man, who lived four miles from Millville, N. J., stationed himself inside the main entrance to the Western Union building one morning in the beginning of February, 1892. He was a big, burly fellow about 50 years old, and in addition to a small satchel slung over his shoulder, carried two large hand-bags. There was a Bible protruding from his coat pocket. The janitor of the building noticed the stranger and asked him his business. Ephraim went away, but came back the next morning, bag and baggage. The janitor insisted on knowing his business. He opened the two big bags he carried in his hands and showed they were empty. He declined to say what was in the satchel swung over his shoulder. The big bags, he said, were to take away $1,500,000 which he expected to get from Mr. Gould as soon as he had talked with him.

The man was finally persuaded to return to New Jersey, and negotiate with Mr. Gould through the mails.

About the same time a crank went into Judge Walter Q. Gresham's court in Chicago, and demanded $5,000, which he said had been sent him by Jay Gould. He gave the name of Martin McCinahay. He made a fight before he could be overpowered. He was sent to an asylum.

"Vice-President No. 71" was the champion dangerous crank of the year 1891. He called on Dr. Munn, Mr. Gould's physician, one evening in May. He said he belonged to the organization of

CHARACTERIZATION OF MR. GOULD. 197

"Christ's Followers," which was very strong in this country at the present time and was steadily growing. The object of the organization, he said, was an equal distribution of the wealth and property of the country. Among the first property to be distributed was that of Jay Gould, and if any difficulty was to be encountered in carrying out that object, Gould would have to die.

Dr. Munn arranged for the man to call the following evening. He called as agreed and found Inspector Byrnes waiting for him, with Detective Sergeants Frinck and McCloskey. He was taken to headquarters, where he claimed that a former employer had sent him some weeks before to a place known as Owl's Head, on the Canadian border, near Buffalo. There he was to meet friends and receive instructions. Arriving at the appointed rendezvous in the night-time he was surrounded by a band of about 50 men, all heavily masked, who compelled him to kneel in their midst, the band forming a circle around him. While in a kneeling attitude he was compelled to take a solemn oath, which was administered with much pomp and ceremony, and he from that time forth was a member of the order of "Christ's Followers."

The object of the order was explained to him, and after various business transactions, which he declined to explain, he was finally, on April 15th, ordered by the Arch Council of the organization to come to New York. His mission was to obtain an

198 *LIFE OF JAY GOULD.*

interview with the money king, Jay Gould, or with some of his most intimate friends, and through them to lay the decree of the order before Gould. He was instructed to say to Gould that the order demanded that $5,000,000 of his money be set apart and sent at once to the headquarters of Christ's Followers. Then, within the next ten years, $15,000,000 more was to be sent to the same destination, and at his death the will must be so made that only $1,000,000 was to go to each of his sons, and $1,000,000 to the widow. All the rest of the vast property was to be set aside for charitable purposes, or for such other purposes as the order might decree.

This crank went to an asylum.

Of all the schemes of cranks and crooks to beat Gould one of the few to prove successful was carried out in February, 1881. There had been a great war between the up-town and the down-town brokers.

Heading the up-town boys were Messrs. Cammack, Osborne, and Travers, who made their head-quarters about the Windsor. They used often to watch the telegraph wires running into Gould's house, across the way, and wonder what they were saying to the crafty little man.

During the Western Union Telegraph manipulations the up-town boys were shut out of the deal. The stock was selling in the neighborhood of eighty and the "points" were thick to go "short" of the

A CHARACTER ESTIMATE. 199

stock, that the bottom would soon fall out of it. All the verdant ones quickly sold the stock, but the older heads of Twenty-third Street suspected that there was a cat under the wheel.

Now it happened that the great storm occurred at this time and Mr. Gould's private wires went down with the rest, despite the owner's apparent omnipotence. It was absolutely necessary that Gould should continue in communication with his downtown people, and for that purpose he made arrangements with the American District Telegraph Company to furnish him with a number of their very best messengers. The boys came and the gang at the Windsor watched the proceedings with no little interest.

Among the messengers was a tall, slender lad, nearly grown to manhood. The brokers were struck with a happy thought. They got him into the hotel, bribed him to lend them his messenger uniform, and into it they placed a very bright clerk in their employ. The messenger was given a private room at the hotel and fed on the fat of the land.

In the meantime the bright clerk was playing messenger, and all the messages he took to Mr. Gould were first opened and read in the Windsor. The boy kept his eyes and ears open while at Mr. Gould's house, too, and nothing escaped him.

The conspirators at first thought that their trick would only be for a day, but owing to the power

200   *LIFE OF JAY GOULD.*

and duration of the storm, their clerk was enabled to play his part for four days. For Mr. Gould had engaged the boys until the wires should again be put up, and had especially arranged that they should not be changed until that time.

Mr. Gould and his friends never suspected what was beneath that tall boy's uniform. The bright clerk was entirely familiar with everything pertaining to stocks, and faithfully transmitted his knowledge thus acquired to his employer. In this way the Twenty-third Streeters became convinced that a great "bull" was about to be made in Western Union, and they consequently covered and bought in all the stock they could from 80 to 85. The stock advanced rapidly to 120, and the conspirators not only recovered their former losses, but cleared more than $500,000.

The real telegraph boy was kept in the Windsor Hotel for four days, while his place was filled by the stock clerk. The outside clique presented the messenger with $500 cash, and got him a good appointment. Operators say this is the cleverest trick ever recorded in the annals of the street. And for the first time the boys got to the windward of Jay Gould.

The cranks were out on the day of Mr. Gould's funeral, and this is a pen picture of one of them:

There was one man in the crowd on whom the detectives kept a close and wary watch. He seemed to be a full-fledged anarchist. He wore a pair of skin-tight trousers, and flaunted the socialistic colors

A CHARACTER ESTIMATE.

in a huge red handkerchief about his neck. He was unwashed, unshaven, and as scurvy a looking fellow as you could find in Fifth Street or Avenue A. He scowled upon the big house, but made no other demonstration until a reporter asked him if he spoke English, and then he broke out into a string of shocking language, and retreated up the avenue snarling like a dog of evil temper.

As he was shambling across the avenue this unmistakably bad citizen was nearly ridden down by a carriage in which John Jacob Astor and his young wife were riding. He turned and cursed them, too, but he would have cursed them a thousand times more bitterly if he had known that it was the wheels of the Astors which so narrowly missed him.

NEWSPAPER CHARACTERIZATION OF MR. GOULD.

[From the New York Sun.]

WHETHER the death of Mr. Jay Gould is a loss or a gain to the community is a point upon which public opinion will be divided. By the great majority he has long been viewed as the incarnation of all that is evil and mischievous in his sphere of activity, and his removal will, therefore, be hailed as a blessing. A smaller number, equally alive to his faults, will also remember his financial ability, his enterprise, and the splendid services which he has rendered the country in developing its material resources and increasing the productiveness of its industry. With the cessation of his impelling energy they apprehend a slackening of the onward movement, if not the possible failure, of various schemes, which, if he had lived to carry them on, would have proved highly useful to the general prosperity.

It was Mr. Gould's misfortune to have surpassed the crowd of men by whom he was surrounded and with whom he had his dealings, not in audacious unscrupulousness, but in skill and in success.

[From the New York Tribune.]

However men may choose to agree or differ as to the life which has ended in peace after multifarious exploits and mutations, there is no doubt that it

A CHARACTER ESTIMATE.

was profoundly interesting. Perhaps not more than half a dozen persons have lived in our day whose names and activities have been so familiar to the civilized world, and who at the same time have been personally known to so few of their fellow-beings. His persistent reticence, cultivated and applied for his own purposes, may have concealed traits and emotions which actually existed in the man. But though he truly loved his own family and fireside and inspired a tender attachment in return, he gave few signs of longing for the affection and praise of mankind, or even of the community in which he lived. It was his business to utilize for personal ends the follies and passions of his fellow-men, and he probably accepted philosophically whatever penalties his vocation imposed. He at least preserved an outward serenity which did not suggest the idea that he was pained by obloquy, or shared in any degree either the bitterness which he provoked or the suffering which he sometimes inflicted. And certainly, whatever feelings he may have indulged in private, he rarely permitted them to interfere with the execution of his designs. And yet, though Mr. Gould was widely accused of failing to keep faith, there were many among his harshest critics who were ready to admit that he seldom, if ever, turned upon an associate without having had previous reason to believe that the associate was turning upon him. The man who set out to play that game with Mr. Gould needed to move with lightning rapidity. He gathered about him a large number of devoted and faithful followers. They rarely failed to speak of him as always courteous, always considerate, and often generous, and the friendship of many of them he retained through numerous stormy periods and great vicissitudes. He had also a few associates almost as powerful pecuniarily as himself, with whom relations of mutual support and unbroken confidence subsisted for many years.

Mr. Gould accumulated enormous riches, but it is easy to believe that he enjoyed their possession far less than the acquisition of them. He loved to surmount and circumvent barriers, to make a conquest of adverse forces, to conduct a complicated campaign, to apply all his strategic powers to the resolution of difficulties, to employ all the weapons of aggression and defense in his armory, and finally to win a victory which he thought worthy of his powers. And then he loved to seclude himself from the public gaze among flowers and books and pictures, with the few whom he loved around him and the world at a distance. He had cultivated tastes and varied information, but he was not desirous of imposing or incurring social obligations, nor solicitous of distinction in any spere of action except the one which he dominated. He was apparently contented to be what he was—the most daring, brilliant, and triumphant speculator of the age in the eyes of the world, and the most loyal and devoted husband and father in the eyes of his wife and children.

A CHARACTER ESTIMATE.

205

[New York *Recorder*.]

One of the phenomenal men of his time has just passed into history. Jay Gould is dead, and there is no financial panic, nor is there any likelihood of one. There was a time when the announcement of his death would probably have been the signal for a convulsion on Wall Street which would have been sympathetically echoed in all the stock exchanges of the world. But that time has passed. The Jay Gould properties are no longer in the creative and speculative stage; they are on a solid footing, and the life of their creator is not now essential, as it once was, to their development.

Harsh things were said of this remarkable man while he lived, and there will be a flood of severe moralizing over his career now that it is closed. It is easy to say that he was a man with but one all-absorbing passion—the acquisition of wealth for its own sake and the sake of the power which it gave him over the great material enterprises of his day. It will have to be conceded, no doubt, that his character, as a whole, was not one to be held up for emulation and imitation to the youth of America. There were not enough of human sympathy and philanthropic impulse in it for that.

Nevertheless there were strong lines of purpose and faculty in the intellectual make-up of Jay Gould which give him rank among really great men. He had courage, grit, insight, foresight, tireless energy, indomitable will—all great qualities. He conceived

LIFE OF JAY GOULD.

his gigantic operations boldly and executed them with consummate coolness and skill. He was the peculiar and unprecedented product of a peculiar and unprecedented epoch of material growth, expansion, enterprise, and development. No other country and time than the United States during the past thirty years could have evolved him. It was a period of colossal undertakings, of enormous railroad construction, of vast telegraphic and telephonic enterprises. Speculation was its keynote —bold, vast, hazardous, and, to the losers, often enough ruinous speculation. Jay Gould was the master mind of this period. He won where others lost ; and those who lost hated and denounced. The game was desperate and merciless, and if the tables had been turned, and the losers had been the winners, we should have heard far less about Jay Gould's sordid and soulless nature.

It is eminently a case for the old proverb—*De mortuis nil nisi bonum.* Jay Gould played a great part in a great age. He was neither a saint, a reformer, nor a philanthropist, and he made no pretensions to be. But at least it must be said of him that, with untold wealth at his command, his private life was clean and reputable, and his moral example as a husband and parent was wholesome. It has been widely insisted that the accumulation of stupendous fortunes is one of the prime evils and dangers of modern American life ; but, even if this be true, Jay Gould was not alone in his offense. In

A CHARACTER ESTIMATE.

common fairness it may properly be borne in mind that he was neither the first, the only, nor will he be the last, of our multi-millionaires. Byron's line on Napoleon fits him—" Neither the greatest nor the worst of men."

[Chicago *Evening Post*]

Is it not about time to give the clay of Jay Gould a rest? This query is suggested by the Christmas sermon I listened to on Sunday. The congregation was select and large; the altar hidden and the officiating minister nearly so behind a profusion of beautiful floral decoration. The tones of the organ pealed forth sweetly in unison with the violin, and soloists and quartette were all that could be desired. In keeping with the occasion and the accompaniments, Parson Henson's discourse was characterized by that homely, moving logic and racy illustration with which he is wont to inspire the hearts of his auditors and bring to their eyes the glistening evidences of charitable emotion.

Never was religious service more soul-expanding —until, unhappily, the good pastor felt himself called upon, pursuant to the fashion of the times, to stoop, drag forth from the grave, and hold up to the gaze of his congregation all that was most unsavory of the dead millionaire. Could he not have alluded to Stanford, Rockefeller, Armour, and the other living worthies just as kindly without villifying the dead Gould? Was it so necessary to effect an odious comparison as to justify—exaggeration? Was it

208   *LIFE OF JAY GOULD.*

not, in fact, a flagrantly intemperate and inexcusable misuse of language to characterize Gould as a " cut-throat "?

There is a hitherto unpublished story told of General Grant: that one day during his last illness, he was observed to be deeply engrossed with some problem. His pencil was kept in motion and his pad gradually became covered with evidences of calculation. At length he called his wife, and, with unmistakable signs of gratification exhibited the results of his figuring. It was an estimate of the number of people outside his own family who would be profited or be given employment by reason of the issuing of his memoirs—publishers, printers, binders, general agents, clerks, stenographers, canvassers, packers, etc. The thought that lucrative employment would come to many through his own painful labors gave him exquisite pleasure.

Judged from that standpoint, Jay Gould need not have feared the summons of his Master to answer for his stewardship in this world. On that line where is the preacher, where the man, who can point to a nobler record? And that is not all the good that might be said of Gould. I knew him, and I knew many who were closely associated with him. None of these ever to my knowledge spoke harshly of him. On the contrary, they said he was of kindly, gentle heart, doing numberless good deeds without blare of trumpet and unheralded by a brass band.

He grew rich, but he kept his means fully em-

A CHARACTER ESTIMATE.

ployed for the building up of the material interests of his country. Seeing his sons following dutifully and ably in the path his example had marked out with such beneficent results, what wonder that he thought the great fortune he was about to relinquish would be, if left to them, more likely to be used for the best interests of mankind than if left to some institution, religious or otherwise, abounding or not, as the case might be, with sinecures and fat salaries?

[London *Telegraph*]

SIR:—I see that Jay Gould is dead. I painted him while I was in America, in 1883, and I have been wondering if some notes on my knowledge of him would be interesting now.

He declined to sit at first, but when a friend of mine told him he had made a mistake in refusing to sit to me, he said: "Oh! what do you know about him?" When assured that I was a safe man he offered to visit my studio and see this friend's portrait. He spoke little at that visit, only really asking what the portrait would cost, and how long it would take to do. These questions being answered satisfactorily, he said: "I guess I'll be done;" and we arranged the sittings.

Fifteen minutes before the last sitting was over, he said: "You have still a quarter of an hour, according to our agreement. Shall you get done?" "Yes," I said (for I knew my man and took good care to be well ahead of time). He was satisfied with the result, but I am sure he was more impressed by my having been "on time" than by the artistic value of the work.

During the sittings he conversed easily and readily about his accomplished deeds. He was especially pleased to talk about his laying of two big cables across the Atlantic: "Having got the topography of the ocean bottom I laid them in a valley, and not from point to point." He told me how he arranged the whole transaction for the making of this new cable in a couple of days by telegraph with Siemens & Co., for, as he remarked, "I can't wait."

But Jay Gould probably never before or since my sittings allowed himself to be looked at as I was obliged to look at him for my painting; for I had him in strong light, while I was in shadow. This order of position it was his study to reverse in life. I saw painful expressions pass over his face as of deep-seated troubles lingering in his mind, and it is a fact that he never came to the sittings without a detective following him.

He had a happy knack of thinking of methods for bringing to justice people who tried to injure him, which was well illustrated by an incident of which he told me. Having received some letters threatening his life and as these letters were always posted in New York, he arranged to have all the pillar boxes watched, and when a letter was dropped into one of them it was taken out at once and examined. It was in this way—a costly way, indeed—that he ran to ground the person who wrote them.

A CHARACTER ESTIMATE.

When others wondered where his power ay, as there was so little outwardly to indicate his great ability in certain directions, I felt the true index was his fine fibre and sensible nerve structure.

Undoubtedly he was a student of human nature, and based his operations on his judgment of men more than on his judgment of events.

HUBERT HERKOMER.

DYREHAM, BUSHEY, HERTS, Dec. 3d.

[Interview in New York *Herald*.]

"Mr. Gould's external appearance affords a fair notion of his mental make-up. His face always wears a contemplative expression. It is a fact that he is thinking incessantly. His interests are so vast and his schemes so complicated that his mind must be bent upon them all the time. Mr. Gould's eyes are seldom turned upon the face of a person with whom he is talking. He will now and then cast a glance at his questioner, but generally he is looking in some other direction. This peculiarity of Mr. Gould's is not because he is unable to look anybody in the face, but because he is meditating while he is conversing. He never lets his gaze rest on any object more than a moment. If he did it would distract his thoughts. His hardest thinking is done when his eyes are wandering off into space.

"Mr. Gould is a man of few words. To every inquiry he responds in the briefest manner. If 'yes' or 'no' is a sufficient answer, only the one

LIFE OF JAY GOULD.

word escapes him. It is remarkable how much he can say in one or two of his terse sentences. He speaks in a low and rather soft voice, without inflections or gestures. Unless he is the questioner, he does not talk even for the sake of enlivening a dragging conversation. When seated Mr. Gould invariably throws one leg over the other and leans back in the chair. When standing he likes to rest his hand upon something. When at the 'ticker' reading the quotations of the stock market, which the machine prints on a paper tape, he generally sits on the arm of a chair. As a rule he has something in his hand, either a letter, a scrap of paper, or a pencil, which he twirls almost incessantly, though not nervously. He seems to be lost unless his hand is occupied in this way. It is an unconscious occupation and merely represents the force of habit.

"In all his ways Mr. Gould is exceedingly plain and quiet. Bluster, show, or an exhibition of importance is wholly foreign to his nature. Perhaps one reason for his great success is that people with whom he has dealt have not accorded him the measure of his ability, and in consequence he has got the best of transactions. The old saying applies to Mr. Gould. He is smarter than a steel trap, and a steel trap is supposed to lie low and say nothing."

[Memphis Appeal]

"The intelligence of the death of Jay Gould was bulletined here this morning, and there were general expressions of regret from leading merchants

A CHARACTER ESTIMATE. 213

and citizens. The people of Memphis have not forgotten that in 1879, when Memphis, after being scourged with yellow fever in 1878, was again visited by an epidemic of the same disease, Mr. Gould, hearing of the exhausted condition of the treasury of the Howard Association of Memphis, sent by telegraph $5,000, and authorized the association to draw on him for as much more as was needed to aid the association in its work of nursing the sick and burying the dead.

"Mr. Gould came to Memphis on October 21st, 1886, and a public reception was tendered to him on the floor of the Memphis Merchants' Exchange. On the large blackboard of the Exchange was written in chalk his memorable telegram, and as he entered the room his eyes caught the few brief words his generous nature had prompted him to send, and which have ever since been held in grateful remembrance."

CHAPTER X.

LAST WILL AND TESTAMENT.

MR. JAY GOULD had with him for eighteen years, in the most confidential relations, a remarkable man, G. P. Morosini, Esq., who kept his accounts in wonderful order, and submitted them to him in a style that was a combination of consummate book-keeping and art. Mr. Gould received from the hands of Morosini every first of January a yearly history of his affairs in a volume bound in morocco, and it had to be without blot or blemish, clear as print, and a perfect record of the year's business. There is a great deal of history in those volumes, and they would be more interesting than a romance. There was one account in them that would perhaps command wider attention than any other, and of it Morosini speaks in guarded general terms. It seems that he and Mr. Gould did not care to call all the money that was given away charity. Therefore it was not a charity account that was kept, but an account of "Beneficence." Mr. Gould did not give in very small sums. He did not trouble himself to give less than two hundred dollars. "What is this, Mr. Gould?" Morosini would ask, "is it a loan?" "Yes, it is a loan," Gould would say,

214

LAST WILL AND TESTAMENT. 215

" one that I shall not see again." It was recorded as a " Beneficence." The last year that Morosini kept the books was 1885, and the sum of Mr. Gould's benefactions that year he says was $165,000, figures that speak very handsomely for themselves.

That the benefaction account still was on and the distribution is in good and generous hands this local article from the *New York Evening Advertiser*, December 27th, 1892, is testimony :

"Miss Helen Gould was the good Santa Claus to the children in the Home for the Friendless yesterday. She gave them a Christmas tree, a big turkey dinner, toys and dolls by the hundred, with oranges and candy besides. As a result the children were in a delirium of happiness from long before daylight until they were tucked into their little trundle beds last night.

" Miss Gould announced some time ago to the managers of the Home, which is at No. 29 East Twenty-ninth Street, her desire to give a Christmas tree and a Christmas dinner to the little ones in the institution, and her offer was accepted and preparations were made accordingly. Dolls of all sizes, complexions, shapes, and materials were bought for the girls and any number of toy dishes, Noah's arks, alphabet blocks, puzzles, and other toys were also quietly smuggled into the Home. The walls of the dining-rooms, nurseries, and chapel were decorated with festoons of evergreen and wreaths of holly.

" On Sunday night all the children, not only in the

216   *LIFE OF JAY GOULD.*

nurseries, but in the hospitals, were told that Santa Claus had sent word that he was coming to pay them a visit, and for them to be sure to hang up their stockings. The announcement created a furor. The tots hung up so many stockings that the walls around the stoves were actually covered with them, and it was so late before they all got asleep that the attendants under Matron Rudgers had hard work to make the necessary preparations.

"The stockings were filled to overflowing, and a Christmas tree was set up in the middle of one of the nurseries. At exactly 4 A. M. the first little girl woke up, and reaching out to her stocking on the bed post, and finding a doll sticking out, with an orange way down in the toe, she set up such a shout of delight that all the rest of the children sat up in bed in a jiffy, and then ran for their stockings too. There was no more sleep in the Home after that.

"When breakfast was over the Christmas tree was despoiled of its treasures, all the children were taken to the chapel with their arms full of toys, and there in the big warm hall, with the sunshine streaming through the great windows, they romped until the aroma of fricasseed turkey, coming from the kitchen, called them to dinner. For a time toys were forgotten, and forming in separate lines, the boys and girls marched to their five dining-rooms.

"Gravely, but with very bright eyes, the little ones marched in, and after grace had been said there arose a prodigious clatter of knives and forks and a

LAST WILL AND TESTAMENT.

chatter of tongues, and the way that fricasseed turkey and 'stuffin',' and those mashed potatoes and good wholesome bread and butter, and oranges and apples and candy disappeared would have testified eloquently enough to the giver, had she been there to see, that the good things were duly appreciated. Finally the little ones gave up the battle, and the turkeys, though frightfully disfigured, remained the victors.

"After dinner the children went back to the nurseries and danced around the Christmas tree, went visiting with their dolls, 'marched the animals one by one' into the arks, and played housekeeping until bed-time came, and then, after a long and happy day, thanks to their benefactress, their Christmas celebration came to an end."

Last winter the Rev. Dr. John Paxton inadvertently spoke of a meeting which had taken place in Jay Gould's house, at which meeting Mr. Gould had subscribed $10,000 for Church work.

The meeting was that of the Committee of the Presbytery of New York on Church Extension and Sustentation. The meeting, it was said, was held at Mr. Gould's house at the request of the committee, and nearly all the members—a hundred or more —were present. It was held on the evening of February 23d. Mrs. Gould had been dead then more than a year. Mr. Gould and his daughter Helen received the guests, and his sons Edwin, George, and Howard assisted in entertaining them. The

LIFE OF JAY GOULD.

Rev. Dr. Paxton took the floor and made a short speech for Mr. Gould, saying that Mr. Gould's modesty prevented him from speaking for himself.

Mr. Paxton said that Mr. Gould had told him that the Presbyterian Church was the best and truest religious organization in the country, and that its work of Church extension was wise and hopeful for humanity. Other clergymen made speeches, including the Rev. Dr. John Hall and the Rev. Dr. George Alexander. At the close of Dr. Alexander's speech, Mr. Warner Van Norden, the treasurer of the committee, said that subscription cards would be distributed, and he hoped all would give liberally. He announced that he had already received subscriptions of $500, $100, $1,000, and $2,500, one of which, he said, was from Miss Gould. A few minutes later Mr. Van Norden spoke again, saying that a number of $1,000 subscriptions had been handed to him, and that the host, Mr. Gould, had subscribed $10,000.

The unkindly comment on this incident was very disagreeable to Mr. Gould and his friends.

The Atlanta *Constitution* said of Mr. Gould, on the eve of his death :

" The trouble with Mr. Gould was that he did not make arrangements with the newspapers to herald his deeds of benevolence, and the result was that no one outside of his small circle of intimates and familiars knew the extent of them. He went about his charities as he did about his business, silently and

LAST WILL AND TESTAMENT. 219

shrewdly. In this day, benevolence that hides itself from the eyes of the quick-witted reporters is open to the charge of eccentricity.

Jay Gould's will was filed for probate in the surrogate's office December 12th. In an affidavit accompanying it the total value of the estate is estimated at $72,000,000—$2,000,000 in real estate and the remainder in personal property. The collateral inheritance tax, which will go to the State, will amount to about $700,000. If paid within six months the law allows a rebate of five per cent., or $35,000. Comptroller Myer's fees for collecting the tax were about $10,000.

The names of the heirs and the estimated amounts they will receive are:

George Gould about $15,000,000. Of this $5,000,000 is a specific bequest in payment for his services in managing his father's business.

Edwin Gould, $10,000,000, and the house where he lives, valued at $60,000.

Helen Gould, $10,000,000, besides the family residence on Fifth Avenue, the use for life of the country house, and $6,000 a month for household expenses.

Howard Gould, $10,000,000.

Anna Gould, $10,000,000.

Frank Gould, $10,000,000.

Jay Gould, son of George, $500,000.

Sarah Northrop, sister, $25,000 cash, a house valued at $15,000, and a life annuity of $2,000.

220   LIFE OF JAY GOULD.

Anna G. Hough, sister, $25,000, and a life annuity of $2,000.

Elizabeth Palen, sister, $25,000, and a life annuity of $2,000.

Abraham Gould, brother, $25,000, and a life annuity of $2,000.

The will is dated December 24th, 1885. There are three codicils, the first made shortly after the death of the testator's wife. The others were added November 21st, 1892, only a few days before Mr. Gould's death. Indications are that they were prepared in a hurry. The will and the first codicil evidently were drawn carefully by a clerk from some rough draft. The last two codicils were written roughly, and the signatures of Mr. Gould were scrawly and almost illegible—very unlike his unvarying, well-balanced autograph as attached to the will itself.

It is easy to imagine that on that day in November, Mr. Gould believed his end was close at hand and sent post-haste for his lawyer. The disposition of his entire estate had been made in the former codicil, providing finally that the residuary estate be divided between the sons and daughters. But as a farewell token to his kinsmen, it would seem, Mr. Gould added first an annuity of $2,000 each for his brother and three sisters, and then came the bequests to his little grandson and namesake and to George and Helen. This codicil was signed and sealed, and the witnesses were Mr. Dillon, the

THE LAST WILL AND TESTAMENT. 221

drawer; Dr. Munn, the family physician, and Margaret Terry, a servant.

Later in the day it must have occurred to Mr. Gould that he had omitted something, for the second codicil was drawn leaving the contents of the Fifth Avenue house to his daughter Helen, and giving his son Edwin the house in Forty-seventh Street.

Mrs. Gould, brother-in-law Daniel S. Miller, and Thomas T. Eckert were to have been among the executors under the original will. The death of Mrs. Gould changed the disposition of the estate entirely.

The following is the text of the will and codicils in full:

In the name of God, Amen: I, Jay Gould, of the city and State of New York, do hereby make, publish, and declare this my last will and testament, in manner and form following:

First.—I direct that all my just debts and funeral expenses be paid as soon after my decease as can conveniently be done.

Second.—I give and devise unto my wife, Helen D. Gould, for and during her natural life, the dwelling-house in which I now reside, known as 579 Fifth Avenue, in the city of New York, and also my country place, commonly called Lyndhurst, situated at Irvington in this State, with any additions I may hereafter make thereto, together with all the hereditaments and appurtenances thereunto belonging.

And upon the death of my said wife I give and

LIFE OF JAY GOULD.

devise the said real estate to such and so many of my children, and upon such terms as shall be appointed and determined by my said wife in and by her last will and testament duly executed; and in the event of her death without having made such testamentary appointment and determination, then the said real estate shall go to and be divided among my surviving children and the issue of any deceased child, share and share alike, *per stirpes* and not *per capita.*

I also give and bequeath unto my said wife all the household furniture, plate, printed books, pictures, and other works of art, chattels, and effects (excepting, however, money, securities for money, evidences of debt and of title and accounts and vouchers) which shall be in my said houses or either of them at my decease, together with my horses, carriages, and carriage and stable appurtenances, and also all the live stock, contents of conservatories, implements and articles in use on my said country place.

Third.—I also give and bequeath to my said wife an annuity of $100,000 per annum during her natural life, to be computed from the date of my decease, and paid to her in equal semi-annual, quarter-yearly, or monthly payments thereafter, as she may elect; and I order and direct that sufficient of my estate to produce said annuity be set apart and at all times kept safely invested for that purpose by my executors and trustees hereinafter named during the life of my said wife.

THE LAST WILL AND TESTAMENT. 223

All taxes, assessments, and charges which may be imposed upon the real estate devised to my wife for her life as aforesaid, together with the expense of the necessary insurance thereupon, shall be a charge upon my estate, and sufficient thereof shall be set apart and kept invested by my said executors and trustees for that purpose.

Upon the death of my wife I direct that the principal sum so set apart for her use in and by this third paragraph of my will shall be divided among my several children and their issue in such proportions as my wife shall by her last will and testament duly executed appoint and provide, and in the event of her failure to make such testamentary appointment and provision I direct that the same be divided among my children then surviving and to the issue of such of my children as may then be dead in the proportions provided in and by the statutes of this State in cases of intestacy.

Fourth.—I give and devise to my sister, Mrs. Sarah B. Northup, the three certain lots of ground situated on Penn Street, in Camden, N. J., with the buildings now or hereafter to be erected thereon, to have and to hold the same during her natural life, and upon her decease I give and devise the same to such of her danghters as shall then be living, share and share alike.

I also give and bequeath to my said sister, Sarah, the sum of $25,000 cash.

I also give and bequeath to my sisters, Mrs. Anna

224   *LIFE OF JAY GOULD.*

G. Hough and Mrs. Elizabeth Palen, and to my brother, Abraham Gould, the sum of $25,000 each.

Fifth.—I give, devise, and bequeath all the rest, residue, and remainder of my estate, real, personal, and mixed, of every name and nature whatsoever and wherever situate, of which I shall die seized or possessed, or to which I may be entitled at the time of my decease, unto my executrix and executors hereinafter named as trustees, the survivors and survivor of them in trust for the uses and purposes following—that is to say:

1. To hold or sell, convey or dispose of the same at public or private sale, at such time or times and on such terms as they or the survivor or survivors of them in their or his or her discretion shall deem advisable.

2. To divide said real and personal estate or the proceeds thereof into seven equal parts or shares, and to designate, hold, and invest one such part or share for my said wife, and to collect and receive, and pay or apply the rents, interest, and income of the part or share so set apart for my said wife to her for her use during her natural life, and upon her death to pay, assign, transfer, and convey the part or share so held in trust for her to such persons and in such proportions as she shall appoint and direct in and by her last will and testament; and in case of her failure to make such testamentary appointment, then to my children then surviving and to the issue of

RUSSELL SAGE.

THE LAST WILL AND TESTAMENT. 227

any deceased child, share and share alike, *per stirpes* and not *per capita.*

3. To designate, hold, and invest one other such share for each of my children, George J. Gould, Edwin Gould, Howard Gould, Frank Gould, Helen M. Gould, and Anna Gould, and to collect and receive and pay or apply the rents, interest, and income from the part or share so set apart for each child to his or her use during his or her life; and upon the death of any such children to pay, assign, transfer, or convey the part or share so held in trust for him or her to his or her issue in such proportions and at such times as he or she shall appoint in and by his or her last will and testament; and in case of failure to make such testamentary appointment, then to such issue absolutely in the proportions provided in and by the statutes of this State in cases of intestacy.

4. In the event that any of my children shall die without issue, then to pay, assign, transfer, and convey the part or share of the one so dying to my surviving children and to the issue of any deceased child, share and share alike, *per stirpes* and not *per capita.*

Sixth.—I direct that all securities in which said trust funds shall from time to time be invested be taken and held by said trustees to their name as trustees for the parties respectively for whose benefit the funds are severally set apart and held, so that each of the trust funds herein provided for

228   *LIFE OF JAY GOULD.*

shall be kept separate and distinct from the others, and the accounts thereof shall be separately kept; and I authorize and direct my said executrix and executors and trustees to employ and pay out of the funds of my estate all the clerks and book-keepers that may be necessary for this purpose.

Seventh.—I direct that no deduction shall be made from any of the legacies herein contained by reason of any gifts or advancements I have heretofore made or may hereafter make to or for the account of either or any of them.

Eighth.—The provision hereinbefore made for my wife is to be in lieu of all right of dower in my estate.

Ninth.—I authorize and empower my executrix and executors and trustees hereinafter named, and the survivors or survivor of them, to sell and dispose of all or any of the real estate devised to them by me in their discretion, at public or private sale, at such times and on such terms and conditions as they, the survivors or survivor of them, shall deem meet or proper, and to execute, acknowledge, and deliver all proper writings, deeds of conveyance, and transfers therefor.

Tenth.—I hereby direct that all stocks, bonds, and other securities belonging to me at my decease shall form part of the trusts created by this my will, at such values as shall be placed upon them by said executrix and executors and trustees; but I hereby authorize them, the survivors and survivor of them,

THE LAST WILL AND TESTAMENT. 229

to sell and dispose of the same, or any of them, whenever in their discretion they think proper.

And I expressly direct that my executrix and executors and trustees, the survivors or survivor of them, are not to be held responsible or liable for or charged with any loss or depreciation that may arise by holding such securities, or any securities forming part of the trust created hereby ; and I hereby empower them, the survivors or survivor of them, to make such investments and reinvestments of the trust moneys in securities other than those in which trustees are authorized to invest by law, in the absence of testamentary direction, as they may think proper ; and I further authorize and empower them, the survivors and survivor of them, to call in, change, invest, and reinvest the said securities and investments and proceeds thereof whenever and as often as they may deem necessary.

In the event of any differences of opinion among my executrix and executors and trustees as to the holding and retaining of securities or investments, or as to the calling in or making investments and reinvestments and management of the estate and of the trusts therein created, I direct that so long as they shall be five in number the decision of four of them shall be conclusive, and when and so long as their number shall be reduced to four, that then the decision of three of them shall in like manner be conclusive.

Eleventh.—I nominate, constitute, and appoint my

230 LIFE OF JAY GOULD.

wife, Helen D. Gould; my brother-in-law, Daniel S. Miller; my son, George J. Gould; my friend, Thomas T. Eckert, and my second son, Edwin Gould, when he shall have reached the age of twenty-one years, executrix and executors of and trustees under this my last will and testament; provided, however—and the appointment of trustees in this my will is subject to this exception—that neither of the persons herein named as trustees shall be trustee of the fund, share, or portion hereinbefore directed to be set apart and to be held for him or her or for his or her benefit; but as to such fund in the case of each of the beneficiaries who is also made a trustee herein, the trust shall vest in and be executed by the others of the trustees herein named and the survivors and survivor of them.

Twelfth.—I further direct that in case any vacancy shall happen in the number of my executors and trustees above named by death or otherwise, if such vacancy shall happen during the lifetime of my wife, that the same shall be filled by the appointment of whichever of my two sons, Howard Gould and Frank Gould, my wife shall designate in writing over her hand and seal, and upon such designation I appoint such son, provided he shall have arrived at the age of twenty-one years, one of my executors and trustees as aforesaid.

And in the event that my said wife shall not be living at the time such vacancy occurs, I direct that such vacancy shall be filled by the appointment of

THE LAST WILL AND TESTAMENT. 231

In the Name of God amen=

I, Jay Gould of the City and State of New York do hereby make, publish and declare this my last Will and Testament in manner and form following. -

First I desire that all my just debts and funeral expenses be paid as soon after my decease as can conveniently be done

☆ ☆ ☆ ☆ ☆ ☆ ☆ ☆

In Witness Where of I, Jay Gould, have to this my last will and testament subscribed my name ana set my seal this twenty fourth day of December one thousand eight hundred and eighty five

232

LIFE OF JAY GOULD.

my third son, Howard Gould, and upon that contingency when he shall arrive at the age of twenty-one years I hereby nominate and appoint him one of my executors and trustees as aforesaid.

And in the event another vacancy shall happen in the number of my executors and trustees as aforesaid, if such vacancy shall occur during the lifetime of my wife, I direct that my other son, who shall not theretofore have been designated and qualified as executor and trustee, shall be and I hereby nominate and appoint him executor and trustee as aforesaid when he shall have arrived at the age of twenty-one years, if she shall so elect and designate in writing over her hand and seal.

Thirteenth.—I desire and direct that in lieu of the commissions provided by statute to be paid to executors and trustees, there shall be paid to my said executrix and executors and trustees for their services the sum of $10,000 per annum each so long as they shall respectively act in the capacities aforesaid ; provided, however, and said appointments of said executrix, executors, and trustees are subject to the further condition, that no commission or compensation shall be charged by or allowed to any of them for their services as executrix, executors, and trustees other than as above provided ; and if either shall decline to serve on said condition, his or her appointment as executrix or executor and trustee shall cease and terminate.

Fourteenth.—Should any of the provisions or di-

THE LAST WILL AND TESTAMENT. 233

rections of this will fail or be held ineffectual or invalid for any reason, it is my will that no other portion or provision of this will be invalidated, impaired, or affected thereby, but this will be construed as if such invalid provision or direction had not been herein contained.

Fifteenth.—I hereby revoke all former or other wills and testamentary dispositions by me at any time heretofore made.

IN WITNESS WHEREOF, I, Jay Gould, have to this, my last will and testament, subscribed my name and set my seal, this 24th day of December, 1885.

Subscribed, sealed, published, and declared by Jay Gould to be his last will and testament in our presence and to us, who at the same time at his request, in his presence and in the presence of each other, have hereto, at the end of such will and testament signed our names as attesting witnesses this 24th day of December, one thousand eight hundred and eighty-five.   (Signed)

ALMON GOODWIN, residing at No. 128 West Fifty-ninth Street, New York.

HENRY THOMPSON, residing at No. 244 East Eighty-sixth Street, New York.

HERMAN W. VANDER POEL, residing at No. 36 West Thirty-ninth Street, New York city.

234   *LIFE OF JAY GOULD*

THE CODICILS.

I, Jay Gould, of the city and State of New York, having on the 24th day of December, A. D. 1885, subscribed, sealed, published, and declared my last will and testament, hereto annexed, do now hereby make, publish, and declare the following codicil thereto, to be taken as a part of the same, that is to say:

First.—My wife, Helen D. Gould, having died since the making of said will, I give, bequeath, and devise unto my executors and trustees hereinafter named, all of the property, real and personal, mentioned, described, or referred to in articles second and third of my said will, to hold in trust for the uses and purposes in the said will and in this codicil expressed and declared, and the same shall be considered and treated in all respects as if the same had originally fallen within the terms of article fifth of my said will and had been part of the property, real, personal, and mixed, given, devised, and bequeathed by the said fifth article of my said will to my executors and trustees upon the trusts therein created, expressed, and declared, subject, however, to the following proviso, qualification, and exception, viz.:

That any of my household furniture, plate, printed books, pictures, works of art, household or stable effects may by my executors and trustees be set apart for, divided among, and delivered absolutely to my said children free from the trusts of my said

THE LAST WILL AND TESTAMENT. 235

will, an equal amount thereof in value, as near as may be, to each child.

After satisfying the dispositions made above and the bequests contained in the fourth article of my said will, I direct that all of my residuary estate, real, personal, and mixed, of whatever nature and wherever situate, be held upon the trusts created, expressed, and declared in my said will and in this codicil, but the fifth article of said will is hereby modified so as to require the said estate to be divided into six (6) equal parts or shares instead of seven (7), one of which parts or shares is to be held, designated, and invested for each of my children as in said will, and in this codicil expressed and provided. And the said shares and the accounts and transactions pertaining thereto shall at all times be kept entirely separate and distinct, and shall never be mixed or mingled.

Second.—In the place of the executrix, executors, and trustees named in the eleventh article of my said will, I do hereby nominate, constitute, and appoint my brother-in-law, Daniel S. Miller; my sons, George J. Gould and Edwin Gould, and my daughter, Helen M. Gould, and my son, Howard Gould, when he shall have reached the age of twenty-one years, the executors and trustees under my said will and this codicil thereto.

In case any vacancy shall happen in the number of said executors and trustees above named by death or otherwise, I appoint my son, Frank Gould, to be

236   *LIFE OF JAY GOULD.*

executor and trustee to fill such vacancy when he shall have reached the age of twenty-one years; and in case any other vacancy shall happen by death or otherwise, I appoint my daughter, Anna Gould, to be executor and trustee to fill such vacancy when she shall have reached the age of twenty-one years.

Third.—I direct that no bond or undertaking shall be required of my said executors and trustees, as a condition of qualifying and acting as such under my said will and this codicil.

Fourth.—That there be added to the tenth article of my said will the following: if at any time the number of my executors and trustees shall be reduced to less than four, the decision of a majority of them shall be conclusive.

In addition to the powers which one or more co-executors may lawfully exercise without the concurrence of all, I especially direct and provide that deeds, sales, contracts, conveyances, and other instruments, executed by a majority of the executors and trustees shall in all cases be as binding in favor of third persons acquiring property or rights thereunder as if they were executed by all of the executors and trustees.

Any one or more of the said executors and trustees may authorize by instrument in writing, duly executed and acknowledged, any co-executor and trustee to act in his or her or their place and to execute in his, her, or their name any instruments which he, she, or they might personally have executed.

THE LAST WILL AND TESTAMENT. 237

In no case shall any purchaser of property from the executor and trustees or other persons dealing with the said executors and trustees be bound to see to the application of the purchase-money or other property or funds under the trusts of my said will.

Fifth.—The beneficial interest of each of my daughters in the trust property and in the trusts hereby created is hereby declared to be for her sole and separate use, entirely free from any right, estate, or control of her husband, and her separate receipt and acquittances shall be sufficient without the assent or joinder of her husband.

No beneficiary under my said will and this codicil shall have any power to dispose of or in any way incumber or charge by way of anticipation or otherwise the rents, interest, and income from the part or share set apart for his or her benefit, or to dispose of, charge, or incumber the part or share itself or his or her interest therein or in any part thereof, nor shall the same or the income thereof or any beneficial interest therein or right thereto be liable or chargeable in the hands of the executors and trustees for any debt or liability of such beneficiary, nor shall the same at any time so liable or chargeable prior to the actual receipt thereof by such beneficiary from the executors and trustees under and pursuant to the terms and provisions of the trusts created and declared in that behalf in my said will and this codicil thereto.

Sixth.—Except as herein modified, my said will

238 *LIFE OF JAY GOULD.*

and all of the provisions thereof remain in full force and unaffected, and the said will is hereby ratified and confirmed in every respect except so far as the same is inconsistent with this codicil.

IN WITNESS WHEREOF, I, Jay Gould, have to the foregoing codicil to my last will and testament subscribed my name and set my seal, this 16th day of February, 1889.

Subscribed, sealed, published, and declared by Jay Gould, the testator, to be his last will and testament and codicil thereto in our presence and to us who, at the same time, at his request and in the presence of each other and of said testator, have hereto at the end of such will and testament and codicil thereto signed our names as attesting witnesses, this 16th day of February, 1889.

(Signed)

JOHN F. DILLON, residing at No. 671 Madison Avenue, New York.

WINSLOW S. PIERCE, residing at No. 208 Lefferts Place, Brooklyn, N. Y.

GEORGE S. CLAY, residing at No. 161 Monroe Street, Brooklyn, N. Y.

I, Jay Gould, of the city and State of New York, having on the 24th day of December, 1885, sub-

THE LAST WILL AND TESTAMENT. 239

scribed, sealed, published, and declared my last will and testament, hereto annexed, and also a codicil thereto on the 16th day of February, 1889, hereto annexed, do now hereby make, publish, and declare the following additional codicil thereto, to be taken as a part of the said former will and codicil, that is to say :

First.—To my sisters, Mrs. Sarah B. Northrup, Mrs. Anna G. Hough, and Mrs. Elizabeth Palen, and to my brother, Abraham Gould, each, and in addition to the bequests in my said will, I give and bequeath the further sum of two thousand dollars ($2,000) annually during the term of their respective natural lives, payable in equal quarterly payments by my executors and trustees ; and I direct my said executors and trustees to set apart from my estate devised to them in trust, bonds, in separate trusts for each, the interests of which shall be sufficient to pay the said respective bequests to my said sisters and brother, which said bonds shall, on the death of said legatees respectively, fall into the residuary estate from which they were taken.

Second.—To my son George J. Gould I give and bequeath the sum of five hundred thousand dollars ($500,000), in trust, however, for the use and benefit of my namesake, Jay Gould, son of the said George J. Gould. Said George J. Gould, trustee, may apply the same, in his discretion, to the support and education of my said grandson during his minority, and when the said grandson shall attain the age of twenty-five

240 *LIFE OF JAY GOULD.*

(25) years the said trustee shall pay over to him one-fourth of the said bequest, and when he shall attain the age of thirty (30) years another fourth, and when he shall attain the age of thirty-five (35) years the remaining half thereof; but subject to the power in the said trustee to pay over the same, or any proportion thereof, at an earlier period or periods after my said grandson shall attain his majority, if in the judgment of the said George J. Gould he deems it wise and best to do so.

Third.—To my daughter Helen M. Gould I give and devise in fee simple absolute my house No. 579 Fifth Avenue, New York city.

Until my youngest child arrives at the age of twenty-one (21) years, I give to my said daughter Helen M. the use of my residence at Irvington, commonly called Lyndhurst, free of taxes, also the use of all horses and carriages, and also the use of all the furniture, books, paintings, and household contents in said house No. 579 Fifth Avenue, and said house called Lyndhurst; and until my youngest child arrives at the age of twenty-one years, I give and bequeath to my said daughter Helen M. the sum of $6,000 per month, to be paid to her by my executors and trustees, commencing at the time of my decease.

While I declare no trust in this regard, this payment is directed in the expectation that my minor children, Anna and Frank J., as well as my son Howard, will, during the period above pro-

THE LAST WILL AND TESTAMENT. 241

vided for make their home with my said daughter Helen.

Fourth.—I give and bequeath to my daughter Helen M. Gould, the portrait of myself by Herkomer, which is in my house No. 579 Fifth Avenue, New York city.

Fifth.—I hereby appoint my son, George J. Gould, and my daughter, Helen M. Gould, the guardians of my minor children, to wit, Anna Gould and Frank J. Gould, during their minority, no bonds to be required.

Sixth.—In the place of the persons named as executrix, executors, and trustees in the second article of the first codicil to my will I hereby nominate, constitute, and appoint as executors and trustees of my said will my sons George J. Gould, Edwin Gould, and Howard Gould, and my daughter Helen M. Gould; the other provisions in the said second article of said codicil to remain in full force.

Seventh.—I hereby declare and provide that if any of my children shall marry without my consent during my lifetime, or thereafter without the consent of a majority of the then executors and trustees under this will then and in that event the share allotted to the child so marrying in and by said will and codicil shall be reduced one-half, and the principal of the other half of the said share shall be paid, assigned, transferred, or set over to such persons as under the laws of the State of New York would take the same if I had died intestate.

LIFE OF JAY GOULD.

Eighth—My beloved son, George J. Gould, having developed a remarkable business ability, and having for twelve years devoted himself entirely to my business, and during the past five years taken entire charge of all my difficult interests, I hereby fix the value of his said services at five millions of dollars ($5,000,000), payable as follows:

Five hundred thousand dollars ($500,000) in cash, less the amounts advanced by me for the purchase of a house for him on Fifth Avenue, New York city, and such amount as I shall hereafter advance to purchase stables; five hundred thousand dollars ($500,000) in Missouri Pacific Railway Company six (6) per cent. consolidated mortgage bonds; five hundred thousand dollars ($500,000) in St. Louis Iron Mountain and Southern Railway Company consolidated five (5) per cent. bonds; five hundred thousand dollars ($500,000) in Missouri Pacific Railway Company trust five (5) per cent. bonds; ten thousand (10 000) shares of the stock of the Manhattan Elevated Railway Company; ten thousand (10,000) shares the stock of the Western Union Telegraph Company, and ten thousand (10,000) shares of the stock of the Missouri Pacific Railway Company—all the foregoing bonds and stocks to be treated as worth par; and the receipt of the said George J. Gould in full for the said services and all other services down to the time of my death, not otherwise paid for by me during my lifetime, unless I shall hereafter by a different testamentary provision provide, shall be

CORNELIUS VANDERBILT.

THE LAST WILL AND TESTAMENT. 245

all the voucher required by my executors and trustees.

Ninth.—The better to protect and conserve the values of my properties, it is my desire, and I so direct and provide, that the shares of any railways and other incorporated companies at any time held by my executors and trustees, or my said trustees, shall always be voted by them or by their proxies at all corporate meetings as a unit; and in case my said executors and trustees, or my said trustees, do not concur as to how said stock shall be voted, then, in view of the fact that my son George J. Gould has for years had the management of said properties, and is familiar therewith, and with other like properties, I direct and provide that in such event his judgment shall control, and he is hereby authorized and empowered to vote the said shares in person or by proxy in such manner as his judgment shall dictate.

Tenth.—Except as herein modified, my said will and the first codicil thereto and all the provisions thereof shall remain in full force and unaffected, and said will and said codicil are hereby ratified and confirmed in every respect, except so far as the same are inconsistent with this codicil.

IN WITNESS WHEREOF, I, Jay Gould, have to the foregoing codicil to my last will and testament subscribed my name and set my seal, this 21st day of November, 1892.

15

246 LIFE OF JAY GOULD.

Subscribed, sealed, published, and declared by the said Jay Gould, the testator, to be his last will and testament and codicil thereto, in our presence, and to us, who, at the same time, at his request, and in the presence of each other and of said testator, have hereto, at the end of such will and testament and codicil thereto, signed our names as attesting witnesses this 21st day of November, 1892.

JOHN F. DILLON, residing at No.671 Madison Avenue, New York city.

JOHN P. MUNN, residing at No. 18 West Fifty-eighth Street, New York, N. Y.

MARGARET TERRY, No. 15 Tompkins Place, Brooklyn.

I, Jay Gould, do now make, publish, and declare the following additional codicil to my last will and testament, to wit:

First.—I give and bequeath to my beloved daughter, Helen M. Gould, absolutely all of the furniture, books, paintings, statuary, silver, plate, and household contents in my house No. 579 Fifth Avenue, New York city, and I modify and change the third article of the foregoing second codicil to my will accordingly; all of the rest of said will and codicils to stand except as thus modified.

Second.—I give and devise to my beloved son, Edwin Gould, in fee simple absolute the house and lot in the city of New York in which he now resides, numbered No. one (1) East Forty-seventh Street,

THE LAST WILL AND TESTAMENT. 247

together with all of the furniture and household effects therein belonging to me.

Third.—I reaffirm my will and the codicils thereto in every respect except as modified and changed by this third codicil.

In Witness Whereof, I, Jay Gould, have to the foregoing codicil to my last will and testament sub·scribed my name and set my seal this the 21st day of November, A. D. 1892.

Subscribed, sealed, and published and declared by the said Jay Gould, the testator, to be his last will and testament and codicil thereto, in our presence and to us, who, at the same time, at his request and in the presence of each other and of the said testator have hereto, at the end of such will and testament and codicil thereto, signed our names as attesting witnesses this the 21st day of November, A. D. 1892.

John F. Dillon, of No. 671 Madison Avenue, New York.

John P. Munn, residing at No. 18 West Fifty-eighth Street, New York, N. Y.

Margaret Terry, No. 15 Tompkins Place, Brooklyn.

248

LIFE OF JAY GOULD.

Mr. Gould's will is remarkable as a legal structure, and while it has been sharply criticised there is no question that it is characteristic of his sagacity, his family affection, his self-respect, and his serene silence in the matters that concerned his personal relations with the public. First he gives due recognition to the services of his oldest son, but he does not place his younger sons in a dependent or inferior position. He does not seek to evade the public policy of the country, and conform to the laws of primogeniture for the conservation of great estates as in England. He gives the oldest son a few millions for that which he has accomplished, but after that the younger sons and the beloved daughters share and share alike. The sons and the daughter who have reached the age of full responsibility are formed into a family council with power to enforce respect but not to make disobedience synonymous with impoverishment. Those who do not heed the admonition of the loving consideration of brothers and sisters, suffer losses, but are not disinherited or outlawed. It was reasonable judgment that the admonition would be sufficient. Mr. George Gould had earned the special mention he received, and the designation of beloved son. He, as the head of the family, was not exalted that others might be humiliated, but in his hands were placed trusts that years of experience had proved he was competent to administer. In the last resort, in cases of differences of opinion, the decision of the oldest son is to be

THE LAST WILL AND TESTAMENT. 249

conclusive. Authority must be fixed somewhere. In private affairs there must ultimately be a despotism. A perfect democracy would result in permanent division and possible dissension.

The family sentiment is clear in the touching bequest to Miss Helen Gould, who is to have an ample income to keep house until the children attain their majority. The home is to stand the castle of the family, and the younger children to be in the care of the elder sister, who has been to them as a sisterly mother since the mother herself was called away. This arrangement is the most solemn testimony of Mr. Gould's tender and loving family sentiments, and the cool, prescient judgment that his antagonists dreaded, but never denied. It is said he gave no great charitable bequests, and failed in his duty in that respect. His justification is found in his experience in giving $10,000 to charity in the church of which his wife and daughters were members. He found those he desired to help embarrassed by uncharitable commentary upon the bounty he bestowed. It was the better way, he thought, to leave to his children the works of benevolence that were not allowed him without reflections upon his motives and actions as to the origin of his means that would have discredited him if the public as well as himself had not regarded them as inapplicable. He was sure his daughter Helen had continued the benefactions that his gentle wife knew so well how to administer. There could have been no happier

LIFE OF JAY GOULD.

solution of the problem of the indebtedness of the rich man to the poor consistent with the maintenance of his great fortune as the inheritance of his children.

It is in evidence from the lips of those most intimately associated with Mr. Gould that what he did in the case of the yellow fever plague in Memphis was an illustration of his method. "I will," said he, "give $5,000 to the help of the people at once, and as much more"—he was speaking to General Eckert—"when it is wanted, if you will fix it so that my name shall not appear in the transaction." He did give much more, and was remembered for it by a grateful community when he died, for after all the secret was not well kept. On one of his yacht trips he stopped at Mt. Vernon and heard the ladies having in charge the home and tomb of Washington were disturbed because there was a purpose to purchase land for sale in the neighborhood, and establish a saloon. Mr. Gould bought the land and gave it to the ladies, and is held by them in grateful remembrance. No one has a right to reproach his memory for lack of charity.

In spite of Jay Gould's many millions, he was down on the tax lists for very modest amounts. He seems to have had as much ability in keeping down his taxes as in piling up his millions. Despite his immense accumulations he paid taxes on only $500,-000 in personal property. The real estate in New York city on which he paid directly was confined to

THE LAST WILL AND TESTAMENT. 251

the Grand Opera House, of which he was the owner, and to his home on Fifth Avenue. At one time he also paid the taxes on his son's home on East Forty-seventh Street, but after that formally passed out of his possession he was, of course, relieved from paying any further taxes on that property.

Notwithstanding the very conservative estimate placed upon the value of his personal holdings, Mr. Gould tried a few years ago to escape paying any personal taxes at all in this city. He urged the plea of outside residence, and because he paid personal taxes in Westchester County on his belongings at his country home at Irvington insisted that he was being unfairly treated in being compelled to pay on $500,000 of personal property in New York city. He did not press the matter, however, and continued to allow his personal property to be placed on the tax list at $500,000.

The Commissioner of the Tax Department has said that it was impossible to tell just what Mr. Gould's holdings in real estate in New York really amounted to.

"Real estate," the Commissioner explained, "is entered on the books of the tax department by number only. The only way to get any idea there as to the ownership of a piece of property is to see who paid the taxes on it. According to this test the real estate on which Mr. Gould paid taxes in New York is confined to his residence. The Manhattan Railroad Company and the Western Union Tele-

252

LIFE OF JAY GOULD.

graph Company are large holders of real estate, but the companies pay their own taxes, of course, and the only place Mr. Gould's name appears on the tax department books is in relation to his residence, and the admitted $500,000 of personal property."

The peculiarity of the matter is that Mr. Gould was never really in business in New York city. His wealth was very largely in stocks that had no particular value by themselves and that were not even on the market. He made his money by taking hold of almost bankrupt companies, getting control of the common stock that had no particular value beyond its voting power, and then by manipulating things to his own interest.

Besides, his various railroad stocks, like the Union Pacific, Wabash, Texas, and Kansas Pacific, were not assessable. The bonds that were assessable were generally those of roads that had been reorganized and reorganized till any estimate of value became a pure matter of guesswork.

Twenty-five thousand dollars a year is said to be an ample estimate for the entire amount of annual taxes Mr. Gould paid on his variously estimated millions.

Under the laws of 1892 property bequeathed to Mr. Gould's children was liable to a tax of one per cent. Section 2 of chapter 399 says:

"When the property or any beneficial interest therein passes, by any such transfer, to or for the

THE LAST WILL AND TESTAMENT. 253

use of any father, mother, husband, wife, child, brother, sister, wife or widow of a son, or the husband of a daughter, or any child or children adopted as such in conformity with the laws of this State, or to any person to whom any such decedent grantor, donor, or vendor for not less than ten years prior to such transfer stood in the mutally-acknowledged relation of a parent, or to any lineal descendant of such decedent grantor, donor, or vendor born in lawful wedlock, such transfer shall not be taxable under this act unless it is personal property to the value of $10,000 or more, in which case it shall be taxable under this act at the rate of one per centum upon the clear market value of such property."

The next section makes the tax a lien upon the property until it is paid. The tax is to be collected by the Controller of the county. Payment within six months gives a discount of 5 per cent.; if it is not made in eighteen months a penalty of 10 per cent. is provided. The Controller's fee is 5 per cent. on the first $50,000 of the tax, 3 per cent. on the second $50,000, and 1 per cent. on the rest. The balance of the tax is to be paid into the State Treasury.

A tax of 1 per cent. on the estate yielded about $720,000. The Controller accordingly would receive a fee of about $10,000.

CHAPTER XI.

MR. GOULD'S COLABORERS.

NATURALLY the fellow-workers in the same field with a man of gigantic undertakings and colossal successes are subjects of no small interest on the part of the people. With Mr. Gould in his meteoric career have been associated some brilliant men of affairs. This chapter will give sketches of their lives and connections with Mr. Gould.

DR. NORVIN GREEN.

Dr. Norvin Green, a distinguished citizen of New York, and President of the Western Union Telegraph Company, was born April 17th, 1818, on the northern bank of the Ohio River, where the flourishing manufacturing city of New Albany, Indiana, now stands, opposite the lower part of the city of Louisville, Ky. His father, Joseph Green, was born in Kentucky, near Louisville in 1799, was a volunteer in the War of 1812, and fought under Jackson at the battle of New Orleans on January 8th, 1815. After this brilliant victory, at the age of 19, Joseph Green returned to Kentucky, where he was soon after employed by Mr. John Speed, father of Attorney-General James Speed, and of many other worthy sons and daughters, to manage his salt works at Man's Lick, near Louisville. He did not remain long in this employment, as he fell in love with, and within two years married, Miss Susan Ball, a young lady of that neighborhood.

Immediately upon this marriage, Joseph Green removed with his young wife across the Ohio, and took a prominent part in organizing the new County of Floyd, of which he was made the first sheriff, and Norvin Green, their first born, was one of the earliest native-born citizens of that county.

In his childhood, Norvin Green had the educational advantages of the ordinary country schools, and no more. During this period his father removed to Breckenridge County, Kentucky, and in the many intervals between the short terms of the country schools in which he wrestled with the rudiments, he learned from practical experience the, truth of the old song:

> " For to plow and to sow, for to reap and to mow,
> Is the work of a farmer's boy."

According to his strength, whatever a boy, and a bright, well-grown one, too, could do of the work of a farm, he did his share. This work, and the knowledge and the skill he then acquired, stood him in good stead at an age when few boys are called on to exercise any judgment in their own affairs. It was not a hard life, and the young lad could and did join the Breckenridge County boys

256

LIFE OF JAY GOULD.

in their games of ball and other sports, and held his own. Kentuckians have always been fond of horse-races, and in those days every community had its own race-track, where, for men and boys, was found their principal amusement. Every promising foal was prepared and tested with the neighbors, and strangers would soon be accommodated with a match. Plucky, agile, always fond of a good horse, understanding and sympathizing with his mount, with a fine instinct of time and a sharp eye on the "other fellows," young Norvin Green became the favorite rider for his father, and gained some local reputation for the skill with which he would bring his horses out ahead at the finish. He was also able to greatly assist his father in more serious matters, for about this time the latter, in performing his duties as sheriff of the county, had to collect the State and county taxes. Norvin, then only 13 years old, rode about over the county, from house to house, collecting taxes, giving receipts, and faithfully keeping an accurate record for the official reports and accountings.

At the expiration of the term, Joseph Green engaged in quite a number of business ventures; keeping a tavern, a country store, a wood-yard, a wool-carding machine, a horse-power grist mill, and a blacksmith shop, and Norvin kept the accounts of all these, with no preparation other than that acquired from his arithmetic in the country school. The prices of everything were in pounds, shillings,

MR. GOULD'S COLABORERS. 257

and pence, six shillings to the dollar, which complicated the young bookkeeper's labors in no slight degree.

In 1833, Joseph Green resolved to concentrate his energies, his fortune, and his credit upon a serious venture, and, to carry this out, bought a small fleet. The Mississippi River, and its tributary, the Ohio, was almost the sole highway of commerce, and these broad waters teemed with life and business. The favorite vessel was the broad flat boat, without keel, stem, or stern-post, adaptable to almost every conceivable purpose. He fitted up three or four of these for a large number of horses, their food, attendants, etc. He took charge of these himself, while another was fitted up and stocked with the multifarious assortment of a country store, including hardware and candy, dry goods and bacon, knick-knacks and grind-stones, school-books and stogy boots, and practically every movable thing that could not be produced on a farm. This boat he placed in charge of his son Norvin, and the fleet was pushed out into the stream, for it was on the current alone they relied for power of locomotion. They did not remain long in company, inasmuch as the father proceeded without delay to the distant Southern market, while Norvin made frequent and protracted stops along the shore, disposing of his wares. Some four or five months after, they met again in Natchez, Miss., where the son, full of exultation over the successful and profitable disposition of nearly all his

LIFE OF JAY GOULD.

stock, sought his father to learn of the main venture.

Very different had been the fortunes of the main fleet. Keeping in the current to make as rapid progress as possible, they had met with adverse fortune along their way, and in the broad water near Grand Gulf had encountered a cyclone that came near swamping the entire fleet, crew and cargo. They, however, escaped with the total loss of one boat and cargo of horses ; a serious loss indeed, but a relief from the overwhelming catastrophe threatened. In consequence of the arduous toil and exposure of this voyage, Joseph Green, on arriving at Natchez, was laid up with a dangerous fever, and, to crown his misfortunes, the remainder of his fleet and shipment were seized to satisfy a surety debt he had incurred by becoming the bondsman of a faithless administrator.

Cast down, but not discouraged by this sudden and severe blow, Norvin Green set about at once to build up the fallen fortunes of the family. As soon as his father's health permitted, he took the whole family to Cincinnati, where, with the proceeds of his first venture on a store-boat, he purchased another and a larger boat, fitted it up as a dwelling and a store, bought a stock of goods, paying one-half cash and giving his promissory notes without security at six months for the other half. These notes were made on April 11th, 1834, just one week before he was 16 years of age.

MR. GOULD'S COLABORERS. 259

Once again, with undaunted pluck, Norvin Green looked fortune boldly in the face, and her frowns vanished like frost before the climbing sun. Slowly floating down the stream, stopping wherever business could be done, until the people's wants were supplied, at length the mouth of the Kentucky River was reached, and the boat tied up on the opposite shore.

The location was found to be of such excellence that he resolved to establish a permanent business here; so he leased a farm, built a store and a warehouse, and did a most prosperous business, not only selling goods, but bartering for and buying all sorts of farm produce, oats, corn, potatoes, bacon, live stock, etc., which, from time to time, were floated off to Southern markets. In three years he made profits enough to pay off his own and the remaining debts of his father in Breckenridge County, and to buy a farm on the Kentucky side, a few miles below the mouth of the Kentucky River.

The country was well wooded at that time, and he made a contract to deliver 1,200 cords of wood at Madison, Ind. Securing the hired labor necessary, he threw into this the earnestness and thoroughness which has since characterized his work. Taking his own axe with him into camp, he added his own labor, while supervising that of his hired assistants. With such management, the contract could not fail of a good profit, and with this in his pocket, his father's family again prosperous, he felt at liberty to choose for himself a pursuit in life.

260   *LIFE OF JAY GOULD.*

He decided upon the noble profession of medicine,
and in the next spring, 1838, he began his studies
under Dr. Mason, of Carrollton, Ky., continuing them
in the University of Louisville, where he graduated
in March, 1840, the entire expenses being met from
the profits of his wood contract.   These two years
were devoted to hard and unremitting study, not
only of the text-books and lectures of his profession, but of the rudiments of Latin and English
Science and Literature.   In the medical school he
developed a rare quality of memory, being able, by
his power of concentration, to memorize and repeat
or write out the most scholarly lectures, upon a
single hearing, unaided by a written memorandum
made at the time.

Soon after graduation, Dr. Green married Miss
Martha English, the daughter of Captain James W.
English, who served in the War of 1812, under
General Harrison, in the Northwest, and had settled
down as a well-to-do farmer near Carrollton, Ky.
For 13 years Dr. Green devoted himself to the
practice of medicine, in which he succeeded.

He took an active interest in politics, and served
two terms in the Kentucky Legislature, in the
second term being a candidate of the Democratic
party for speaker.

At this period of his life, Dr. Green presented a
striking appearance.   Tall and slender, his bearing
was at once easy and dignified, and he seemed rather
more than less than his six feet in stature.   Indeed.

CYRUS W. FIELD.

MR. GOULD'S COLABORERS.

his "presence," most difficult to describe, was such that he was always regarded as a tall man among a people noted for their unusual height. His complexion was pale, but set off by his hair of a raven blackness and fine as silk, with a suspicion of a curl, and the ever-varying expression of his dark eyes, and flexible, smooth-shaven lips and chin. In the canvasses of those days a much greater part was done by public speeches than nowadays, and nearly all the voters attended the political debates. At times these gatherings were so large that but few voices were strong enough and clear enough to reach the most remote, and at such times without strain or huskiness, Dr. Green would pitch his voice in a high, clear tone, and electrify the crowds by his ringing enunciation of terse, succinct, and clear statements of the questions of the day. After the close of this brilliant canvass and the inauguration of President Pierce, he was appointed Commissioner and Disbursing Agent for the construction of the new Post Office and Custom House building at Louisville, in May, 1853.

In the following year, Dr. Green became interested in the telegraph, a business with which his name is inseparably associated. The outlook for this infant industry was then very unpromising. Although Professor Morse's wonderful invention had long been demonstrated to the scientific world, the problem of its daily use in application to the ordinary business of life was yet to be solved. The re-

264   *LIFE OF JAY GOULD.*

quirements of construction were imperfectly understood and worse carried out. Worst of all, the transmission was subject to long interruptions and delays.

In 1854, a syndicate was formed to lease the united lines of the Morse system from Cincinnati to New Orleans, and the O'Reilly lines between the same points. Norvin Green was the new blood in this syndicate, which was incorporated and afterward more widely known as the Southwestern Telegraph Company. A new policy was adopted, a new and better system of construction instituted, the locality changed almost throughout, to get on the lines of the railroads then being rapidly projected in that section, a quicker and more reliable service in transmission enforced, together with a better economy of office expenditures, and very soon the new company was enabled to do what the old ones never had done—make profits over expenses. The reform came too late for these to benefit by, as they were both hopelessly insolvent, and all their properties and interests were sold out under decrees for judgment creditors, the new company ultimately becoming the purchaser.

Much as had been done, it was but the beginning of the vast labors that were to follow, to remove the exasperating delays and build up for the telegraph a popular confidence in its speed and reliability, which is the very breath of its life. In 1857, Dr. Green came to New York, and succeeded in gathering there a conference of the Presidents of the six leading telegraph companies, and laid before them a plan for improving and increasing their work. This was the first telegraph "deal," as it was the most important of all; it was a contract for thirty years, expiring about 1885, and was never broken. It was the beginning of all telegraph consolidation, and all that have followed have been upon the principles set out in it.

The immediate consequences of the Six-Party-Contract—the first embodiment of the idea of a continental telegraph system—were a prompter and better service, and a speedy response from the public, in the form of increased and profitable business.

Nine years afterward, the benefits of this alliance were so obvious that all the parties, doing business exclusively in the United States, united in one company, selecting the Western Union, as holding a charter better adapted for the purpose, and their stocks were exchanged for the stock of that company, which had been increased for the purpose. In this deal, as in all the subsequent ones, Dr. Green took the active part, drafting the provisions on the most difficult points, and, in the preliminary negotiations, being often made the referee on contested matters, not only because of his thorough mastery of the questions in dispute, but because of his well-earned reputation as a fair man and a just arbitrator. Clear-headed and patient to an unusual degree, Dr. Green never becomes excited in negotiations though they involve millions, and never provokes antagonism from those representing conflicting interests. It has frequently devolved upon him to settle disputed points contended for by men of the most aggressive bent of mind, and his great ability in devising a common plane on which all can meet without sacrificing principle, has made him the central figure in these vast transactions, and has added, in every instance, to the respect he has earned from those associated with him in important affairs.

A full biography of Dr. Norvin Green would involve the history of the telegraph in America, a subject much too large for this sketch. But great as has been his influence in the direction and control of that new and mighty industry, he has not been confined to it, nor even continuously in its active control. In 1867, his neighbors in Louisville elected him to the Legislature, and informed him of it the next day as a surprise. He served, and a large number of his fellow-members came near electing him to the United States Senate, a place equally unsought by him.

He was largely interested in the Louisville, Cincinnati & Lexington Railroad, and, at the urgent request of the stockholders, in 1870 he accepted the presidency and active management of its affairs.

It is in the development of the telegraph that Dr. Green's best work has been done, but he has done enough outside of that to show that he would have taken a corresponding position in any line of work he should lay his hand to.

MR. GOULD'S COLABORERS.

Dr. Green's reputation, and the respect and honor accorded as his due, are not confined to this country. All the administrations of telegraph in the nations of Europe send him their official reports as they are published, and many of them send to him inspectors and other high officials to investigate and report upon the details of the organization which has grown up under his hands. Handling more messages than any three of the Continental nations, at a profit and not at an annual deficit, and extending every year in advance of the construction of new railroads, his administration is regarded by them as a model of efficiency, elasticity, and economy. In 1883 he visited England, where he was welcomed by the magnates of states and cities. The Hon. Henry Fawcett, the great Postmaster-General, presented him with a circular letter to all telegraph offices, commanding them to transmit all messages for him free. This document is unique, the only one of its kind ever issued by the government of Great Britain, and was intended as the highest compliment to the great telegrapher.

And now, any day and every day, Dr. Green may be seen seated in the large room, which is at once his office and the place of meeting of the multitudinous boards of directors, committees, and conferences over which he presides, by which the affairs of the Western Union and its many subordinate corporations are conducted. His appearance has greatly changed in the last 20 years, mainly through an increase of weight. While his flesh is by no

268

LIFE OF JAY GOULD.

means a burden to him or too much for his large frame, yet a double chin and an amplitude of waistcoat make a great difference from the slender figure of his earlier manhood. With the fuller habit his complexion has also changed, and presents a healthy ruddiness. His hair has become very thin, and there are now but few left of the orignal raven hue, and his mouth is shaded by a heavy mustache entirely white. His ante-room is generally occupied by persons waiting their turn to see him on the widest range of subjects, and without hurry or rush of any kind each one is admitted and his business promptly considered.

Imperturbable and completely at his ease in the midst of a great whirl of business, Dr. Green always has time for a pleasant word with a friend.

Courteous and kindly to all, Dr. Green has been noted for more than a third of a century for his countless acts of friendship and benevolence to his fellow-workers of the telegraph, from the messenger's bench to the director's chair. It will be a sad day of parting to thousands of these when he leaves forever the well-worn chair at the broad President's table, which he has filled so long and so well.

THOMAS THOMPSON ECKERT.

Thomas Thompson Eckert, who holds to the foremost place in the active conduct of the Western Union Telegraph Company, now vast and interna-

MR. GOULD'S COLABORERS. 269

tional, was born April 23d, 1825, in Steubenville, Ohio. He learned the telegraphic art in 1848, and on the following year, having been appointed Postmaster at Wooster, Ohio, opened up the first postal telegraph service by receiving the Wade wire into his office, and uniting the duties of postmaster and operator.

J. H. Wade, now one of Cleveland's most wealthy citizens, was, at that time, building telegraph lines westward, with Denis Doren as his chief of construction. He saw in young Eckert's aggressive vigor and industry a man he needed. Without much hesitation he offered him the superintendence of the "Union Telegraph Lines," then being extended from Pittsburgh, Pa., by way of the Fort Wayne & Chicago Railroad to Chicago. The Union Telegraph Lines were operated in connection with the Wade, Speed & Cornell lines, then somewhat extensively in operation throughout the Northwest. They were of the gossamer order, and all needed whatever support an earnest man could give them. Mr. Wade having identified himself with the Western Union Telegraph Company soon after its formation, his lines, one by one were absorbed thereby, and formed the basis of his fortune. Superintendent Eckert thus came into the service of the company, over which in later years he was to become the managing head. In his new relations he became soon known for his energy, good judgment, and capacity of labor. Yet, in 1859 he

LIFE OF JAY GOULD.

resigned and went to superintend the affairs of a gold mining company in Montgomery County, N. C. Here he remained until the breaking out of the war in 1861, when he returned North, and resided in Cincinnati, Ohio.

He was not long permitted to be idle. A few months after his return to Ohio, Colonel Thomas A. Scott, Assistant Secretary of War, called him to Washington, where he was placed in charge of the military telegraph at the headquarters of General McClellan. In 1862 he accompanied General McClellan to the Peninsula as Superintendent of the Military Telegraph Department of the Potomac, with the rank of Captain and A. Q. M.

In September of the same year he was recalled to Washington to establish the Military Telegraph Headquarters in the War Department Buildings, and was promoted to be Major and A. Q. M.

In this service General Eckert was thoroughly at home. His duties placed him in the most intimate relations with President Lincoln and Secretary of War Stanton, by whom he was highly trusted and esteemed. An evidence of this confidence was shown by his appointment, at a very delicate stage of the war, to meet the leaders of the Southern Confederacy at City Point, in January, 1865, a mission which he performed with discretion, intelligence, and fidelity. It was not the only service thus discreetly and successfully rendered during the long night of the nation's peril.

MR. GOULD'S COLABORERS. 271

It is one of the unwritten facts connected with that period that General Eckert, on his way back from City Point, after his interview with the Confederate chiefs, was met by gentlemen from New York who offered him, but in vain, a large sum of money to give them the result of his mission.

On the afternoon when the message came from the army in Virginia, "We are in danger; send Sheridan," Stanton and Sheridan were in the War Department in anxious council. Instantly General Eckert took possession of the Baltimore & Ohio Railroad, ordered it cleared, and a special engine made ready to carry Sheridan to Harper's Ferry. It was soon ready. All through the night it sped, while every operator remained at his post, guarding the road until the iron horse flew past. At break of day the car entered the depot at Winchester, and there pawing the ground and ready for the great ride to the field, stood the gallant horse that was to make "Sheridan's Ride" famous in all coming history.

In 1864 General Eckert was breveted Lieutenant-Colonel and soon after to Brigadier-General. The same year also he was appointed Assistant Secretary of War, which position he held until August, 1866, when he resigned to accept the office of General Superintendent of the Eastern Division of the lines of the Western Union Telegraph Company. This included the entire territory between Washington and Cape Breton, including all the New Eng-

LIFE OF JAY GOULD.

land States, the State of New York, and Eastern Pennsylvania, a position which assumed unusual importance and responsibility on account of the opening up of the transatlantic correspondence, which followed the successful laying of the Atlantic cable.

He carried into this work much of the discipline, vim, and thoroughness which characterized him in the War Department as assistant to his great chief and friend, Edwin M. Stanton. As President of the Atlantic and Pacific and American Union Companies, notice has already been taken. Mr. Gould's chivalric friendship for General Eckert, which appears in connection with the latter company is curious and interesting. It secured for him a post of honor and of responsibility as General Manager of the greatest industry of the world. No one believes that Mr. Gould erred in his choice. General Eckert was a force he needed, and whom, therefore, he selected and held.

As a man, General Eckert has personal qualities which endear him to his friends. He is at the prime of life, at a period when years mellow without weakening. His physique is powerful, well formed, and indicative of self-reliance and capacity of resistance. His feelings are strong, alert, and sensitive. As an officer, he is punctilious, insists upon recognition, on prompt obedience and respect. He has, however, beneath his official vigor a wealth of consideration and kindness which renders him

MR. GOULD'S COLABORERS.

gentle and approachable, and secures him a large circle of devoted friends. In the service of the War Department this was indeed noticeable. It was just the character of labor in which the fellowship of men become strong, fraternal, and affectionate. It often challenged heroic devotion. It awoke in the sense of danger the profoundest sentiments of sympathy, respect, and love. His most trusted lieutenants are the men who served him in the war.

General Eckert has at his side in the conduct of his executive work a gentleman, whose ready pen and literary ability greatly facilitates its prompt and graceful performance. He is Thomas Frederick Clark, General Eckert's private secretary.

Mr. Clark has shown great ability in wielding a fluent and graceful pen. It is easy to see how valuable readiness of composition is in connection with so large and varied and exacting a service as belongs to the general managership of the Western Union Telegraph Company.

Close to him was also placed a man which the general manager knew he could trust. The lines now consolidated cover the entire country. They had been built by men more or less capable, but required the oversight of some competent man accustomed and capable to control. Each of the 20 Superintendents of Districts had under him gangs of men under foremen of more or less experience, constantly adding or renewing the lines. The cost

274

LIFE OF JAY GOULD.

of ordinary repairs alone was millions a year. On the honesty and promptness of their work much of the success of the company depended. These needed a head that could catch with a firm hand this important class of labor.

Gen. Eckert was ever one of the most esteemed of Mr. Gould's colaborers.

G. P. MOROSINI.

One of the closest of Mr. Gould's friends—many years in his confidence—enjoying and reciprocating his highest consideration, is G. P. Morosini. He is a man of striking presence and romantic history. Mr. Gould first met him in the Erie Railway service, finding him chief clerk in the Auditor's office. Morosini is a native of Venice, and was one of the young revolutionists in northern Italy when the grandfather of the present King was overpowered by the Austrians. Morosini had received a military education and was surrendered a prisoner of war. He was a follower and friend of Garibaldi, and when his country became an Austrian conquest, became a sailor.

He was tall, muscular, full of courage, and seasoned in adventure. One day, taking a stroll on Staten Island, his ship at anchor in the bay, he happened to encounter a small mob of roughs abusing a boy, who was defending himself to the best of his ability but badly hurt, bleeding and struggling, asking for mercy and shouting for help.

MR. GOULD'S COLABORERS. 275

The tall, young Italian sailor rushed headlong to the rescue, knocking down two or three of the first of the ruffians, who were a gang of stout boys; and when they in turn assaulted him he drew his sheath knife, which sailors carried afloat and ashore, and held the pack at bay. The rescued boy was still an object of vengeance, and Morosini saw him well on the way home, followed for a considerable distance by his enemies, who were only held back by the certainty that they would be knifed if they ventured within reach. A few days after the boy he had befriended sought him out and brought his father to thank him. The father was Nathaniel Marsh, Secretary of the Erie Railroad Company, and he offered the gallant sailor money, which was declined. Then Mr. Marsh wanted to know whether there was anything else he could do. Morosini said he was tired of the sea, and would be glad to find employment in New York. Mr. Marsh managed that, and Morosini, May 29th, 1855, entered the service of the Erie Company and remained in it until six months after Mr. Gould retired from it, and then he was employed by Mr. Gould as a confidential secretary. In this capacity he was of great service to Mr. Gould, and won for himself an enviable reputation.

Mr. Morosini's name has been intimately associated with that of Mr. Gould for years. When Mr. Gould would not talk to the newspaper representatives and others, Mr. Morosini was ever ready to extend such courtesies as would not conflict with sound policy.

LIFE OF JAY GOULD.

At a meeting of the Directors of the Western Union Telegraph Company, immediately after Mr. Gould's demise, the President, Dr. Norvin Green, formally announced the death of Mr. Gould, saying he had been a powerful and enthusiastic supporter of the Company, and a loyal and whole-souled friend of all who had been associated with him. Mr. Samuel Sloan offered a memorial, which was adopted with unanimity, as follows :

"Jay Gould died at his residence in the city of New York on Friday, December 2d, 1892, in the fifty-seventh year of his age. He had been a director of this Company for about twelve years, and was such at the time of his death. It is fitting, therefore, that it shall place upon its record its estimate of Mr. Gould's character and services and its sorrowful sense of its great loss in his death.

" Familiarity with him, acquired through years of constant intercourse, enables the members of its directory to speak concerning him with knowledge and confidence. What follows are words, not of eulogy, but of just and considerate estimate.

" Among the many eminent men who in the history of this Company have had a place in its counsels Mr. Gould was in some respects the most remarkable. The intellectual qualities to which he owed his almost unexampled success are not far to seek. Underlying all was his faith in,the continued growth, advancement, and prosperity of our country. He forecasted the future with confidence. and saw in

MR. GOULD'S COLABORERS. 277

their earlier stages the value of such properties as the Union Pacific, Kansas Pacific, Missouri Pacific, Manhattan Railway, and Western Union. He boldly risked all on the soundness of his judgment. His judgment concerning the value of corporate properties singly, and of their possibilities for profitable combination amounted to positive genius—a genius in these lines probably never surpassed, if equalled.

" Acquiring these properties, he gave his energies to their development. This was not the hasty work of a day, but the slow work of years. He was not merely or chiefly a speculator. He was at home in every department of the service. He knew his properties intimately. He could instantly detect anything wrong. He inspected them in person regularly. He gave to his properties the benefit not only of his genius, but of his diligence and industry, which, until his health gave way, never tired. He did not always receive the praise to which he was entitled. He did not invest his wealth in lands, or buildings, or governments, or established securities, and content himself with idly receiving their income. His industries gave daily employment to more than one hundred thousand men and support to their families. His enterprise contributed more largely to the opening and development of the western and southwestern parts of our country than that of any other man.

"At his death probably no man in the United States possessed more power. His word was law

278   *LIFE OF JAY GOULD.*

throughout the vast interests in his control established in many States and Territories—almost from ocean to ocean. But with all this he ever bore himself modestly, without any ostentation or vulgar display of wealth or power. He was a model of parental and domestic virtue. So much is known of all men.

"But the members of this body desire to record their knowledge of the warmth and steadiness of Mr. Gould's friendships, of his noble impulses, and disinterested and generous deeds, some of which, without murmur or complaint from him, were popularly distorted so as to become matter of blame instead of praise.

"*Resolved*, That in the death of a counsellor so wise, sagacious, and faithful as Mr. Gould ever proved himself to be, this Company feels it has sustained not only a deep but an irreparable loss; that it tenders its sincerest sympathy to his surviving sons and daughters; that its directors will attend his funeral in a body; that this minute be spread upon its records, and that a copy thereof suitably engrossed and authenticated, be sent to his children."

The Board of Directors of the Manhattan Elevated Railroad Company adopted the following preamble and resolution:

"The President of this Company has been taken from it. Elected on the 9th day of November, 1881, to be its official head, Jay Gould has uninter-

LORD ROTHSCHILD.

ruptedly from that time to this given to the service of this Company a large part of his thoughts and of his interest. No one of the many other great enterprises in which he was concerned enlisted to a greater degree his close attention and best energies. Although in many States of the Union locomotives rode on railways he had contributed to construct, the corporation that furnished him with the means of daily access to his home had no superior in its rank in his mind. In the management of its affairs he displayed the qualities to which he owed his success in many fields. He was clear in his perceptions, swift in judgment and prompt in action. Patient in investigation and in the accumulation of details, his mastery of them was complete and his memory accurate and tenacious. He was self-reliant, yet ever seeking information and correction of his views from others.

" While disposed to adhere strongly to his own plans and ideas, he was always ready to yield his judgment to a superior reason. He expected full performance of his duty from each one who undertook responsibility, but he fully trusted those who were engaged in the duties of execution, and left them large latitude in the discharge of their functions. Never elated by success, he was cool and courageous in defeat. He acted in accordance with well-considered and far-reaching plans, and possessed the strength of will to adhere to his purpose through difficulties and apparent repulses. In his

282

LIFE OF JAY GOULD.

personal intercourse with those who were associated with him in his great endeavors he was kind and considerate, a good listener, and willing to modify his plans to serve the common interest. He found the Manhattan Railway Company in the hands of receivers, substantially bankrupted, and in a condition where it was doubtful whether or not its system was to be disintegrated and resolved into its original elements. He leaves it prosperous, in excellent physical condition, its different lines consolidated and indissolubly bound together, performing an indispensable service to the public in the city of his business life.

" In his home life and in his relations to his children he found his happiness. As fellow-directors with him, he insured the companionship and the affectionate support of his sons in his business hours. To his sorrowing family, and especially to the members of this board who have lost not only President, but an affectionate and tender father, whose domestic circle furnished him with his only solace amid responsibilities greater than those that have been borne by many rulers of empires, the sympathy of this board is tendered.

"*Resolved*, That the foregoing minute be adopted and inscribed in the minutes of this board of directors, and that a copy thereof, duly certified, be sent by the Secretary to the family of the deceased President.

MR. GOULD'S COLABORERS.

"*Resolved*, That the general offices of the company be closed on the day of the funeral, Monday, December 5th, 1892."

RECOLLECTIONS OF SURVIVING FRIENDS.

A letter written by Mr. Gould when a mere boy of eighteen years has been published at Kingston, N. Y., by Mr. S. B. Champion, the editor of a local paper there. Mr. Champion was an intimate and personal friend of Mr. Gould in his younger days, and the veteran editor received numerous visits from the great financier all through his life. Mr. Champion was not much older than his friend, but was often able to give him the benefit of his experience in the form of sound advice. Mr. Gould often worked in the line prescribed by the advice of his friend Champion with success. When they were together evidences of friendship were not lacking, and when separated they invariably corresponded. Mr. Gould was engaged upon his Delaware County map and was recovering from a severe illness at the time the following letter was written.

"ROXBURY, December 28th, 1854.

"*S. B. Champion, Esq.*

"FRIEND CHAMP :—How shall I commence a letter to you? Would you believe me were I to say I was puzzled whether to commence with a broad business letter caption 'Mr.,' etc., 'Dear Sir,' etc., or whether to sit down and imagine an actual mouth-to-mouth chat proceeding? Well, you see that at the top of my letter is that cold, formal commencement, but just then the recollection of the pleasant times we have had together, and the time for which I hope is not altogether past, put every shadow aside, and I almost imagine myself in *The Mirror* office at this moment. It is a long time since I have heard from you, except by Mr. Peters, a week since. But through the weekly invitation of *The Mirror* I commenced to write last week, but my hand shook so that I had to give it up. Now, Champ, you are a man of newspapers and advertisements, and proprietor of *The Mirror* office. I want you to study up something for me to do. The doctor stands over my shoulder and criticises every movement as an alarming symptom. His orders are, for the present: 'Live on soups made of shadows.' To say the word map requires a potion of castor oil, and the thought of transacting any kind of business is equal to jumping into a mill-pond in winter-time. But I have dismissed their sympathies, and regulate my own diet. I find health and strength to improve in consequence. I have cutter and harness, and if you will only furnish sleighing I am at your service. Now, Champ, if you have time to answer this, tell me a good funny story. I have hardly raised a smile for five weeks. Yours respectfully.

" JAY GOULD."

This anecdote is related of Gould's relations with Mr. Champion:

In his youth Mr. Gould's vaulting ambition was to be an editor. He ventured over the hills from Roxbury up to Stamford, the beauty spot of Delaware County, while he was yet in his teens, to get

LIFE OF JAY GOULD.

the chance to learn the printing business. Venerable S. B. Champion, then a hustling journalist hardly much older than young Gould, gave the lad the chance he sought. Mr. Gould tied on his apron, rolled up his sleeves, and went at it.

Champion is full of anecdotes of that apprenticeship time. There is a tradition that, in addition to setting type, the apprentice was permitted to look somewhat after the editorial side of the paper.

Early in Mr. Gould's career Mr. Champion's journal was able, for one week, at least, to attract considerable and rather unusual attention. "Champ" went one day to a political convention, held over in an adjoining town, and young Mr. Jason Gould was left in charge on publication day to close up the forms and generally look after such important matters as addressing wrappers and seeing to it that the office towel was kept standing safely in its accustomed corner.

But the future master of the railway world was ambitious. He bethought himself to scan the editorial, more or less fervid, in which "Champ" was extolling the party's nominees. Somehow it seemed to the budding genius that that editorial lacked something.

After consideration, he came to the conclusion that he ought to round the rhetoric out; that he ought to supply the virtues which were lacking. He did. Mr. Champion came home to find his eulogistic

MR. GOULD'S COLABORERS. 287

periods slightly changed. Only slightly. Mr. Gould had only taken the liberty of writing in an occasional " not " here and there.

That was the week that " Champ " learned to swear. It was also the week that Mr. Jay Gould became an ex-editor.

There is this clever story that Mr. Gould was superstitious. He did not bother, perhaps, over beginning things on Friday, and the new moon over his left shoulder may not have disturbed him. But only a few weeks before his death he rather insisted upon having a superstitious weakness. He was on his way down town, when he came across a Wall Street friend, with whom he kept up conversation down the avenue. In the course of the chat Mr. Gould expressed himself as feeling physically much stronger than for a long time. His eyes were clear, his countenance was ruddy; he did not look like a sick man.

"I am getting along famously," he said. "My appetite has come back. I feel like a new man. Why, last night I ate two bowls of bread and milk, went to bed at eight o'clock, and slept through till eight this morning."

There was as much enthusiasm in the tone as if a record was being made of some stock market transaction with a million profit in it. But the cheerfulness disappeared when Mr. Gould's companion asked:

" How old are you, Mr. Gould ?"

LIFE OF JAY GOULD.

"Oh! I'm a young man yet," answered the millionaire.

The evasion was noticed, and for politeness' sake the questioner remarked, blandly:

"Pardon my inquiry, I only happened to be thinking of an odd thing I heard yesterday. Did you ever hear, Mr. Gould, that once every seven years a man runs extraordinary risks, and that whenever a man has a birthday divisible by seven he is in danger?"

"No—I never heard of that," said Mr. Gould. Then he turned to his *Times*. The elevated train ran down two or three blocks further. Mr. Gould was scanning the death notice column.

"The stock market looks well," remarked the other gentleman.

"How strange!" quoth Mr. Gould. His gaze went on through the death notices.

"I think stocks are going a good deal higher," was further remarked.

"It's really true," said Mr. Gould.

"Still," went on Mr. Gould's companion, "the bears are well organized and they are confident."

"My gracious, it's so," said Mr. Gould.

His neighbor looked at him a little astonished. Mr. Gould had finished the death notices, and was looking out of the window. There was not much glisten in his eye. The countenance wasn't ruddy. He had been dividing by seven the ages recorded in those death notices.

MR. GOULD'S COLABORERS.

"Western Union ought to go a good deal higher, oughtn't it, Mr. Gould?" said the other man.

And Mr. Gould's answer was: "It may be odd, but really I never heard before about this dividing your age by seven."

"Oh! that's only a foolish superstition," was the soothing reply.

"Oh! of course," said Mr. Gould; "of course!"

Then the chat went on of stocks, of money rates, of all the fol-de-rol of Wall Street.

"Cortlandt next!" yelled the elevated railroad guard.

"It's odd, isn't it," said Mr. Gould, as if in a reverie, and he arose to leave the train. "Do you know," said he, "eight sevens make fifty-six—and fifty-six, sir, is just my age."

The *World* has given accounts of instances of their experience of getting news from Mr. Gould that contain most interesting information. Mr. F. P. Hastings says in November, 1883, after the elevated railroad hearing, he was directed to see Mr. Gould, who had been on the witness stand two consecutive days, standing the legal firing as calmly as if questioned by one of his clerks. The courtroom was packed to suffocation by persons brought there through curiosity to see Gould. Several times he passed his hand over his brow, and the judge ordered the windows lowered to give more air, particularly as it seemed at one time that the witness would faint.

LIFE OF JAY GOULD.

A couple of days later rumor had it that Mr. Gould was sick, but all reporters were met by George Gould, who gave the assurance that his father was quite well. I called at the Fifth Avenue mansion the following afternoon, having been cautioned by my city editor not to come back without positive information.

I was shown into the reception-room on the left of the hall and the servant took up my card. Presently George Gould entered and said his father was dressing to go out, asking if he could be of service to me.

Telling him of the disquieting rumors concerning his father, he said they were false, absolutely false. "But," said I, "if Mr. Gould is not sick cannot I see him, just to convince myself?"

"I'll see; excuse me a moment," said George, and he ran up-stairs.

About five minutes later in walked Mr. Gould, and, extending his hand, which I took, he gave mine a gentle shake, and in a modulated voice asked:

"Do I look as if I were ill?"

George had apprised his father of my mission, and he came charged. He didn't look like a sick man. Bidding me be seated, he let himself down gingerly upon a small straw-bottomed chair.

Mr. Gould sat with his side to the window, a little to my right, facing me, so that I could observe every play of his countenance. Crossing his legs, one foot resting squarely on a fox skin, he ran both thumbs over his gold watch-chain, and said:

MR. GOULD'S COLABORERS.

"Well, what can I do for you?"

Telling him the object of my call, which so far had been satisfactory, I asked him if it was true that he had been squeezed to the extent of millions in Wall Street, as reported.

"Haven't heard of it," he replied, in the same low tone and slowly.

"But there are rumors that you lost heavily."

"Yes?"

"Is that true?"

"I can't say," and he dropped one hand on his knee, while with the other he toyed incessantly with the small charm suspended from his watch-chain.

"What is your opinion of the course of the stock market within the next fortnight?" I then ventured.

"I can't say," he replied, as his black eyes darted from the floor into my face as if he intended reading me through.

"Do you anticipate a large grain movement this fall?"

"Perhaps, yes."

"And that will, of course, advance the granger stocks, won't it?"

"Yes."

Seeing that he was not disposed to let himself out to any great extent on finances—not that he need have feared my taking advantage of his information—I went on another tack and said it was rumored that he was about to go away on a cruise aboard his yacht.

LIFE OF JAY GOULD.

"Yes?" he answered with an attempt at a smile.

"Then you do contemplate going?"

"No." And he twirled the little charm around his thumb with increased vigor.

"You do not intend leaving the city?"

"No."

Then his right foot apparently got asleep, for he stood up suddenly, stamped the foot a couple of times and resumed his seat, crossing his left leg over the right this time.

"Mr. Gould," I then said in desperation, as I was getting tired of doing all the talking, "then I can safely report you as quite well, and that you do not intend to take a trip on your yacht?"

"Yes," and he inclined his head gently while closing his eyes.

"Are you going down-town to-morrow?"

"Perhaps."

Being asked where his yacht then was, he dropped his watch-charm and exclaimed:

"Well, ask George"

Mr. George W. Blake says:

"The excitement attending the elopement of the daughter of Giovanni P. Morosini with coachman Schilling had pretty nearly died away when there came a rumor that Mr. Gould had determined to carry Mrs. Schilling to Europe in his steam yacht. The rumor said that the misguided girl was even then on board of the yacht, which lay in the Hudson a mile south of Irvington. I had been engaged in

MR. GOULD'S COLABORERS. 293

trying to solve the seeming mystery of Mrs. Schilling's disappearance, and this rumor sent me hurrying up to Irvington to ask Mr. Gould about it.

"A warm afternoon was dying when I reached the puzzling structure known as Mr. Gould's summer home. It was my first visit, and I looked in vain for a door pretentious enough to indicate that it opened into some room not occupied by the servants. I finally came to a ginger-bread door that was half glass. I rapped on the glass, and pretty soon the door opened about an inch. Before I saw who was on the other side I asked:

" 'Is Mr. Gould in?'

" The door slowly opened wider, finally disclosing Mr. Gould himself. He wore a shabby coat and had on slippers. His eyes twinkled merrily as he looked cautiously around and then said:

" 'I don't believe he is in!'

" This surprised me very much, but as it seemed to tickle Mr. Gould I gave no sign that I had ever met him before and asked:

" 'Do you expect him in before long?'

" 'I really cannot say,' replied Mr. Gould, with a brighter twinkle than ever in his eyes. 'What did you want to see him for?'

" I explained the object of my errand, and Mr. Gould said:

" 'I am sure that Mr. Gould doesn't know anything about Mrs. Schilling, and that he has no intention of taking her to Europe or anywhere else.'

294   *LIFE OF JAY GOULD.*

"'I am very much obliged to you, Mr. Gould,' I said.

"He started abruptly, and then laughed right out and said, 'You are perfectly welcome, young man, I'm sure.'"

Mr. Louis J. Lange says:

"If Jay Gould knew and trusted him, a newspaper reporter rarely failed to secure an interview with him. I had, perhaps, a half-dozen talks with the dead financier, and in each instance Mr. Gould conversed freely upon a great variety of subjects.

"The first time I was assigned to see Mr. Gould was during the exciting days succeeding the election of 1884. It had been charged that he was instrumental in holding back the Presidential election returns, which were passed over the Western Union wires, either in the interest of James G. Blaine, the Republican candidate for the Presidency, or to secure himself from loss in the stock market should a raid be made upon his holdings after the declaration of Mr. Cleveland's triumph.

"While a maddened crowd was threatening to sack the *Tribune* building, and was hooting Gould's name, the financier was reported to be under guard in the Western Union building, apprehensive of mob violence. Being unable to secure any satisfaction as to his whereabouts at the Western Union offices, I called at his house, at Fifth Avenue and Forty-seventh Street. The butler told me Mr. Gould was not in, and probably was out of the city.

I suspected that the butler was fibbing. On entering the Windsor I happened to meet a broker who had large business dealings with Mr. Gould, and, besides, was his personal friend. I explained to him the situation. He gave me a note of introduction to the Wizard. It got to Mr. Gould, and word came back that he would see me in the reception-room.

"I was ushered into a richly-furnished but small apartment on the left of the hall. It was just after 7 P. M., and the gas burned brightly from a cut-glass chandelier. Soon there appeared at the door a man of exceedingly small stature, with very black hair, beard, and mustache, dressed in dark trousers and vest, and wearing a modest smoking-jacket. Slippers which looked like Russian leather incased his very small feet. He wore a plain, white collar, with a little black bow tucked under it. He said, quietly:

"'You wish to see Mr. Gould. I am he. What can I do for you?'

"As he spoke Mr. Gould rolled an easy chair to the grate, and rested his feet on the tender, behind which a fire was blazing brightly.

"'Mr. Gould,' I said, 'they are saying down-town that you are holding back the election returns. Crowds have gathered in front of the Western Union and *Tribune* buildings, and are singing "Hang Jay Gould to a sour-apple tree."'

"Mr. Gould smiled rather coldly, and then fixing his eyes upon me, said quietly: 'If I denied all the lies

296 LIFE OF JAY GOULD.

circulated about me I should have no time to attend to business. Of course there is no truth in this. I do not care one rap of my finger whether Cleveland, Blaine, Butler, or any one else has been elected. I doubt if the administration of either would imperil the prosperity of the country.'

"Then Mr. Gould proceeded to explain that all the time he had been reported to be guarded by police officers in the Western Union building he had been at his home nursing a slight cold."

INSIDE THE GREENHOUSE.

CHAPTER XII.

MR. GOULD'S GREATEST ENTERPRISE.

IN the later years of Mr. Gould's life his attention was more especially turned toward the telegraph, for he recognized that it was becoming as important to the country and was as rich a field for cultivation as the railroads had been in the days when his attention had been entirely directed to them. It is therefore fitting that the last chapter of this volume should contain somewhat of a history of the evolution of the telegraph in general, and of the Western Union Telegraph Company in particular.

The first thought of the *bon vivant* as his eye twinkles through a fresh sample of his favorite wine, which with dexterous thumb and finger he holds up to the sunlight is "how old are you?" "Where grew the grapes that made you?" And he is but a type of an age that seems bent on tracing all things to their origin, of hunting them backward to their primal nest.

The more remote the seed, the further removed and dimmer the dawn, the deeper and more pervading is the fascination. The telegraph has had just such a scrutiny. It has even been suggested that its origin was in Eden on some such a far-fetched

LIFE OF JAY GOULD.

argument as this: The word which in France expresses the English term magnetism is "aimentation," from the word "ainer" to love. Of course, we are told in the Book of Books that there was love in Eden, and the persistent arguer thinks that he can trace the telegraph back by this means.

So far as we have any knowledge, the earliest method of signalling, all of which have come to be classed in with the general term, telegraph, were of a very simple character. Among savage tribes, and indeed largely among civilized nations, these signals were by fires. As civilization advanced, torches, flags, birds, drums, trumpets, and other modes of conveying the vocabulary of signalled thought and information were employed. The Indian mounds on our Western prairies give evidence of having been beacon bearers in years gone by. Gradually the unfolding intelligence of the ages revealed itself, and it became possible to spell out words and to elaborate thought by the same comparatively primitive modes of signals. Mr. Schaffner, in a very intelligent manual on the history of telegraphy, has with wonderful industry prosecuted his researches as far back as 1084 B. C. He gives a remarkable illustration of the capacity for signalling, which was the telegraphy of the ancients about that time. He says that the announcement of the fall of Troy at the Palace of Rome was by beacon lights from Ida to Lemnos; from thence to Athos, Mount of Jove; thence to the watch-towers of Masistus, Messapius,

MR. GOULD'S GREATEST ENTERPRISE. 301

the crag of Cithaeron, and the mount Ægiplanctus; thence to the Arachnaen Heights, and finally to the roof of the Apreidæ.

The first description of what is called a "telegraph," although that word belongs to modern times, as it really means " writing at a distance," was a system of wooden blocks of various shapes to indicate letters, arranged by Dr. Hooke in 1684. A century later, in 1794, three brothers named Chappé were confined in schools in France, situated some distance apart, yet within sight of each other. Free communication, under the rigorous rules of these schools, was denied them. They yearned for intercourse, and finally affection suggested a plan by which a pivoted beam could be used to convey the signs of letters by pointing it in different directions. The variety of signals was enlarged by adding small movable beams at the end of the main beam. In this way these brothers arranged the remarkable number of one hundred and ninety-two different signals, and by correspondence relieved the tedium of their confinement.

Curiously enough, what was thus contrived under the spur of brotherly affection proved the future of our modern telegraphic signals. After the release of the brothers the system they had devised for communication with each other was exhibited to the government of France and adopted as a service of signals. One of the brothers Chappé became telegraphic engineer for the government. Semaphoric signal houses and signals were rapidly established

302   LIFE OF JAY GOULD.

along the whole French coast in 1803, with Chappé as manager. These were continued in use for a number of years till electrical discovery provided the modern means for that purpose. Even in this infantile state the telegraph began to be useful. As an evidence of its value, even in the crude state in which it then was, it is stated that the very first use made of the Chappé signals was to announce an important victory gained by the French army. This message was transmitted with surprising promptness to the French Convention then in session, direct from the French frontier. The code of signals had been perfectly arranged and there was no error whatever in the sentences transmitted.

Just before this, in 1795, Lord George Murray, of England, had improved somewhat on Chappé's original plans by using two frames in which six Venetian blinds were inserted, thus adding greatly to the ease in operating and translating, as well as to the variety in signals. Lord Murray's system was adopted by the government about the close of the last century and continued in use till about 1816.

Prussia did not adopt the system until it was nearer perfection; that was about 1832, and four thousand and ninety-six complete signals could then be transmitted by the system, and the service was rapidly extended all over the kingdom.

In Russia all along the great arteries of travel the old Semaphoric signal towers were erected for that purpose and may still be seen. Over two hundred

MR. GOULD'S GREATEST ENTERPRISE. 303

of them were erected at an enormous cost. Of course the towers are no longer used but are preserved as mementos of times bygone.

General Pasley and Sir Home Copham contrived modifications of the Chappé and Murray systems. Jules Guyot, of France, and Treutler, of Berlin, also perfected similar systems, but there was little practical advantage in these over the ones in use. They were, however, quite ingenious inventions.

Coming down to our own country we know that during the Revolutionary War one of the signals employed was a flag-staff surmounted by a barrel, beneath which a flag, a basket, and a lantern could be so interchanged and combined that a number of announcements could be in that manner communicated. It will be remembered also how the farmers of Middlesex, Essex, and Worcester on the night of April 18th, 1775, sprang to arms to meet the foe, having been aroused by Paul Revere, who having seen the signal agreed upon in the North Church Tower which told the movement of the British troops from Boston, had started on his famous ride to warn the people that "the storm had burst."

> " He said to his friend, if the British march
>   By land or sea from the town to-night,
> Hang a lantern in the belfry arch
>   Of the North Church Tower, as a signal light,
> One, if by land; two, if by sea;
>   And I on the opposite shore will be
> Ready to ride and spread the alarm
>   Through every Middlesex village and farm
> For the country folk to be up and to arm."

304 · LIFE OF JAY GOULD.

Jonathan Grout, Jr., a Massachusetts man, filed an application with the United States government in 1800 for a patent on a telegraph which he operated between Boston and Martha's Vineyard, a distance of about ninety miles, from hilltop to hilltop, and which was sighted by the aid of telescopes. About the same time a certain Christopher Colles, of New York, exhibited from the top of the Custom House on Tuesdays, Thursdays, and Saturdays in the afternoons a system which he explained as follows: "Eighty-four letters can be exhibited by this machine in five minutes to the distance of one telegraph station averaged at ten miles, and by the same proportion a distance of two thousand six hundred miles in fifteen minutes and twenty-eight seconds." For this exhibition an admittance fee of fifty cents was charged.

Of course, this was nothing but an American adaptation of the Semaphoric system already used in Europe, but the fact that Colles worked the signals for a number of years between New York and Sandy Hook showed that American inventive genius was beginning to take hold of the subject of telegraphy and apply it to American needs.

Perhaps there is no class of business or professional men to whom the telegraph to-day is more valuable than the brokers and bankers. It is a curious circumstance that as late as 1846 signals on the Murray plan, erected on high or prominent points of land. were used between New York and Philadel-

MR. GOULD'S GREATEST ENTERPRISE. 305

phia by some enterprising street brokers, to aid them in their business. They kept the matter a secret for a long time, using it even after the introduction of the Morse electric telegraph. Their means of information was for a long time a subject of much mystery to the members of the stock exchanges in both cities. One of these enterprising men was the famous "Bull" Bridges. He took great enjoyment in these private lines of his, and was probably the first man in the country, certainly the first man in Philadelphia, to take the Morse characters by sound.

In all ages men have resorted to signals to quicken intelligence, and they have longed for something better and speedier. Various expedients for enlarging the vocabulary of signals have been adopted by different nations and races as they were best suited to the languages spoken. To the Scotchman the burning brand by which the Highland chieftain gathered his clans to battle as it flamed through the Scottish mountain, borne by men swift of foot was a most eloquent signal. The signal fires of the Sioux and Blackfoot Indians curling up from the mounds of our Western prairies were equal in eloquence to them. Both were only hints of a time coming when an instrumentality which was to bring men all over the earth side by side was also to be the agency to a larger degree of universal peace and of magnificent commercial and diplomatic operations.

Power, especially when associated with mystery,

306   LIFE OF JAY GOULD.

has never failed to fascinate. It inspires the realm of the imagination. This gives life to many of its charms. It is easy to see why the subject of electricity has, in all ages and among all classes, captivated the human mind, for where it did not impel to investigation it has excited curiosity. Aside from this, however, electricity as a science has powers to greatly stimulate and delight. Its demonstrations are unique, brilliant, and startling. No branch of experimental philosophy is so replete with surprise and with pleasing results. It is so identified with the great and sublime agencies of nature; demonstrates the possession of such mysterious power; so affects the animal frame; so trembles through the human body; so roars through the sky; so bounds from the human finger out over the earth; taking as its path the deep caverns of the sea and the highest altitudes of the mountains, that there seems no wonder that its fascination has been absorbing and complete.

Early in the seventeenth century, Dr. Gilbert, of England, and still later in the same century, Boyle, Guericke, Newton, Hawksby, and Dr. Wall variously experimented in the rapidly dawning science, and very important facts became known. Gilbert noted the influence of dry north and east winds in producing rapid electrical excitement under friction. Guericke constructed an electrical machine which became the basis of the discovery of electric lights. He also discovered that when once a light body was attracted by an electric body it was also repelled by it, and was incapable of a second attraction until it had been touched by some other body. Newton substituted glass for sulphur, and showed that electricity could be excited on the side of the glass opposite to the side which had been rubbed. Wall, curiously enough, speaks of thunder and lightning as suggested by the sounds, and light produced by the friction of amber. The seventeenth century, however, concluded with comparatively little definite knowledge on electrical subjects, but with very widely awakened interest therein.

With the eighteenth century came Stephen Gray, a man of wonderfully clear head and indomitable perseverance, who bent his whole mind to the discovery of the nature and powers of the new agents which appear to have dawned somewhat definitely on the scientific world. He found, after a variety of experiments, that electricity was easily producable from a vast variety of objects; by the friction of feathers, of hair, of silk, linen, paper, and other substances. He found, also, that electricity communicated itself to bodies incapable of excitement at distances of several hundred feet. He next proved the conducting power of fluids and of the human body; he also proved, by a series of very interesting experiments, the important fact that electrical attraction was not proportioned to the mass of matter in a body but to the extent of its surface. He then discovered the insulating qualities of silk.

308   *LIFE OF JAY GOULD.*

hair, glass, and other substances, and he discovered the fact of induction, although he seems to have been unable to explain it. Stephen Gray, therefore, made the first grand advance in definite electrical knowledge, and the rudimentary facts which he well established were suggestive and valuable, and furnished the most important basis for further observation and experiment.

Dufaye, a man possessed of Gray's perseverance, and blessed with a mind of greater analytic power and sagacity, discovered, about the middle of the eighteenth century, that electricity had two distinct forms or modes of development ; namely vitreous and resinous, and by other experiments took close glance into the laboratory of nature. About this time a curious discovery was made : it was found that bodies quickly lose their electrical virtue when exposed to the atmosphere. An attempt was therefore made to surround them with an insulating substance ; water contained in a glass bottle was accordingly electrified, but nothing remarkable followed this until the holder of the bottle attempted to disengage the wire connected with the prime conductor, then greatly to his alarm and to the amusement of his friends, he received a genuine electric shock of no gentle kind. He was indeed seriously alarmed, and describing the effect produced upon him by one of his experiments, Munschenbroek, the shocked philosopher, says that he felt himself struck on his arms, shoulders, and breast so that he lost his breath and

MR. GOULD'S GREATEST ENTERPRISE. 309

it was two days before he recovered from the blow and the terror.

So thoroughly astonished and frightened was he that he declared he would not take another for the kingdom of France. A genius by the name of Boze, however, whose desire to be famous, or perhaps to subserve France seemed to have been stronger than the love of life ardently desired to be killed by electric shock, so that his demise might furnish the subject of an article for the memoirs of the French Academy of Science. History does not inform us that he was gratified in his unselfish wish, although others at a later date, much against their expectations and wishes, have suffered as he desired to suffer.

The effect of the shocks received by different parties at this time was amusingly magnified on every hand, and connected the subject of electricity in many minds with a diabolical agency. These experiments were the result of the discovery of the Leyden jar by Von Kleist, Cuneus, and Muschenbroek, although the first named seemed best entitled to the credit.

The most important record of this period in the history of an experiment adjusted to the rapid advance which had been made in electrical inquiry and which excites surprise that its employment in telegraphy, which is so clearly foreshadowed, has been so long withheld from the world.

In making experiments with the Leyden electrical phial Wilson of Dublin described what is known as

310   *LIFE OF JAY GOULD.*

the lateral shock. He had observed that a person standing near the circuit through which the shock is transmitted would sustain a shock if he were only in contact with or even placed very near any part of the circuit. This immediately, of course, started inquiry as to how far the shock could be transmitted, and very numerous experiments were made to determine the matter. Herrick has said, "Nothing is so hard but search will find it out." The series of investigations in electrical and telegraphic matters have proven how true a saying was that of Herrick's.

Dr. Watson of England took a prominent part in the investigation to which the inquiries following the discoveries of Wilson lead. In July, 1747, he succeeded in conveying an electrical charge across the river Thames at Westminister Bridge ; a few days afterward he caused it to make a circuit of two miles at the New River at Stoke-Newington. In August of the same year he sent it over a circuit of four miles. Two miles of the distance were of wire and two of dry ground. He proved also that the passage of electrical matter through 12,276 feet of wire was instantaneous. Here was a vast step taken almost a century before a practical telegraph was perfected and put into public use. It was just at this interesting juncture that America first stepped into the arena of European philosophical investigation under the keen leadership of our renowned and revered Benjamin Franklin.

In 1747. Mr. Peter Collinson, a fellow of the

Royal Society of London, in a communication to the literary society of Philadelphia, gave the earliest impetus worthy of note to electrical inquiry in the United States. It stirred Benjamin Franklin to a series of experiments and to a correspondence with the scientists of Europe which at once evoked universal admiration. Perhaps nothing was ever written on the subject of electricity which was more generally read and admired. It is not easy to say whether the people of that time were most pleased with the simplicity and versatility with which the letters were written, the modesty with which the author proposed every hypothesis of his own, or the noble frankness with which he related his mistakes when they were corrected by subsequent experiments.

The part taken by Franklin in electrical discovery and discussion was in truth a genuine surprise to the scientific world. Nothing had been expected from the "new land beyond the sea," where the Indian was still generally supposed to be master, and the tomahawk the emblem of the law; and thus it happened that when with acute and rigorous analysis, with delightful humor, and with exhaustive experiment, in language most lucid, terse, and simple our great Franklin modestly questioned the correctness of existing theories then held by the foremost thinkers of the world, and entered with bold yet modest adroitness into the field of electrical discovery and made those brilliant experiments which

312 LIFE OF JAY GOULD.

still cling to his name, Europe was forced to make her first bow to the young empire, and felt the first token of its coming influence on the world of civilization.

Franklin claimed the existence of but one electric fluid so called; his idea was that all bodies in their natural state were charged with a certain quantity of electricity. In each body the quantity is of definite amount. Some have it in excess and in a condition to impart it readily to other bodies having less, and which are in a condition to receive it. Franklin applied this principle to the Leyden jar; the inner coating of tin foil being charged with more than its natural quantity of electricity was regarded as positively electrified. The outer coating having its ordinary quantity reduced was named the negatively electrified. The discharge was made by a conductor connecting the two. He showed that a series of jars may all be charged at once by suspending them on the prime conductor. With jars thus charged he constructed a battery by separating them, and then putting their insides and outsides in metallic connection. There seems to be in this ingenious and suggestive arrangement the first outline of our modern batteries.

In 1749 Franklin proved the identity of lightning and electricity. He said: "The electric spark is zig-zag and not straight; so is lightning. Pointed bodies attract electricity; lightning strikes mountains, trees, spires, masts, and chimneys. Electricity

MR. GOULD'S GREATEST ENTERPRISE. 313

chooses the best conductor; so does lightning." Of course, it will be remembered that these remarks of his were made in 1749, and his hypothesis was established in 1752 by his famous kite experiment.

There was one sentence in his letter to European scientists describing this famous experiment which opened the eyes of the world wider than they had been for many years. It was as follows. "When a gun-barrel, in electrical experiments, has but little electrical fire in it, you must approach it very near with your knuckle before you can draw a spark. Give it more fire, and you can draw a spark at greater distance. Two gun-barrels united and as highly electrified will give a spark at still greater distance. But, if two gun-barrels electrified will strike at two inches distance and make a loud snap, at what a great distance may ten thousand acres of electrified cloud strike and give its fire, and how loud must be that crack?"

After the kite experiment, which led lightning by a hemp cord from the sky, Franklin raised a metallic rod from one end of his house, the first lightning rod ever known. To this he attached a chime of bells, which gave notice of atmospheric change. He now conceived the idea of protecting buildings from lightning, and made possible the much (and often justly) maligned lightning-rod man by inventing something that seemed to the people of that time to be more important than any telegraphic system— that is, the lightning-rod.

314 *LIFE OF JAY GOULD.*

Later Franklin's experiments took more of the nature of applying electricity in other than telegraphic channels, but among his achievements not already mentioned was the transmission of a strong electric current across the Schuylkill River near Philadelphia in 1748.

For nearly half a century after the experiments of Franklin no American record appears of any important advance in the realm of electrical adaptations to practical ends until 1810, when Dr. John Redman Coxe, of Philadelphia, proposed the signal telegraph, using the electrical currents of the recently discovered Voltaic pile to produce electrical decompositions at the end of wire conductors evolving visible gas as signals of letters, and for which he employed thirty-six wires. This was slow and cumbrous, and practically came to nothing, although in justice it must be said that a practical test was not given the system.

No striking advance, it will be seen, had been made in this country, but master minds were at work on the mighty problem in Europe. The reader is perhaps familiar with Volta's splendid discovery of the battery which placed in the hands of scientists the promise of ability to hold in bridle electric currents, and to prolong them. In 1810 the precise thought, out of which grew the modern telegraph, was uttered in the ears of its subsequent inventor by Jeremiah Day, Professor of Natural Philosophy in Yale College. Day's lectures at that

COMMODORE VANDERBILT.

MR. GOULD'S GREATEST ENTERPRISE. 317

date were remarkably accurate, and are justly renowned in history for the maturity of the knowledge of electrical matter they display. Contemporaneous with Dr. Day was a man whose name, by reason of his rich contributions to science, was almost equally renowned to the whole world of learning and science. This was Professor Benjamin Silliman. In company with Dr. Day, he was fully up with the latest and most advanced thoughts on physical and electrical phenomena, to which he gave exhaustive prominence in his college discourses.

In 1827 electrical matters began to assume a shape more definite in the public mind. A practical demonstration of the theories which had been expounded in scientific journals and in college discourses, assumed practical shape in the form of a line of telegraph two miles in length on a race course on Long Island Sound. Mr. Harrison G. Dyar erected this line of telegraph and made himself more or less famous through his work. But he used what is known as frictional electricity, which is at the best, fitful, easily affected by the weather, and unreliable. On a damp day the horses running on the race course were much more liable to get to the end of the two miles than was the message over the wire. Yet Mr. Dyar stood on the threshold of success. Had a Daniell battery been known at that time, he would have undoubtedly made use of it, and he might have anticipated Morse and have worn his laurels. But the knowledge requisite to the perfect

318 *LIFE OF JAY GOULD.*

telegraphic system which we have to-day was to come through Henry and Morse.

One year later, in 1828, another one of the successive important steps in the development of telegraphy, respecting which invention seems to have thoroughly aroused herself, was by the distinguished secretary of the Smithsonian Institute, Professor Joseph Henry. The inventions and discoveries of this profound thinker were too intricate to be described here. He stood on the very verge of one of the greatest inventions in the history of the world, but his success could not be perfect until other links in the chain were supplied by other minds. Although Morse was the inventor of the telegraph, grateful recognition must be accorded Dyar and Professor Henry, for their experiments and adaptations left the best possible conditions for the final invention and perfection of our present system.

With the year 1837 the subject of electric telegraphs seems to have burst upon public attention in America and in Europe as well, and everywhere awakened a deep interest. Two Frenchman, Gonon and Servall, who announced publicly the possession of the system of telegraphy adapted for public use attracted the attention of capitalists in this country, but their system proved to be only a modification of Chappé's Semaphoric telegraph before referred to. Congress was invoked to aid in the erection of a telegraph on this system, but our own grand thinker, Professor Morse, began to have his apprehensions

MR. GOULD'S GREATEST ENTERPRISE. 319

awakened, for he felt sure of ultimate success and did not mean to have the honor of establishing the first practical telegraph in his beloved country relegated to foreigners. He began to devote himself more assiduously than ever to the perfection of his instrument. In the meantime Professor Morse was approached by speculators, who it is believed intended to establish another form of the public lotteries which was rampant at that time, for the construction of a private telegraph line two hundred miles in length; they were quick-witted men and would have been just the ones to bring out the invention had their motives been more honest and sincere for the good of the people. But Morse was not ready at this time to give out his invention in its imperfect state, and it is well in the light of subsequent events that he was not.

It is certainly just to allow an inventor to tell his own story. Morse had to do that very often, but not half so frequently as it has been attempted, and unsuccessfully attempted, for him. The best outline of his invention which Morse gave was in a paper to the International Exposition at Paris in 1868; considerably abbreviated it is as follows: he said, "My aim at the outset was simplicity of means as well as of results, hence I devised the single circuit of conductors from some generator of electricity. I planned a system of signs consisting of dots or points and spaces to represent numerals and two modes of causing the electricity to mark or imprint

320
LIFE OF JAY GOULD.

these signs upon a strip or ribbon of paper. One was by chemical decomposition of salt which should discolor the paper ; the other was by chemical action of the electro magnet operating upon the paper by a lever charged at one extremity with a pen or pencil. I conceived the plan of moving the paper ribbon at a regular rate by means of clock-work machinery to receive the signs ; these processes as well as the mathematically calculated signs devised for and adapted for recording were sketched in my sketch book. I also drew in my sketch book modes of interring the conductors in tubes in the earth, and planned and drew out the method upon posts." This was the general condition of the invention when Professor Morse arrived in New York from a trip abroad on the 15th of November, 1832.

Morse turned his attention to recording electrical phenomena and making observations and experiments with the object in view of perfecting the system of recording messages at a great distance. He turned his attention entirely, or at least almost entirely, from static electricity to dynamic electricity. He says, " The nearest approach to simplicity in recording at distances seemed to be the passing of chemically-prepared papers between two broken parts of a circuit so that the electricity should pass through the moistened paper or cloth; this would mark the point or dart when the circuit was closed, and by rapid closing and opening of the circuit while the paper was moved regularly forward points

MR. GOULD'S GREATEST ENTERPRISE. 321

or dots in any required groups could be made at will."

He originally intended only to indicate words and sentences by numbers. It was a desideratum to arrange the ten digits to be represented by dots or points within as small a space as possible. The first and most obvious mode seemed to be the following:

1	2	3	4	5	6	
.	..	...	....	.....	......	etc.

It did not take long for Professor Morse to discover that after about five or six dots or points the number of dots became inconveniently numerous in indicating the larger digits, and it occurred to him that by extending the spaces appropriated to the five larger digits, giving them greater space value than was possessed by the five smaller digits, he might reduce the number of dots necessary to indicate any of the ten digits within five dots. This was the basis of the present perfected system of telegraphy. It would be uninteresting to the lay reader to follow up in minute detail the elaboration of this scheme. From 1832 to 1838 Morse was busily engaged perfecting his invention. As the old line goes, " 'Tis not for mortals to command success but to deserve it." And so even Morse, the profound thinker, the erudite scholar, found obstacles in the way of success.

21

322

LIFE OF JAY GOULD.

However, he thoroughly completed his recording machinery on the threshold of the new year, 1838.

On invitation of the President, his system was successfully exhibited in the presence of himself and the Cabinet, on the 21st of February that year, and elicited gratified interest and warmest praise. As was before said, he might, in the year previous, have had private telegraph lines erected to serve the purpose of a lottery company, but he had higher aspirations than that. He determined to ask Congress for aid to make a thorough public exhibition of the capacity of his system on an actual line of such length as to make it a positive proof of what might be accomplished by his invention. He received no little encouragement from individuals in this endeavor. Congress was asked to furnish the means to erect an experimental line to prove its value. Morse had some idea and hope of selling his invention to the Government. The officials of the Government were not at all sure that they wanted to saddle such a burden upon themselves. Later, when Mr. Gould had a controlling interest in that gigantic enterprise, the Western Union Telegraph Company, there was no small agitation in favor of the Government buying the corporation. In 1843, just five years to the day from the time that a successful exhibition of the method had been given to the President and his Cabinet, a bill was offered before the House of Representatives, by Hon. John P. Kennedy, appropriating $30,000 to be

MR. GOULD'S GREATEST ENTERPRISE. 323

expended under the direction of the Secretary of the Treasury in a series of experiments to test the expediency of the telegraph projected by Professor Morse.

Morse sat in the gallery during the discussion which followed, quiet, but intensely anxious; the crisis of his life had come. His invention was in the hands of the nation's representatives. If the members of that Congress could only have anticipated the wonderful events which transpired during the next twenty-five years, how ready, how enthusiastic, would have been the response to that bill, and how different would have been the vote on it! While Professor Morse and his system received the hearty co-operation of a few men who were more advanced than their fellows, they were at the same time the subjects of no little ridicule on the part of others. The debate was sharp, the attacks on the invention and the inventor were cruel, but victory was at hand, even though it was not a brilliant one. The vote was finally taken on the 23d of February, and resulted in ninety for and eighty-two against the passage of the bill. New York and Pennsylvania, which have benefited more by the telegraph than any of the other States, it may be remarked, cast the highest number of votes in favor of passing the bill. So far, success seemed to be dawning, but the bill, it must be remembered, had only passed the House of Representatives, and the crucial test still remained to be made, for the Senate must yet act

324 *LIFE OF JAY GOULD.*

on the bill. The Senate was inclined to procrastinate, and it seemed as if the bill was doomed to failure. Morse was a constant attendant on the sessions of the Senate, and on the day of the last session, when but two hours intervened before the final adjournment, one of the Senators, who was a friend of Morse's, came to him and said: "I advise you to go home, and think no more of your invention." He took the advice, went to his hotel, and, with what little money he had remaining, paid his bill and purchased a ticket for New York. His heart was heavy, but he was a trusting, Christian man. He felt that he had done all that he could to place before the world an invention, which he knew needed only a trial to prove its success, an invention which meant more rapid advancement for his country and the world than had been made because of any previous invention. He knelt, poured out his overburdened heart in prayer, and laid down to the peaceful sleep of one who is conscious of having done his duty.

Next morning, refreshed by rest yet grave and thoughtful, he came down from his room, wondering how the thirty-seven cents in his pocket was to pay for his meals for that day and his lodging for another night. While seated at the table partaking of an humble meal, a visitor was announced. It was Miss Annie G. Ellsworth, the daughter of the Commissioner of Patents. She grasped him by the hand, exclaiming in a voice full of unconcealed joy, " Pro-

MR. GOULD'S GREATEST ENTERPRISE. 325

fessor, I have come on purpose to congratulate you."

"Congratulate me, for what, my dear friend, can you offer me congratulations."

"Why," she exclaimed, gayly, as she enjoyed the Professor's wondering surprise, who was not at the time really in the fittest mood for pleasantries, "on the passage of your bill. The Senate last night voted you your $30,000." She then informed him that her father remained in the Senate until the close of the session and that in the very closing moments, the Telegraph Bill, to his great surprise and delight, was passed without division or debate. On reaching home he had communicated the news to his family, all whom were greatly attached to the Professor, and his daughter begged the favor of being allowed to impart the good news.

Had Morse lived in the days of the Western Union Telegraph Co., in its present perfection of operation, and had his invention been of another character, a dispatch announcing the passage of the bill by the Senate would have reached his hotel in New York before he arrived there on the train. As it was, the instinctive impulse of a warm-hearted woman led her to be the first to communicate the grand news to the disheartened inventor.

So overcome was Morse at the good news that for a time he could not speak. His first words were: "Annie, you are the first to inform me of this great event, which means so much for me and our country. I was until now utterly unconscious of the

326   *LIFE OF JAY GOULD.*

fact, and now I am going to make you a promise. When the line is completed, the first dispatch sent upon it from Washington to Baltimore shall be yours."

"Well," she replied, "I will hold you to your promise."

Morse now arranged for the construction of the line. The Government allowed him a salary of $2,500 per year during the test. Unfortunately, his mind seemed prepossessed in favor of underground lines. They gave to him the general impression of safety and permanence, and unlike his usual cautiousness, he adopted this method without experiment. A cable was laid from Baltimore to a point some seven miles distant, but a test of it proved that its abandonment was an immediate necessity. More than half of the appropriation of $30,000 had been spent. Another dark hour had come. Morse's mind was fearfully agitated at the result of his error, but he bravely set to work to place the wire upon poles, and the line between Baltimore and Washington was finished in that way.

Morse was not an apt mechanic and was consequently dependent even in his grandest conceptions upon others. He knew what he wanted, and his conceptions of his wants were perfectly practical, but it was laborious for him to adapt mechanisms to his conceptions. Hence, the great value to him of men like Alfred Vail and Ezra Cornell, who had become associated with him, will be readily seen.

MR. GOULD'S GREATEST ENTERPRISE. 327

In about a year after the passage of the bill the line was completed, and the first office in Washington was in a small room on the East front of the Capitol and afterward in a room over the City Post Office. True to the promise he had made to his friend, Miss Ellsworth, Professor Morse now sent for her. She was invited to give a message for transmission. This was promptly done in language which has become historic, and which expressed just what the inventor himself would have suggested. It was "WHAT HATH GOD WROUGHT?"

The message was at once sent successfully over the wires, and the strip of paper on which it was imprinted was claimed by the Governor of Connecticut in honor of the lady, who was a native of his State, and of the inventor who received therein his collegiate education.

The first use to which the Chappé semaphoric telegraph system had been put in France after its adoption by the Government had been to transmit an important message from the French frontier to the Capitol city, and it immediately aroused universal interest. Just so one of the first messages sent over Morse's line from Baltimore to Washington, after the word sent by Miss Ellsworth, brought the telegraph into instant public recognition in this country. The National Convention to nominate a President was in session in Baltimore. James K. Polk had been nominated President and Silas Wright, then in the Senate and in Washington, was

328   *LIFE OF JAY GOULD.*

named for the Vice-Presidency. Mr. Vail, one of Morse's assistants, communicated this over the wires to Morse at Washington, who immediately told Mr. Wright. In a few moments the Convention was astounded to receive a message from Mr. Wright respectfully declining the nomination. The presiding officer read the dispatch and he refused to believe its authenticity, but adjourned to wait the report of a committee sent to Washington to confer with Mr. Wright. The committee confirmed the telegraphic message. This led to a conference between the committee and Mr. Wright over the wires. The fact was, of course, soon known, and the fame of the telegraph was established forever in the country.

It is related about this time a distinguished functionary asked an assistant how large a bundle could be sent over the wires, and if the United States mail could not be sent that way, and a noted wag of the time straddled a pair of begrimed boots over the wire and then told his friends, as he pointed to them, how they had become so spoiled in his rapid flight over the wire from Baltimore to Washington.

On April 1st, 1845, the line which had been worked as a curiosity and experiment was opened for public use. The Postmaster-General, who had control of the telegraph, fixed the tariff at one cent for every four characters. During the first four days the receipts of the company amounted to just

MR. GOULD'S GREATEST ENTERPRISE. 329

one cent. What a contrast to the receipts of the company in which Mr. Gould has left millions of dollars invested! On the fifth day 12½ cents was received. The sixth day was the Sabbath. On the seventh the receipts ran up to 60 cents; on the eighth day to $1.32; on the ninth day there was $1.04—not a very dazzling prospect. But watchful eyes and keen minds saw the value of the system. It is recorded that at about this time a certain good dame, whose idea of discipline was somewhat stern and fundamental, after surveying a pole recently erected near her door, placing her hands on her haunches, exclaimed somewhat bitterly: "Now, I suppose no one can spank their brats without it's being known all over creation."

The telegraph was now fairly started, and it spoke for itself with no uncertain tongue. Professor Morse offered it to the Government for $100,000. The offer was refused upon the ground that the operations between Baltimore and Washington had not proved that lines of telegraph could be successfully operated on a paying basis. It was a fortunate fact for the inventor, for the country, and for other nations that the American Government did not take up Morse's offer. From this time on the American telegraph improved with great rapidity, and the inventor had the satisfaction of seeing, long before his death, his system acknowledged and in use in all parts of the world. The alphabet used in the Morse system is wonderful in its simplicity and availability.

330

LIFE OF JAY GOULD.

It can be used by sight, by sound, by touch, by taste, by sense of feeling. Men can wink it with their eyes, can beat it with their feet, and dying men have used it to speak when vocal organs and strength to write were exhausted. The prisoner can tap it on the wall or grating of his dungeon. Lovers in distant rooms can converse by it on the gas pipe. Its uses are endless. It is a universal language for the world. The telegraph was the offspring of a century of thought. It was the finest and grandest gift of the human brain, and Professor Samuel B. F. Morse had the great honor to lead it forth for the admiration and use of mankind.

The Government having refused Morse's offer to sell his invention, it was at once determined to present it to the public and to endeavor to enlist private capital in its development. In 1843 Professor Morse engaged Hon. Amos Kendall, of Washington, as his agent for the purpose of securing capital. Mr. Kendall is well known in American history. He was General Jackson's Postmaster-General, and was an incorruptible, able, clear-headed, methodical, and ingenious lawyer of fine education; but he lacked the *bonhomie* which in those days seemed necessary to any great business success in the seaboard cities.

Commerce between New York and Philadelphia has always been large and the intercourse by telegraph it was presumed would be proportionately large and valuable alike to the country and those making use of its wires. It was, therefore, thought best to attempt construction of telegraphic lines between the two cities first, and Mr. Kendall took steps to organize a company for that purpose, requesting only capital enough for the probable cost of construction. To aid in securing capital Mr. Ezra Cornell and Mr. O. S. Wood went to New York to exhibit the Morse machinery upon an experimental line strung over housetops in New York city. Such violent opposition was developed that it was found necessary to pay Professor Silliman, before mentioned, $50 for an opinion as to safety of stringing wires on insulators over the housetops.

A great mistake was made right here. An office was secured at 112 Broadway, almost within shadow of the present fine offices of the Western Union Telegraph Company, and the instruments were arranged in such a position that a large number of spectators might witness the receipt of messages to be sent from another office which had been set up in another portion of the city. An admission fee of twenty-five cents was charged to see the invention operated, but there were not visitors enough to pay the expenses of the exhibit. Everything seemed to trend toward poverty and ultimate failure. The men interested in the venture were almost ready to accept charity as a means of keeping body and soul together. The princely founder of Cornell University was at that time glad to make his breakfast on what he could purchase with a shilling picked up from the sidewalk on Broadway. He afterward

332 *LIFE OF JAY GOULD.*

said this was really one of the most sumptuous meals that it was ever his pleasure to partake of.

Fifteen thousand dollars was needed to erect a telegraph line from Fort Lee to Philadelphia, and capitalists were importuned to furnish the money necessary for the venture. They carefully and searchingly scrutinized the aspect of affairs from the poverty-stricken inventor and his assistants to the ticking instrument which they by no means comprehended and the straggling wire running from the humble and ill-furnished office to the housetops of the city, and refused to have anything further to do with it. But, if capitalists were not willing to invest in the enterprise, shrewder men of smaller means were ready to embrace what they knew must soon be recognized an absolute essential to the successful operations of commerce. One of the first men who started the subscription list of $15,000 was the proprietor of a small eating house in Nassau Street, in which a meal could be obtained for fifteen cents.

It was provided in this original subscription that the payment of $50 should entitle a subscriber to two shares at $50 each; therefore, when $15,000 had been subscribed, $30,000 of stock had been issued. To the patentees $30,000 of stock was issued in exchange for their invention, thus the capital was in total $60,000. Messrs. W. W. Corcoran and B. B. French were made trustees to hold the patent rights and property, and an act of incorporation was granted by the Legislature of the State

LINDEN TREE AT LYNDHURST.

MR. GOULD'S GREATEST ENTERPRISE. 335

of Maryland, which was the first Telegraphic Charter issued in the United States. In it the incorporators were named as follows :—S. F. B. Morse, D. B. French, George C. Penniman, Henry J. Rogers, John S. McKim, J. R. Trimble, W. M. Swain, John O. Sternes, A. Sydney Doane, and associates under the title of the Magnetic Telegraph Co.

The telegraph now started on its wondrous career in this country, let us turn to the inventor and note some of the environments which seemed to have molding influence on his life, the faculties which earliest developed, his instincts and companionships, and his labors and researches.

Character not infrequently runs through generations of men like a golden cord, and is as marked as the whiteness of a dove or the blackness of a raven's wing. Such is the influence of a noble origin, for "blood is thicker than water," and "blood will tell." There is a chivalry in the blood of some families which beams and scintillates down through the ages. Among the great blessings which come to men in this world, and the stimulant to action and endeavor, which is the highest valued and the most important, is an unsullied and honorable descent. There is a proper curiosity to know the possible influences which produced a man whom fame and fortune delighted to favor, and the benefit of whose brain work can never properly be estimated.

The Morse family were of English origin. His long line of ancestors were not distinguished as

336 LIFE OF JAY GOULD.

nobles, or as royal families, but as men and women of courage, enterprise, and integrity. Morse's mother's name was Breese. She was born in New York, not a stone's throw from where the first telegraph office, made possible by the inventions of her illustrious son, was opened in that city. Among her ancestors might be named one of the Presidents of Princeton College, Samuel Finley, and other men of great ability and extensive learning. She was a woman of superior character, and beyond doubt the inventor inherited from her his calm judiciousness and his faculty for cautious reflection. From such a stock sprang Samuel Finley Breese Morse, who first saw the light of day at Charleston, Mass., April 27th, 1791. This place was about a mile from where Benjamin Franklin had been born and Morse's birth occurred about a year after Franklin's death.

Morse began his education in his fourth year. His first instructor was an old and crippled lady of frail body but sound mind. Although she could not walk about the school-room she had a long rattan which answered in place of locomotion, and young Morse often felt that rod suddenly descend upon his head in punishment for some act prohibited in the school-room. An especially severe blow was received one day when it was found that he had scratched with a pin a likeness of his venerable teacher on a chest of drawers. Three years later he entered the preparatory school at Andover, and was known as a conscientious, persevering student.

MR. GOULD'S GREATEST ENTERPRISE. 337

That grand book, Plutarch's *Lives of Illustrious Men*, which has done so much to lure budding geniuses on in the path of endeavor, was one of Morse's constant companions. He read it and reflected over its contents, and it seemed to touch his ambition and inspire him with a desire to do something noble. At thirteen years he wrote the *Life of Demosthenes*, which was not published, but which is preserved by his descendants in the original manuscript. One year later he entered the Freshman Class of Yale College.

It was at this famous institution of learning that Professor Day, before mentioned, first instilled into the young inventor's mind the rudamentary principles, as well as some of the more elaborate facts, of that most charming science, electricity.

At that time it seemed questionable whether the æsthetic side of his nature or the inventive should have sway. He was about as much inclined toward nature, painting, and sketching as toward inventive research. The famous lecture of Professor Day had a wonderful effect on Morse's mind. He says of that lecture: "The fact that the presence of electricity can be made visible in any part of the circuit was the crude seed which took root in my mind and grew into form and finally ripened into the invention of the telegraph." About this time Morse formed some especially advantageous friendships with men as much interested in science in general, and electricity in particular, as he was himself. They have

338   *LIFE OF JAY GOULD.*

described him as a youth of remarkable personal beauty, of very attractive manners, of most enthusiastic temperament, of pure heart and blameless life. They have commented on his ardent patriotism, and have said that it knew no bounds and sometimes even endangered his personal safety. It was this patriotism that developed later into the refusal of an offer to sell his invention to a lottery company for what was then a handsome sum. He had determined that the Government should profit by his work, or, at least, should have the first opportunity of doing so.

At Yale young Morse felt the inconvenience of an empty purse. His first effort at self-support was painting portraits on ivory of some of his more wealthy companions at five dollars each. This work almost entirely paid for his college expenses. At that time, notwithstanding his ardent love for the study of electricity, his ambition was to become a popular and successful artist, as it seemed to him that there was more promise of financial success in that line. As soon as he graduated, in 1810, at the age of nineteen he resolved to place himself under the tutorage of Washington Allston, one of America's most famous artists. Allston learned to love his young pupil and took him to Europe in 1811. Benjamin West was in the zenith of his fame, and it was a proud moment for Morse when he grasped West's hand in the latter's studio. There was a mutual recognition of genius between the two. West imme-

MR. GOULD'S GREATEST ENTERPRISE. 339

diately exercised his influence in Morse's behalf. His passion for art seemed to be as enthralling and as soul-thrilling as was in later years his passion for electricity. He did some good work in art which was praised by his friends in London. While he was successful in art from the artist's standpoint, he was not fortunate enough to make a pecuniary success, and he lived what might have been called a threadbare existence. In his cheery way he would say: "My stockings want to see my mother," when they were really worn out, and then he would sit down and wonder how he'd get another pair.

It seems laughable that a man whose name has been linked inseparably with electricity should have begun his line of inventions by patenting a pump. Nevertheless he did invent an instrument for raising water from depths, and so excellent was it that it was exhibited in model form to classes in Yale College. About this time he first began to think of marriage. He was not pecuniarily able to take this step, but the pump seemed to be the means of fortune. Success to the pump meant union to his beloved. His hopes were inspired by the warmth of reception it met with in scientific circles, but when a practical man, whose opinion after all was worth most to Morse, dubbed it: "*Morse's patent metallic double-headed ocean drinker and deluge spouter valve pump-box*" it began to die a slow death 'stung by ridicule.

On a trip to the South Morse received a large

340 *LIFE OF JAY GOULD.*

number of orders for ivory portraits, and at the end of the first year found that he had $3,000 to his credit. He was immediately married on October 1st, 1818, to Lucretia P. Walker, of Concord, N. H., who has been described as the most beautiful and accomplished woman of her town.

After various experiments Morse settled in New York and founded the National Academy of the Arts of Design, and was annually re-elected its President from 1827 to 1845. Until Morse was forty-one years old his attention was entirely given to matters of art, with the exception of the pump episode, but on his return from a tour in Europe, lasting three years, he at once became engaged in electrical matters. The general condition of his theories of invention at the time of his arriving in New York in November, 1832, from his trip has previously been described.

Reflecting upon the famous lecture of Professor Day, he began to think : "If the presence of electricity can be made visible in any part of the circuit, I see no reason why intelligence cannot be transmitted instantaneously by electricity." This was the second great conception in the line of his invention of the telegraph. Morse began to see in his invention not a crown for himself, but a great aid to human happiness.

Out of the Magnetic Telegraph Co., the foundation of which has been described, sprang various other companies reaching different points in the country,

MR. GOULD'S GREATEST ENTERPRISE. 341

and of various degrees of utility and of success. Such men as Michael Faraday, William M. Swain, James E. Reid, S. B. Gifford, C. G. Merriweather, Hiram Sibley, Jeptha H.Wade, James Gamble, Cyrus W. Field, George G. Ward, A. M. McKay and others became interested in the various ventures. Among the companies formed were the Washington and New Orleans Telegraph Co., the Western Telegraph Co., the Atlantic and Ohio Telegraph Co., the Pittsburgh, Cincinnati and Louisville Telegraph Co., the Southwestern, the Ohio and Mississippi, the Illinois and Mississippi, the Ohio and the Illinois, the Lake Erie, the Erie and Michigan, the Northwestern, the New York and Erie, the New York, Albany and Buffalo, and a host of others of less importance.

What might be considered the real beginning of the Western Union Telegraph Co., which is really made up of numerous organizations combined for utility, economy, and profit, was the American Telegraph Co., which was duly organized with a capital of $200,000, under the Telegraph Law of the State of New York. There had been a series of moves previous to this involving the first organization of the company and then the leasing of minor lines, and the consolidation of them into one company. The headquarters of the American Telegraph Co. were established at No. 10 Wall Street, and the operating department at No. 21 Wall Street. The American Telegraph seemed to suddenly gain an importance, and in 1857, when preparations were being made

LIFE OF JAY GOULD.

for the laying of the Atlantic cable the company seemed to have indeed approached a climax. Its offices were crowded with distinguished citizens who hastened to congratulate the officers on the auspicious event. The American Telegraph Co. had a wise policy which it early adopted, of securing possession of all patent claims and buying all property rights which would be useful to it, or which might form the basis of an antagonistic company.

The well-known inventions of House's printing telegraph system was absorbed by the American Telegraph Co., which, in turn, was absorbed by the Western Union Telegraph Co. One of the immediate results of the purchase, lease, and union of the various interests referred to, was an economy of over $70,000 a year in the single item of rent, as choice offices which had been selected by rival companies in the contest for business had been given up and the offices combined in prominent centres. A marked enlargement of business and increase in the promptness of the service was soon noticed. The wires of the Western Union Co. became full of business, for seven entire years all of the receipts above the actual expenses necessary to carry on the business were expended in strengthening and extending the lines. Victory and grand success is due more to this wise policy than any other step in the history of the company. Stocks of the absorbed companies and the general stock of the Western Union Co. began to climb toward par value and

MR. GOULD'S GREATEST ENTERPRISE. 343

even to exceed par. For instance, the stock of one of the absorbed companies, amounting to $240,000, had been valued at about two cents on the dollar, or about $4,800. In comparatively few years it represented about a million of dollars.

New contracts were constantly made with telegraph companies whose lines were valuable in the extension of the business of the Western Union Telegraph Co., and some minor leases were made. Charles Minor, General Superintendent of the Erie Railroad, appears to have been the first man with sufficient sagacity to see the value of the telegraph in connection with the railroad service. So clearly did he see the value of such connection that he had a line built along the Erie Road before making any contract for machinery to work it. Of course, this employment of the telegraph was immediately recognized to be a matter of prime importance. Right here lay an immense field which required prompt occupation.

As the business of the company developed it became necessary to employ men to take charge of the various departments of the work. This was done by the officers with a fine sense of the ability of the men employed. The business began to develop enormously, contracts were constantly being made for extensions of this line, and the stockholders of the Western Union Telegraph Co. found themselves the owners of exceedingly valuable stock, which it seemed had not even yet reached its

344   *LIFE OF JAY GOULD.*

highest value. A vast accession of strength and prestige was made and the Overland Telegraph Line was added to the Western Telegraph Co., for this was one link needed to connect the Atlantic and Pacific by wire. The business of the company was now large, its outlook especially brilliant, its position practically inpregnable, and its influence immense. It was confessedly one of the most gigantic and comprehensive of the private enterprises of the world, and it was the basis of a number of large fortunes. The entire West with its swelling population and vast possibilities became the field for future developments and power of the company.

There was no territory in the United States apparently needed the telegraph more than the great States springing into life along the Pacific coast. There was a craze in that section for making money in more daring and reckless ways than investing in telegraph lines, and at best the state of society there was in so chaotic state that it could not properly appreciate the benefit of telegraph lines through its domains. Even enough money could not be obtained to run a line from the different mining towns through the West strung on trees, but with some outside aid the project was finally gotten under way. Natural development of the country suggested the idea of perfecting lines to carry large business directly between the Atlantic and the Pacific. This was done, and scarcely had congratulatory messages passed between the Golden

Gate and the Atlantic harbors before a proposition was presented to run an overland telegraph from the United States by way of the Bering Strait and Asiatic Russia to Europe. At that time it was considered a most important part of diplomatic policy to create and maintain peace and friendship with Great Britain and Russia and other more powerful European nations. Russia took up with the project and stood ready to assure the construction of the whole line of seven thousand miles from Moscow to the Pacific. Telegraphic communication with the foreign countries began to be regarded as the best possible means to employ in bringing about a healthful state of commerce and a condition of respect, confidence, and good-will between this country and the European nations. These sentiments seemed to be adopted by the foremost people of our country, and the Russian line at once became the most popular enterprise of the period. Twenty thousand shares of $100 each, of what was known as the Extension Stock were issued by the Western Union Co., and an expedition was gotten ready to prosecute the work. Both land and marine services were organized and careful surveys and estimates of cost were made. During explorations by land the natives in the various sections traversed were found everywhere to be friendly, but few physical difficulties were encountered, and these seemed readily surmounted. The enterprise was favored on every hand and was prosecuted with great zeal.

346

LIFE OF JAY GOULD.

Meanwhile spirited enthusiasm and ardent labor were being exercised in another direction with an ultimate object in view, practically the same as that of the two services already at work. The "Great Eastern" was in an English harbor having coiled into her enormous hold wires for another and final attempt at establishing submarine telegraphy between America and Europe, but few of the enthusiasts interested in the overland scheme of connecting America with Europe, thought that the proposed Atlantic cable would ever amount to anything practical, and they thought if it did its success would be but temporary. This project, therefore, did not greatly disturb the investors in the overland scheme. But the brain child of Cyrus W. Field succeeded. The Atlantic cable was an assured success. The advantage in its two thousand miles of cable over sixteen thousand miles of land line, a big portion of which was along an unpopulated coast, at once became patent to every one. The Western Union people saw that the contest between two such lines would be unequal. They, therefore, recalled the land force and the fleets that were at work and ordered an abandonment of the undertaking. Men everywhere were surprised at the great success of the cable. It was as difficult for some of them to receive with credulity messages over it as it had been for the convention which nominated Silas Wright for the Vice-Presidency to accept that gentlemen's telegraphic declination of the office over the first line run by Morse from Baltimore to Washington.

MR. GOULD'S GREATEST ENTERPRISE. 347

Notwithstanding the fact that enormous outlays had been made in this attempt to establish a land line from America to Europe, the entire expense was footed bravely by the Western Union Co. without so much as a shiver. This was an excellent proof of the strength of the company at that period. The loss to the Western Union Co. was great, but the gain to the world in the benefit accruing from the Atlantic cable cannot be over-estimated.

At the period of the entrance of Mr. William Orton into the management of the Western Union Telegraph Co., a new era in telegraphic history had arrived. He had been Collector of Internal Revenue for the Sixth District of New York. He was young, just passed his thirty-sixth year, of delicate physical organization, but with an intellect unusually alert and keen, and with an industry which amounted almost to ferocity. Four classes of men had already performed their work. These were the first patient pioneers in scientific discovery who had discovered the foundations of natural laws.

Secondly, were the inventors who took up the discoveries of the former class, gave them form, and made them suitable for the service of human industry. Third, were the men, who, with enthusiasm, lacking method, webbed the country with telegraphic lines. A fourth class appeared in those who had brought the weak forces of different telegraphic lines throughout the country into strong systems, made telegraphic property valuable and its employment a national success.

348   *LIFE OF JAY GOULD.*

These men had now largely accomplished their work. The result was a vast organization with its wires extending to the extremities of civilization in all directions. A great work had been accomplished, but there was still much to be done. The administration era was dawning with Mr. William Orton's accession to the Presidency of the Western Union Co. The management of such a gigantic interest was a trust which it was necessary should be held by a man of just such fine brain, administrative faculty, and power of labor as the man who seemed by Providence raised to fill the position. Mr. Orton was a reflecting man, and he accepted the responsibility of the office with the consciousness of its greatness and of its perils. His position was a peculiar one. The enterprise was entirely private in the sense that the capital was furnished by individuals and was managed by the representatives of individuals, and yet it was of national, yes, of international importance and value.

Necessarily policies had to be adopted from which there could be no deviation in any case. At one time, it seemed almost inevitable that a few narrow-minded men, whose financial interests in the company were considerable, would insist on the adoption of a policy which would probably have blighted the future of telegraphy in this country. The principle on which they wished the company operated was, to say the least, a policy of rapacity and selfishness. They wished the tariffs greatly increased in order that what they supposed would be larger revenue,

MR. GOULD'S GREATEST ENTERPRISE. 349

and consequently heavier dividends might be derived, even though the business was greatly cut down. This would have been a direct step in the line of making one of the most gigantic enterprises of the times subservient to the interests of a few instead of the masses. It was necessary now that a nicely drawn line could be found, which would insure the adequate perfection of property on one side and the protection of the people from oppressive exactions on the other.

Without attempting to enter into the history of Mr. Orton's administration other than in this introductory manner, it is certainly permissible to note a circumstance connected with the first year of his incumbency which greatly aided in its development and success. Little attention had been given to electricity as a science, and the character of most of the improvements which had been proposed in connection with telegraphic appliances except in the matter of repeating apparatus were comparatively of a trifling and unscientific character.

There arrived in New York early in Mr. Orton's administration Cromwell Fleetwood Varley, whose accomplishments as a gentleman of education and as a scientist were famous the world over. Immediately upon Mr. Varley's arrival there appeared to be natural attraction for him in the executive chambers of the Western Union Co., where he was warmly welcomed and to which he became a frequent visitor. Animating conversations were held over various

350   *LIFE OF JAY GOULD.*

conditions of the telegraph and possible improvements. It soon became evident to Mr. Orton that earnest inquiry into the American telegraph might prove highly beneficial. He employed Mr. Varley to investigate in the most thorough manner the condition of the lines and services of the Western Union Co., and in that appointment lay the seed of future triumphs. Mr. Varley's reports were a revelation, and were startling enough to command at once the most vigorous efforts to reform the service. To this report may be traced the beginning of the magnificent series of developments and inventions which have made many fames and many fortunes, and which greatly perfected the Western Union's systems.

It now became evident that a unity of administration in the matter of tariffs, rules of order, compensations, methods, and management, must be adopted. The consolidation of so many organizations under one administration had unavoidably brought together some discordant elements. For the sake of perfection in execution of business it was necessary that there be some supreme authority, and through the agency of Mr. Varley's investigations and the fine executive ability of Mr. Orton the desired conditions were brought about. But trouble was in store for Mr. Orton and his associates and a supreme test of their abilities was to be made. On December 8th, 1869, Cyrus W. Field and President Orton sailed for Europe. Mr. Orton's trip was both for rest and recreation. In the absence of the President of the

VIEW OF THE HUDSON FROM IRVINGTON.

MR. GOULD'S GREATEST ENTERPRISE. 353

company, the management largely developed upon the Vice-Presidents, A. B. Cornell and George Walker, and upon Judge O. H. Palmer, Secretary and Treasurer.

Through the struggles of the Western Union Co. and of the other companies which it eventually absorbed, there had been in all departments a disposition to perform labor without even a murmur of discontent and with devotion almost amounting to heroism. But, with the dawn of New Year's morning, 1870, there came the muttering and the murmuring of a storm. Most of America's violent movements have originated in the West, and this storm originated in the same quarter. It rapidly spread eastward through Chicago and New York and diverged to Boston in the East and Philadelphia, Baltimore, and Washington in the South. It was so desolating and so relentless as to make itself memorable. Four years previous the Telegraphers' Protective League had been organized in times of peace between employers and employees, and was therefore not the outgrowth of any grievance. It probably owed its existence to the fact that labor organizations were popular at that time. They had their charm, which lay mostly in the idea of good fellowship and sociability, more than in protection for labor. In 1869 the League embraced a great proportion of the effective working force of the Western Union Co. The headquarters of the League was in New York. To show the principle upon

354 *LIFE OF JAY GOULD.*

which this organization was founded and the animus of its operations the following oath, which every member was required to take, is here given: "You do solemnly swear, in the presence of Almighty God and these witnesses, that you will make common cause with the members of the League, that forsaking your allegiance to corporations and individuals, you will, if necessity requires it, place your time and services at the disposal of the officers of the Telegraphic Protective League and reveal neither the names of officers nor members, nor the purposes of this society. So help you God."

The following pledge was required after taking the above oath:

"I, ————, do hereby acknowledge, that, having become a voluntary member of the Telegraphic Protective League, and being made cognizant with its objects and intentions, I have bound myself with a solemn oath to bear true allegiance to said League, and do hereby pledge my sacred honor that I will aid in whatever manner may be required the advancement and protection of its members," etc. The League was numerous and strong, and the restless spirits which controlled it, desired an opportunity to test its power. Those who were most concerned in its existence were not aware that it had ever been organized. Even those who were aware of its organization had no apprehension of a possibility that it would resort to extreme measures. Its oath obligated the members in such a way as to destroy

MR. GOULD'S GREATEST ENTERPRISE. 355

all legal and legitimate authority of the Western Union Co. over its business and its employees.

President Orton had received intimations of the existence of such a League and its power for destructiveness, but he had no fear of immediate danger, because he believed there was no grievance and could be none which would cause any discontent in the ranks of the League. A few months previous to the opening of 1870 a strike had been declared along the line of the Franklin Telegraph Company, and it had been successful. This seemed to instigate the leaders of the Protective League to declare a strike on the Western Union's lines. A reduction of a few salaries along the Pacific coast seemed to be a favorable opportunity to inaugurate the strike. The following demands were made upon the Western Union Company:

First, that no reduction of salaries be made at San Francisco and that any operatives dismissed there be at once reinstated.

Second, that in case of refusal the grand chief operator order all members of the organization to aid the brethren in San Francisco in the only way possible by immediately suspending work.

In December, 1869, the company had rearranged the salaries along the Pacific coast, with a view to adjusting compensations in such a way as to favor and encourage fidelity. Reductions were made in some cases and increases in others. No general reduction of salaries had any time been contem-

LIFE OF JAY GOULD.

plated or made, but the restless spirits of the organization determined that they must have a standard scale regardless of the abilities of the men.

The above demands were presented to the company, and Judge Palmer, acting in the absence of President Orton, refused to comply with them, as he knew no grievances which the organization could justly urge against the company. With the effort to enlist the sympathies of the public, the Grand Chief Operator immediately issued this manifesto : "We accept the challenge cheerfully. We control all the important points in the United States. We only ask of our brother operators outside of the organization not to come in and fill our places. We are determined that we will be men even while working for a gigantic corporation."

The movement greatly agitated the country. The activity and loyalty of the managers of the company, however, prevented with a single exception complete stoppage of business at any point. This exception was in Troy, N. Y., where the manager joined his staff and closed the office. On the same day that he closed it, another man opened it and kept it opened during the strike. The movement was not a contest against a definite wrong. It was merely a demand that labor should have the right to control and administer the property of capital. Some people were charitable enough to charge the movement to the over-zealousness of young blood, and fidelity to an oath which had been taken without its full significance being understood ; but, generally, universal indignation was aroused against a body of men who would so ruthlessly jeopardize the property and profits of legitimate capital. The intercourse of continents by telegraph in which innumerable industries had learned to depend was put in peril without the least justification.

At the height of the excitement the unintelligent and narrow management which characterized the strike from its beginning permitted a very imprudent circular to be spread broadcast. There were so many uncalled-for and violent criticisms of the policy of the Western Union Company in the matter of tariffs, dividend treatment of opposing lines, issuing of stock, etc., that whatever outside interest and sympathy had been manifested was withdrawn, for the impression was created that the strike was in the interest of opposing lines and not to right a wrong.

The Western Union Company had now become national ; it touched society everywhere. No enterprise entered so thoroughly and penetratingly into the activities of the nation. The management of the company was energetic, successful, and conscientious. The strike which seemed to threaten the company was completely subdued, and it taught the company's employees, as well as the employees in other lines of industry, that the people would not tolerate unjustified interference with the equilibrium of commerce.

358 *LIFE OF JAY GOULD.*

As has been cited in another chapter, Dr. Norvin Green succeeded Mr. Orton in the Presidency of the Western Union Company. He had acted for many years as Vice-President, and had been in many respects to Mr. Orton a strength and guide. He seemed to have a high and natural adaptation to the work of the office, and he had, indeed, a wide and useful experience.

During the struggles and successes of the Western Union Company Jay Gould had had his eye constantly on the rich prize. He had practically owned the Atlantic & Pacific Telegraph Company and had given the Western Union Company a controlling interest in that company. General Thomas T. Eckert had been Mr. Gould's manager and acting President, and he had won Mr. Gould's entire confidence. When the Atlantic & Pacific Company had been turned over in the Western Union, he expected that General Eckert would be placed in a commanding position such as he knew him to merit. In this he had been disappointed. He determined, therefore, to organize a new interest over which he might place his friend. The American Union Company may, therefore, be said to have had its origin in one of those marvelous friendships which now and then relieve the cold and hard sordidness of ordinary life. It is possible and probable that Mr. Gould had in his mind at the time of his organizing the American Union Company the possibility of its some day controlling the Western Union. He realized General

MR. GOULD'S GREATEST ENTERPRISE. 359

Eckert's ability and his intense and justified feeling against the Western Union, and he knew that he could be depended on for a bitter fight against that company if such a course were deemed necessary and advisable.

General Eckert was tireless in his efforts to make the new company a worthy antagonist of the old. In one year the company owned a wire mileage of fifty thousand miles and operated two thousand offices. Valuable contracts were secured with various railroads in different parts of the country and with various minor telegraph companies, and the American Union Telegraph Company, in two years, was a more formidable opponent of the Western Union Company than it had been deemed possible to organize, and the world was so impressed with its capacity and the vigor of its management that a very large business was speedily established. An earning capacity of six per cent. was shown at the close of 1880. It had perfected connection with Europe by the French Telegraph Company, of Paris. Investors began to see that, in a very short time, the new company's earning capacity would be fully six per cent. on $20,000,000 of capital. The board of the company was organized as follows:

JAY GOULD,	THOMAS T. ECKERT,
RUSSELL SAGE,	SYDNEY DILLON,
FRED. AMES,	F. GORDON DEXTER,
ROBERT GARRETT,	W. E. CONNOR.

360 *LIFE OF JAY GOULD.*

THOMAS SWINYARD,   J. J. SLOCUM,
LEVI L. LESTER,   E. H. BATES,
NATHANIEL NILES.

The Construction Company was composed of Washington E. Connor, G. P. Morosini, and Joseph Owen.

Reduced rates were immediately put into effect, and they induced a large class of business to be developed, which was somewhat of a social and domestic nature, and while it did not take away from the commercial patronage of the Western Union Company, it added greatly to the revenue of the American Union Company. But before many months the Western Union Company began to feel that its rival was gaining strong points, and to some extent undermining it. It was doing an enormous business, but its revenues had been reduced over $5,000 a day or $2,000,000 a year. This was attributed to the American Union Co. The stock market was quick to catch the situation, and Western Union stock declined to a very much lower figure than it had reached for years. W. H. Vanderbilt was heavily interested in the Western Union, and he began to see, as did other stockholders, that peace must be had at almost any cost. He therefore wrote a note, on the 9th of January, 1881, to Mr. Gould, asking him to meet him at his house at nine o'clock.

These two men, each with a telegraph company in his control, met, and began to negotiate for peace.

MR. GOULD'S GREATEST ENTERPRISE. 361

Both saw the advantage of amalgamating the affairs of the companies, as had been done in the first place, when the Western Union Co. had absorbed minor companies, and it was agreed to recommend consolidation to the Executive Committee of the Western Union Co. Terms of consolidation were agreed upon in February, 1881, and there was a united capital of $80,000,000. There was considerable trouble in the way of suits and counter-suits over this consolidation, but the union was not affected.

At the delivery of the property the American Union Company showed a milage of ten thousand seven hundred and one miles of poles, and forty-six thousand four hundred and twenty-two miles of wire. The Atlantic & Pacific showed a mileage of five thousand three hundred and thirty-six miles of poles and seventeen thousand eight hundred and sixty-nines miles of wire. Thus in a short time Jay Gould with the assistance of General Eckert had brought up a magnificent property and wonderfully increased its value. From that time on no man was more thoroughly identified with telegraphic interests and systems in this country than Jay Gould. With a far greater range of conception of their importance, he early recognized the railroad and the telegraph as two of the most prominent and permanent industries of the continent so vast in its distances as ours, and he realized the value and necessity of their working hand in hand.

There had been much opposition developed to

362 *LIFE OF JAY GOULD.*

the consolidation of the Western Union and the American Union, and this opposition took the form of legislation at Albany with the intention of sundering the union. An attempt was made by men keen in the art of bleeding to pass a bill which would annul the consolidation. The Western Union Company demanded that it should be heard, and Dr. Green gave his testimony, which contained many important points, the best of which are herewith presented as being of unusual interest. Dr. Green said :

"This bill if passed will not affect the legal status of the consolidation just made. Its legality is beyond question. Outside of its connection with stock speculations there is nothing to complain of. The sum and substance of that stock speculation is this : an opposition to the company I represent was projected and vigorously prosecuted, our stock was run down much below its intrinsic value under the threat of cut-rates. We cut down our expenses and expected a long struggle, but it was found that the other party had accumulated a large part of our stock and were ready for terms of adjustment. In the interest of our stock-holders, we could not forego an opportunity so unexpectedly offered. We accepted the terms proposed and that was the whole of it."

"But, in the continued depression of our stock, a number of speculators confidently expecting a further decline sold large blocks of borrowed stock, anticipating an opportunity to buy back very low. They

MR. GOULD'S GREATEST ENTERPRISE. 363

imagined themselves following an experienced leader; but who instead of selling was buying, and who was, perhaps, not unwilling that these gentlemen should make it easy for him. He had proposed to himself to end telegraphic war by purchasing control. When he had purchased ten millions or more of the stock thus thrown on the market, he agreed to terms of peace. The stock at once rose with great rapidity. Then was heard a howl great and long. These speculators had to buy in their stock and at every bid for it, the market bounded up. Take the matter of speculation out of the case, and what is left? Absolutely nothing."

Mr. Gould himself said on this occasion : "General Eckert was my friend. For him I started the American Union Co. We carried it forward until a proposition was made to merge it into the Western Union Co. As the stock of the latter went down I bought a large interest in it, and found that the only way out was to put the two companies together. General Eckert became General Manager of the whole system, and meanwhile I thought so much of the property and its earning powers that I have kept increasing my interest. I thought it better to allow my income to go into the things I was into myself. I have never sold any of my interests, but have devoted my interests to increasing them."

This attempt at legislation to destroy the consolidation and plunder the Western Union Co. was defeated by the earnest and energetic actions and the

364   *LIFE OF JAY GOULD.*

prompt defense of General Eckert, Dr. Green, and Mr. Gould.

The Western Union Co. gradually became stronger, for its policy throughout the years has always been in favor of consolidation. There was considerable litigation of a protracted nature with rival companies and with individuals in the early years of the presidency of Dr. Green, which had necessarily pressed very heavily upon him. He was capable of great endurance, but, of course, there was a limit to his strength; therefore, in April, 1883, feeling, as his predecessor had done, that he needed rest from the arduous duties of his position, he sailed for Europe.

Dr. Green was cordially and affectionately received by European gentlemen who had visited America and Canada, and had seen the vast scope of the Western Union Co. under the management of Dr. Green. He spent three months visiting different parts of the Continent, accompanied by his son. While Dr. Green was thus enjoying the hospitalities of the Continent, just as in the case of President Orton in 1870, who was absent in England when the operators' strike of that year occurred, the great body of telegraphic operatives in America again became disturbed, and were the source of much public and private anxiety. There were about thirty thousand operatives in various capacities in actual service in the Western Union, and the nation had learned to lean upon it as an

MR. GOULD'S GREATEST ENTERPRISE. 365

actual necessity of commercial and social intercourse.

Immediately succeeding the war there there had been a rapid and a great advance in values and considerable increase in the activity and the number of industries in the country. Every method of gain was pushed to the utmost, and success seemed to be everywhere, but more prudent men began to see that this universal prosperity of so marked a degree must eventually be succeeded by a state of depression fully as marked. The first faint forerunners of coming disaster were appearing. Values began to decline, the railroads that had been built in advance of actual public necessity because of the anticipation of a greater bulk of business could not meet their obligations. Mills and manufactories began to be without orders, great output of cereals in our country was fully matched by an equal output in Europe, so that our grain was not finding its way to the ports. By the casual thinker and observer it might be supposed that the telegraph would thrive equally as well when the country was in a condition of depression or of prosperity. To a certain extent this is so, but it has its limit. By the general depression of the industries, the country began to be thronged with young men and women out of employment to whom the telegraph was inviting on account of its being clean and genteel work and a rapidly-acquired art. These men and women were on the lists of applicants in all the cities for vacancies in the Western Union

366 LIFE OF JAY GOULD.

offices, consequently when vacancies occurred, inexperienced employees were engaged at salaries considerably below the rate which had been paid to those discharged. This was both just and politic. The old telegraph operators began to be alarmed at the state of affairs. Their craft became overcrowded, and the organs of union labor began to urge measures for active resistance. In 1881 at a convention held in Pittsburgh, Pa., the Brotherhood of Telegraphers of the United States and Canada was organized. A year later it claimed a membership of fifteen thousand. It was organized under a charter granted to the Knights of Labor, but was to be separate and independent and known as District Assembly No. 45. The Knights of Labor claimed a membership of eight hundred thousand, which was a strong backing for the Brotherhood of Telegraphy, and a self-support fund was originated, which by the first of July, 1883, amounted to $400,-000. At least, this was the claim of the Brotherhood at that time. The Brotherhood prohibited all instruction in telegraphy, except to members of an operator's family, and a vigorous opposition was made to all telegraph colleges for teaching the art. They failed to appreciate the fact that any attempt to deprive the youth of this land of an education of any kind must of necessity be a failure. They could not hope to succeed in closing the doors of any reputable vocation against energy and ambition.

To render education in telegraphy still more diffi-

MR. GOULD'S GREATEST ENTERPRISE. 367

cult, no member was allowed to teach another telegraphy except by permission of the local assembly, and orders were issued against compulsory Sunday work, eight hours were announced to be the limit of a day's work. Seven hours were to constitute a night's work. Five hours were to constitute the basis of work for an extra day, pay was to be alike for both sexes. Members of the Brotherhood were to strike when ordered, no strike was to be ordered until all attempts at arbitration had failed. Under a strike unmarried persons were to receive five dollars a week and married persons seven dollars a week.

It began to be observed that a crisis was imminent, the tone of the organ of the Brotherhood was especially defiant. The demands which it was intended to make upon the telegraph companies were assuming unreasonable proportion. The Western Union officials kept close watch and were well informed on every movement of the Brotherhood. There appeared to be an element of justice in one of the demands, and to this the Western Union Co. directed its attention. The following order was therefore duly issued and bulletined:

"At all independent Western Union offices which may be required to keep open all day Sunday, nine hours actual service in the day, six days in the week, or seven hours actual service at night, seven nights in the week, will constitute a week's work. All service in excess of the above named hours, includ-

368   LIFE OF JAY GOULD.

ing Sunday, will be regarded as extra, and will be paid for at a regular salary on the basis of seven hours a day."

By some of the more violent of the members of the Brotherhood this order was regarded as an evidence of weakness on the part of the Western Union Co., and an attempt to evade an issue with the Brotherhood. Some of the members of the Brotherhood thought the order very satisfactory and were inclined to accept it. It was determined to inaugurate a strike. The famous contest between labor and capital in 1870 had taken place in January, and the operators had in mind the unpleasantness of those cold, piercing days when no money was coming in to buy clothing and fuel, and although July was a month when the Western Union Co. was not busy comparatively, that month was chosen for the inauguration of the strike, because it was thought that the operators stood better chances of success.

On July 15th, largely attended meetings of the Brotherhood were held in some of the principal cities. The less discreet of the daily papers published the inflammatory speeches which were uttered at these meetings, and made them the basis of attacks on the telegraph companies. Others thoughtfully contemplated the vast injuries to society and commerce which would be sure to follow on the sudden stoppage of telegraphic communication and of hampering the operation of railroads by ordering

JAY GOULD'S RESIDENCE AT IRVINGTON.
South-east View.

MR. GOULD'S GREATEST ENTERPRISE. 371

the operators on a strike, and counciled calmness and moderation.

The movement seemed to be beyond the influence of advice. Men were sent by the Brotherhood to the various cities to present their demands. In the case of the Western Union Co. these were presented to General Eckert, the General Manager, who, after carefully reading them, remarked that he must be assured of the authority of the gentleman presenting the memorial to act for the employees of the Western Union Telegraph Co. The Western Union Co. appointed a committee to inquire into a complaint of irregularities of compensation or conditions of service which might exist, and an invitation was issued at the same time to all to make known their complaints to this committee.

There was, of course, great attempt at concealment of actual preparations for a strike. The very effort was so evident that to the intelligent managers of the Western Union Co. there was no doubt of what was at hand. On the morning of July 19th every one was at his post early, some of the usual late-comers were at work sharply on the hour appointed for duty, every detail of work was quietly and faithfully attended to ; but a number of faces were pale with suppressed excitement, and inquiries were answered with such an excess of respect and such a subdued tone that nervous unrest and expectation were very evident. This was the morning of the day which inaugurated very great peril for the operators of one of the greatest industries in

372   *LIFE OF JAY GOULD.*

the country. The hands of the clock pointed to twelve. Contrary to the expectations of the managers the noise of the instruments went on as before, and nothing was noticeable except the very evident suppressed excitement, but just at 12.12, or what was noon at Washington, every operator in the employ of the Western Union Co. went out from work on signal. Everything was done in an orderly manner, and there seemed to be a concerted plan to prevent any act being performed which should reflect on the craft. This was only one of the attempts made to enlist public sentiment, as it was shortly afterward very largely advertised that no intoxicating liquors whatever should be drunk while on strikes. In the different large cities there were a small number of loyal employees, and the managers had instructed to close the minor offices, and concentrate the force in one principal office for the prosecution of business. This was a stroke of business which astonished the strikers. In addition to this the company announced that all labor would be paid for as extra work on a basis of seven hours a day as a full day's work, and that their regular salaries should be given them as a bonus. A free table with all kinds of excellent food was served by day and night, and comfortable cots and bedding were placed in every available room. The managers and executive officers of the company combined in a working force which proved exceedingly effective.

Much excitement prevailed among the operators.

MR. GOULD'S GREATEST ENTERPRISE. 373

The managers of the strike succeeded in having published in some of the newspapers greatly exaggerated reports of the strike, which were all in their favor, as well as items which were intended to influence the public in their favor, and against the Western Union Co., but here the strikers were met again. The company had a press correspondent, who was given the authority to say to the different press associations and individual publications that the policy of the company was now, and would be throughout the strike, to maintain its rights, if it were necessary to close every one of its offices in order to do so. It must be understood that the strike was a general thing among telegraph companies of the country, and that there was not as much of a union among the companies as there was among the strikers.

The American Rapid Telegraph Company had acceded to the commands of the Brotherhood, and an order was issued to the deserters of that company to return to work. This was only a scheme to secure business, which it was believed would follow when the public knew that this particular company's offices were fully manned, and that there would be no delay whatever in the transmission of messages. It resulted in a considerable number of the strikers finding employment. It was believed that many of the other companies would follow suit, but the large companies felt they could afford to wait, among them the Western Union. Matters

LIFE OF JAY GOULD.

became desperate. Master Workman Campbell issued orders on the 29th of July for railroad operators to refuse Western Union business. This was intended to effectually cut off the communication of the minor towns and cities with the outside world. It had the flavor of dynamite and force about it, and the public mind was unfavorably influenced by it. The "bears" of the Stock Exchange began to take up the thing, and to run the stocks of the telegraph companies down. Cables and wires were cut, and other damage done to the property of the telegraph companies almost nightly. The strikers began to feel the bitterness of defeat and the strike took on an element of absolute unfairness and dishonesty. By August 1st, there was evidence enough that the second strike had failed, just like that of 1870, although every effort had been made to prolong it. On August 15th a committee of the Brotherhood waited on General Eckert to ascertain on what terms the strikers could be reinstated to their positions. Many were not re-employed because of their inefficiency, or because they had made themselves obnoxious to the company. The strike was at an end and nothing had been gained, in fact everything had been lost by it. Many operators had lost their situations and had to seek employment elsewhere and in other lines of industry. Thus the second strike ended in defeat.

Nothing so well illustrates the subsequent progress

MR. GOULD'S GREATEST ENTERPRISE. 375

of telegraphy in America as the massive building which it has been necessary to erect in the city of New York for the headquarters of the Western Union Co. The site on which the building stands cost $900,000 and the building itself $1,300,000. It is in the fifth floor of this building that the Gould offices are situated. It was first occupied February, 1875. Thirty years previous the rent of the leading telegraph company's office in New York was $500 a year and it was a small basement room.

SKETCHES

OF

GREAT FINANCIERS

CONTEMPORARY WITH

JAY GOULD

BY

W. FLETCHER JOHNSON

THE VANDERBILTS

VANDERBILT is a name which, in the United States, has become synonymous with wealth, practically boundless. We shall see, however, as we proceed with the consideration of that family's history, that this wealth has been acquired not by any lucky stroke of fortune, not by a fortunate deal at a gambling-table, not by the wholesale swindling which is so often gilded with the name of speculation, but by a combination of unflagging industry and rare perception of the fitness of means to ends, usually commendable means, and ends almost invariably for the welfare of the community. The family is of Dutch origin, and was first planted in this country early in the last century. For many years its home was on Staten Island, where its members pursued a hardy and laborious out-door life, obtaining through familiar intercourse with the elements acquaintance with hardship in many forms, thus developing characteristic traits of thrift and industry, and obtaining an admirable equipment for the battles of life in the form of sturdy bodies, simple habits, strong wills, and clear perceptions. These traits have been transmitted from generation to generation without impairment, and generally in the

380 *LIFE OF JAY GOULD.*

line of primogeniture. The first famous Vanderbilt, best known as the Commodore, was the eldest
son of an eldest son. His successor in the administration of the great fortune amassed by the Commodore was also an eldest son, and in turn his
eldest son is the foremost figure of the present
generation.

Cornelius Vanderbilt, the Commodore, was born
on Staten Island in 1794, the son of a thriving
farmer, who owned his farm, and carried his produce
to the New York markets in his own sail-boat.
Cornelius was a sturdy lad, a leader in athletic feats
on land and water, a daring rider and great lover
of horses. He would not endure the restraints of
a school-room, and so acquired his education, which
was but rudimentary, on the farm and on the bay.
When he had earned enough money, yet in boyhood,
to buy a sail-boat, he began business on his own account. When he was only eighteen years old he had
saved $500 of his own earnings, and a year later he
was married to his second cousin, Sophia Johnson.
He soon thereafter became the captain of a small
steamboat running between New York and New
Brunswick, N. J., and ultimately placed himself at
the head of a considerable coasting trade. As a
result of this change of business the family moved
to New Brunswick and opened a hotel. Of this
Cornelius became the head, and in these varied
employments was soon on the way to wealth. By
the year 1853 he was a wealthy owner of steam-

THE VANDERBILTS. 381

ships, and, having built the ship "North Star" for the purpose, went with his family on a voyage to Europe. A few years later he built the Staten Island Railroad, and began withdrawing his money from steamships for railroad investments. In 1860 he bought the Harlem Railroad at $6 or $7 a share, a few years later he became President of it, when it was worth $30, and in 1864 it was worth $285. This was the foundation of the great Vanderbilt fortune. The consolidation of the New York Central and Hudson River roads followed, and the entire system became the property of Commodore Vanderbilt.

It cannot be denied that there was a considerable amount of work connected with those operations that would not bear a strict application of the laws of ethics. The stock was "watered" wholesale. Nevertheless, the Commodore was not, like some of his contemporaries, a railroad wrecker. He began at once improving the property, useless expenditures were stopped, waste was checked, improved depots were built, tracks were relaid, and business was encouraged and developed all along the line. When Commodore Vanderbilt died, on January 4th, 1877, he was one of the richest men in America, his fortune amounting to more than $100,000,000, almost entirely in railroads.

William H. Vanderbilt, the Commodore's eldest son, was born at the New Brunswick hotel, and was educated at the Columbia grammar school, in New York city. For a time he worked in a ship-chand-

382   *LIFE OF JAY GOULD.*

ler's shop, and at the age of eighteen became clerk in a bank at $150 a year. At twenty years old he was married to Miss Kissam, and the young couple went to board in East Broadway. After a time he became tired of city life, and bought a farm of seventy-five acres on Staten Island, intending to settle down to humble rural life. His father appears to have had at this time a contemptuous opinion of his abilities. The young farmer needed capital to improve his property. The Commodore refused to advance it to him, thinking it would merely be wasted. So William borrowed $6,000 of a friend, and gave as security a mortgage on the farm. A few months later his father found it out.

"Is it true," he asked, "that you have mortgaged your farm for $6,000?"

"Yes," was the young man's reply.

"You don't amount to a row of pins!" thundered the old man, furiously. "You never were worth your salt, and never will be. You'll never be able to do anything except bring disgrace upon yourself and upon every one connected with you. I'm not going to have anything more to do with you. You can hoe your own row, and go to the devil as you please."

It was in vain that the young man tried to remonstrate, and show that the money was needed for improvements which would make the farm vastly more profitable than before. The enraged Commodore merely growled and grumbled and raged

THE VANDERBILTS. 383

the more; but the mext day he sent the young man a check for $6,000, with the curt command to "Pay off that mortgage, right off!" The young man happily disappointed his father's gloomy prophecies. In a few years he was the owner of 350 fertile acres, which yielded him an annual profit of $12,000. Still the Commodore distrusted him, and thought he never would rise above the rank of a successful farmer, although he had to confess that as a farmer he was uncommonly successful. In 1853 father and son went on the "North Star" voyage to Europe together. Walking the deck one day in mid-ocean, the Commodore noticed his son smoking a cigar.

"Bill," said he, "I'll give you $10,000 if you'll quit smoking."

"I don't want you money," replied the son; "but if you say quit smoking, I'll do it," and he threw his cigar overboard.

The younger Vanderbilt became associated in the Staten Island Railroad, and, when his father allowed it to become bankrupt, he was made its Receiver, and soon restored it to prosperity and became its President. This convinced the Commodore that "Bill" might amount to something after all. Soon after this a younger son, George Vanderbilt, died in Europe. He had been the Commodore's favorite child, and had been educated at West Point for a soldier; he was one of the most brilliant and phys-ically powerful young men ever entered at that school, lifting with ease on one occasion a dead

384   *LIFE OF JAY GOULD.*

weight of 900 pounds. His health was ruined by
his arduous services in the civil war. Cornelius
Vanderbilt, Jr., the second son of the Commodore,
was now leading a reckless life, and had become
estranged from his father. The old gentleman
therefore began to look upon William as perhaps
of necessity his successor in the management of the
great fortune he was building up, and, from month
to month, trusted him more thoroughly. It may be
that his decided fondness for William's eldest son,
Cornelius, had something to do with this change of
spirit.

In 1865 William H. Vanderbilt became Vice-
President of the Hudson River Railroad, and four
years later held the same office over the consolidated Hudson River and New York Central system.
On his father's death he succeeded to the Presidency
of this great railroad, and also of the Harlem
Railroad and the Lake Shore & Michigan Southern
Railroad. Under the Commodore's will, William
H. Vanderbilt received the bulk of the enormous
estate. The will was disputed by other members of
the family, but was sustained by the courts. From
that time until the fall of 1881 Mr. William H. Vanderbilt's history was the history of American railroad enterprise. This was a period of unusual
activity in railroad matters, and he was sufficiently
enterprising to place himself in the forefront. He acquired possession of the Canada Southern Railroad.
In 1877 the great railroad strikes came on ; there

THE VANDERBILTS. 385

were 12,000 men employed on the New York Central and Hudson River lines, and their wages had just been reduced 10 per cent. Mr. Vanderbilt at once sent out word that $100,000 would be distributed as a gratuity among the men and the 10 per cent. restored to their wages as soon as increasing business justified such a step. The result was that while other railroad systems were paralyzed, these lines worked without interruption, less than 500 of the 12,000 men going on strike. From time to time he was forced to engage in rate wars with the competing trunk lines. These he conducted vigorously and with invariable success, and established the policy of protecting his lines and all their branches from the attacks of rivals. In November, 1879, he sold a block of 250,000 shares of stock to a foreign syndicate, with the effect of greatly increasing public confidence in the stability of his roads, and raising the price of all stocks in which he was interested. From the proceeds of this sale and other funds he purchased $53,000,000 of Government bonds.

Realizing the uncertainty of life and feeling his own health weakening, he now began putting his fortune into such a shape that it could readily be transferred to his heirs at his death. This sale of stock and purchase of government bonds was an important step in this direction. In 1881 he began transferring the active management of his railroads to his sons, Cornelius and William K. It was under

386 *LIFE OF JAY GOULD.*

the management of William K. Vanderbilt that the so-called Nickel-Plate road, which was built as a competing line, and the competition of which the Vanderbilts had vainly tried to prevent, was purchased outright in 1883. In that year, on May 4th, William K. Vanderbilt finally surrendered the presidencies of all the roads with which he had been identified. "In my judgment," he said, "the time has arrived when I owe it as a duty to myself, to the corporations, and to those around me upon whom the chief management will devolve, to retire from the Presidency. I do not mean to sever my relations or abate the interest I have heretofore taken in these corporations. It is my purpose and aim that these several corporations shall remain upon such a basis for their harmonious working with each other and for the efficient management of each as will secure for the system both permanency and prosperity." The next day Mr. Vanderbilt, with his son, George, and his uncle, Jacob H. Vanderbilt, sailed for Europe. James H. Rutter, long conspicuously identified with the roads, was elected President of the New York Central, and on his death was succeeded by Mr. Chauncey M. Depew. Thus the great system established by Mr. Vanderbilt has been maintained to the present time.

William H. Vanderbilt died on December 8th, 1885. He was one of the 13 brothers and sisters, and to him had been born nine children, of whom only one died in early life. His eldest child, Cor-

A VIEW OF THE GREENHOUSE AT LYNDHURST.

THE VANDERBILTS. 389

nelius Vanderbilt, has succeeded to the chief management of the great railroad systems, although the second son, William K., is prominently identified with them in official capacities. The third son, Frederick W., is also deeply interested in some of the roads. The youngest, George W., has devoted himself chiefly to a literary career, and is one of the most liberal and discriminating collectors of books in America. It is his ambition to gather one of the largest and most valuable libraries in the world. The four daughters are Mrs. Elliot F. Shepard, Mrs. William D. Sloane, Mrs. H. McK. Twombley, and Mrs. Seward Webb. On his death Mr. Vanderbilt divided the bulk of his fortune between his four sons, handsomely providing, however, for all other members of the family, and arranging for the bulk of the fortune to be kept intact as a family possession. His successors have faithfully followed out his plans and wishes in all respects.

When William H. Vanderbilt was already worth many millions he continued to live in a house which had been given to him by his father at Thirty-eighth Street and Fifth Avenue. From there he moved to a larger and better, yet still unpretentious house, on the same avenue. After his father's death, however, he determined to build what should be the finest private residence in the city. A block of ground was purchased at Fifth Avenue and Fifty-first street, and the ablest artists and architects were instructed to spare no expense in designing and ex-

390 *LIFE OF JAY GOULD.*

ecuting the great work. They were empowered to ransack the world to furnish the palace. On this ground two great houses of brownstone connected by a wing were constructed; one for Mr. Vanderbilt, and one for his two daughters, Mrs. Sloane and Mrs. Shepard. Outwardly they closely resemble each other, but within differ widely in arrangement and furnishing. The one intended for Mr. Vanderbilt himself cost without its priceless picture-gallery more than $2,000,000. It represents the work for a year and a half of more than 600 men on the interior decorations alone. Sixty sculptors were brought here from Europe on large salaries, and kept at work for more than a year. The great front doors of solid bronze are exact copies, reduced in size, of Ghiberti's famous bronze gates in Florence. The great hall extends from the ground floor to the roof, and is surrounded in the upper stories by galleries leading to the various rooms. It is lined with English oak, dark red African marble, and bronze. The great drawing-room has a ceiling painted by Gallaud, of Paris, and the walls are hung with embroidered velvet enriched with crystals. The library is lined with mahogany and rosewood, inlaid with brass and mother-of-pearl. The great picture-gallery is thirty-two by forty-eight feet, and thirty-five feet high, roofed with opalescent glass. In this room Mr. Vanderbilt gathered the costliest collection in America of modern paintings, purchased chiefly in Paris. Here are masterpieces of Detaille, Rosa

THE VANDERBILTS. 391

Bonheur, Meissonier, and Gerome; of Alma Tadema and Louis Leloir; of Millais, Le Fevre, Knaus, Defregger, and J. F. Millet.

Mr. Vanderbilt inherited his father's love for horses. One of his favorite recreations was to go on the road behind a team of swift trotters. He purchased the famous trotter, Maud S., for $20,000; also such horses as Aldine, Early Rose, Small Hopes, Lysander, Leander, and Charles Dickens. In 1877 he went to England to see the great Derby race, and said afterward that the sight of 300,000 persons watching a horse-race was well worth a trip across the ocean. Whenever he visited Saratoga or Sharon Springs, or other watering-places, he always took a number of his favorite horses with him. He built for them a stable in New York, at Fifty-second Street and Madison Avenue, the building costing more than $60,000, exclusive of the land. Its walls within are finished in polished cherry, ash, and black walnut, and the metal work is largely sterling silver. His sons have not altogether inherited this taste, generally preferring yachting. Mr. William K. Vanderbilt spends much of his time cruising about the world in his steam-yacht, which is one of the finest vessels afloat.

The name of Vanderbilt has been pleasantly connected with many great deeds of benevolence. Mr. William H. Vanderbilt gave in the aggregate vast sums every year for charitable purposes, but so quietly that few persons knew of it beside himself.

LIFE OF JAY GOULD.

His father had already given a great deal through the Rev. Charles F. Deems, a Methodist minister, to whom in early life he became much attached. He had given Dr. Deems a fine church in New York city, and had endowed Vanderbilt University, at Nashville, Tenn., with more than $1,000,000. To the latter institution William H. Vanderbilt also gave liberally, and continued to make Dr. Deems the almoner of many of his charities. He secured the transportation, at a cost of more than $100,000, of the famons obelisk known as Cleopatra's Needle, from Egypt to New York, and had it set up in Central Park. It was formally presented to the city of New York on February 22d, 1881, the Hon. William M. Evarts, Secretary of State, delivering the oration. A silver medal in commemoration of the event was struck and presented to Mr. Vanderbilt. In that year the millionaire gave a large sum to the University of North Carolina, and not long afterward another liberal gift to the University of Virginia. He paid $50,000 toward wiping out the debt of St. Bartholomew's Protestant Episcopal Church, in New York city, of which he was a member. One of his most notable benefactions was the gift, on October 17th, 1884, of $500,000 to the College of Physicians and Surgeons in the city of New York, for the purchase of real estate and the erection of buildings to enable it more successfully to carry out the purposes for which it was founded.

Mr. Vanderbilt's four sons have continued to

THE VANDERBILTS.

393

practice the liberal generosity inaugurated by him, and are frequent givers to causes for promoting the welfare of the general public. Mr. Cornelius Vanderbilt has conspicuously identified himself with the work of the Young Men's Christian Association, and has for years been at the head of a branch of that institution existing among the employees of his railroads. He has given $100,000 for the proposed Protestant Episcopal Cathedral in New York, and he and his brothers have been generous patrons of many other religious, educational, and charitable enterprises. Mr. George W. Vanderbilt has endowed a free circulating library in New York, and established and maintained a valuable manual labor training-school. The brothers have spent much time with their families in Europe, but make their home in New York city in the great house built by their father, now the residence of William K. Vanderbilt, and in neighboring mansions on Fifth Avenue, that now occupied by Cornelius being conspicuously elegant. They also possess fine summer residences at Newport.

LELAND STANFORD

LELAND STANFORD.

IT has been of late years a matter of complaint, not always well grounded, that the United States Senate is being filled up with the possessors or representatives of great wealth. It is true that there are many millionaires in that body. It may be true that some of them have obtained their positions merely because of their wealth. But there are some who began in the humblest walks of life, and who attained their fortunes by hard work and unremitting labors for the development of the resources of the country. Reaching mature years, and becoming the possessors of vast wealth and the controllers of enormous industrial interests, they are not the representatives of money-bags merely; they are types of that American pluck and enterprise and those traits of industry that have built up the greatness of the nation. As such, he would indeed be bold who would challenge their right to sit in the highest assembly of the country as representatives of the American people.

Leland Stanford, whose best known memorial is the Pacific Railroad, was born March 9th, 1824, near Albany, N. Y. He was the son of a well-to-do farmer of good old Puritan ancestry, and led the life of a farmer's boy. He grew up sturdy, industrious, and intelligent. After a few winters at the village

398   LIFE OF JAY GOULD.

school, he went, at the age of 17, to Cazenovia
Seminary, where Senator Hawley, Charles Dudley
Warner, Bishop Andrews, Philip D. Armour, and
other men prominent in American business and
literature received their early education. Here he
was known as a careful, industrious student, with a
faculty for taking pains, which has been said to be a
mark of genius. Next he went to Albany and
studied law, but after three years there, went to the
West. He stopped for a time in Chicago and might
have settled there for good, but one day he was
assailed by a perfect cloud of bloodthirsty mos-
quitoes, for which he had a special aversion, and that
trifling circumstance impelled him to pack his trunk
and leave the place at once. He next, stopped at
Fort Washington, near Milwaukee, where he practiced law for three years and managed to save some
$2,000, nearly all of which he invested in a library
of law books. One night his office took fire, and,
with its contents, was entirely destroyed, leaving
him almost penniless. He sold out a little timber
land which he had purchased, and managed to raise
nearly $1,000. With that, in 1852, he set out for
the Pacific coast.

His first settlement there was at Sacramento,
where he opened a general store. Those were
flush times in California, and within three years he
had made more than $10,000. He kept on at the
same business a while longer, steadily increasing
his fortune, and in ten years was worth about

LELAND STANFORD.

$100,000. In 1861 he was chosen Governor of California, and then struck out for a wider field of activity. In his earlier years he had heard an Albany engineer talking about the feasibility of constructing a railroad in Oregon. Indeed, he had even hinted at the construction of a railroad line clear across the continent. Of course, such schemes were then considered chimerical, but now that young Stanford was actually on the ground and appreciated the needs and the possibilities of the Pacific coast, he recalled these hints with interest. He began talking with surveyors and engineers about the feasibility of such plans. He talked on the same subject with his brothers and with Messrs. Collis P. Huntington and Charles Crocker, who also were storekeepers at Sacramento, and were intimate friends of his.

His idea was to build a railroad from Sacramento over the Coast Range and Sierra Nevada mountains to the mining camps on the borders of Nevada. At that time the rates of freightage on all supplies for the camps were enormously high, and it was evident that if such a railroad could be built it would be exceedingly profitable. One engineer looked over the proposed route and said he thought the road could be built. Thereupon Mr. Stanford organized a company under the California State law, and with Messrs. Huntington and Crocker went on horseback over the route. When they reached the top of the mountains they stopped, dismounted, and sat

400　LIFE OF JAY GOULD.

down to discuss the situation. At their feet was a precipice dropping perpendicularly down a quarter of a mile. The idea of building a railroad through such a region was startling; such a thing had never been attempted in the world. One of the little company said that they would have to build a derrick by which to lift the cars up to the top of the mountain, but Mr. Stanford was confident that although the difficulties were enormous the road could be built and operated successfully. The grade would be very steep, and the road would be an expensive one to build, yet the profits, once it was opened, would be correspondingly great.

They returned to Sacramento and arranged for the construction of the road. As projected, the line was about 150 miles long. To build it took the labor of 3,000 white men and 10,000 Chinamen for four years. Indeed, without " Chinese cheap labor " the road probably could not have been built at all. But it was finished, competed successfully with the mule teams and oxen that had formerly carried supplies to the camps, and soon became enormously profitable. With this done, the Government was encouraged to go forward with its trans-continental railroad schemes. With these Mr. Stanford was conspicuously connected, and it was largely due to his energy, enterprise, and enthusiasm that the stupendous task was carried to successful completion. He has also identified himself very largely with other railroad enterprises on the Pacific coast; he is

LELAND STANFORD.

an enormous land-owner, and his wheat farms and vineyards are the pride of the State.

A few years ago Mr. Stanford's only child, Leland, a promising young man of 18 years, died. This was a great shock to Mr. and Mrs. Stanford, and they determined to erect an unequalled memorial to their boy. With this purpose in view, Mr. Stanford called to his aid the best educators, and with characteristic energy completed plans for the "Leland Stanford, Jr., University," with an endowment of more than $20,000,000, in lands and other property, which is sure to increase greatly in value in the next decade. This endowment includes the Vina ranch of 55,000 acres in Tehama County, on which is the largest vineyard in the world; the Girdly wheat ranch in Butte County, comprising 21,000 acres; and the Palo Alto ranch and stock farm of 7,200 acres. The total value of these three ranches is $5,300,000. It is his intention to make at Palo Alto, California, an institution which for literary and scientific learning shall be second to none in the world. It shall afford to its students every opportunity for learning the useful professions, businesses, and trades of American life. A young man will be able there to learn agriculture, mining, engineering, carpentry, and building, the construction of machinery, or any other vocation for which nature has fitted him and to which his tastes attract him. To the development of this magnificent scheme of prac-

402   *LIFE OF JAY GOULD.*

tical philanthropy Mr. Stanford has largely dedicated
the remainder of his life.

Another enterprise with which Mr. Stanford's
name is inseparably connected is the invention and
development of instantaneous photography, especially as applied to the picturing of men and animals in motion. The conventional pictures of
horses galloping and trotting did not satisfy him;
he was convinced that their attitudes as represented
were unnatural and impossible. He therefore sent
for a skilled practical photographer, gave him un-
limited means with which to prosecute his experiments, and himself indicated the lines on which
those experiments should be conducted. The results were astonishing and highly successful; not
only were perfect photographic pictures secured of
horses galloping and trotting at their utmost speed,
but equally satisfactory pictures were produced of
birds flying, of men running, leaping, and wrestling,
and even of a cannon ball in full flight, just as it was
discharged from the mouth of the cannon. These
achievements have been of the highest value to
painters and sculptors, and have almost revolution-
ized the art of illustration.

Mr. Stanford has little taste for public life. He
is essentially a business man and developer of industrial resources. But he was persuaded, in 1861,
to accept election as Governor of California, and
served in that office with ability and distinction.
Two years ago he was chosen a Senator of the

LELAND STANFORD.

403

United States, and in that office he has made his mark, not as an orator or debater, but as a careful, painstaking, and accomplished committee-man; and it is in the committees that the most important work of Congress is accomplished.

He has been a notable and much observed figure on the floor of the Senate; a tall, well-proportioned man, with gray moustache and whiskers; a full, round head, thickly thatched with gray hair; a strong nose; a large and finely-developed forehead, and an expressive and masterful mouth. His whole air is that of a man of resolute action, able to undertake and execute great deeds, and to impress his potent individuality upon all his associates. Despite his great wealth, his life has been always a simple and unostentatious one. He is one of the most plainly dressed men in public life at Washington. His clothes are of plain black material, and jewelry is conspicuous by its absence from his person. It is his habit to rise at a not very early hour in the morning, to eat a hearty breakfast, and then to prepare himself for the labors of the day by an hour of exercise, often taken in the form of a walk across country. He takes a light lunch at noon, and a moderately hearty dinner in the evening, and retires at from ten to eleven o'clock at night.

When in California the Senator spends nearly all his leisure at his country estate. His town house, on the crown of what has been irreverently dubbed "Nob Hill," cost, with its furnishings, not less than

LIFE OF JAY GOULD.

$1,500,000. It is occupied, perhaps, two months in the year by the owner. It is rich in wood-carvings and frescoes, and the art gallery contains the largest collection of old masters outside of a public gallery in this country. He maintains residences in New York and Washington also. His wife, who was Miss Lathrop, of Albany, usually travels with him. She is eminent for her practical charities. Senator Stanford's wealth is estimated at $50,000,000.

JAY GOULD'S RESIDENCE AT IRVINGTON.
North-east View.

CHAUNCEY M. DEPEW

CHAUNCEY M. DEPEW.

PERHAPS the widest conception in the public mind of the subject of this sketch is that of an incomparably witty and versatile after-dinner speaker. He is entitled, however, to at least equal rank as a serious orator on any occasion worthy of high eloquence; as a shrewd and far-seeing politician, a broad-minded statesman, a successful business man, a skilled lawyer, a polished man of society and of the world; and, above all, in all the private relations of his life, a thoroughly manly man, a natural gentleman.

Chauncey Mitchell Depew was born on April 23d, 1834, the reputed anniversary of Shakespeare's birth, at Peekskill, Westchester County, New York. His father was of Huguenot descent and his mother Puritan. Isaac Depew, his father, was descended from a family which settled at New Rochelle, New York, more than 200 years ago, a man of great physical and mental strength, with an indomitable will but a tender and generous heart. It has been well said of him that he ruled everybody and everything about him, but his wife ruled him. He was a man of considerable wealth, owning a number of village stores and a small fleet of sloops on the Hudson. His wife, the mother of our hero, was Martha Mitchell, a granddaughter of the Rev. Josiah Sher-

410   *LIFE OF JAY GOULD.*

man, who was a brother of the illustrious Roger Sherman. Thus, Mr. Depew is related to General and Senator Sherman, and, through them, to Senator Evarts and Senator Hoar. Mr. Depew was from the first his mother's own child, inheriting from her tact, grace, and kindliness, humor, adaptability to circumstances, and a most versatile nature. From his early boyhood he was highly popular with all his neighbors, and soon acquired reputation as a brilliant and almost exhaustless story-teller. Sitting of an evening in the village store, he was sure to be the centre of a circle of admiring and applauding men and boys. No social gathering was complete without him; he was a fine singer, a graceful dancer, and always ready to be at the head of whatever schemes of entertainment his companions might desire.

His early education was acquired at Peekskill Academy, where he was fitted for entrance to Yale College. Entering that venerable institution in 1852, he continued his reputation as a "royal good fellow," but it is confidently asserted that his health was never injured by over-study. He was, however, a wide reader, a brilliant speaker, and on one occasion captured a debating prize. One of his classmates has borne concerning him this high testimony: "Depew was a man of high mark for quick intelligence, fine character, and most delightful good fellowship. In the class of 1856 he was one of the best known, most cordially liked, and most thoroughly respected men of his time there. A young man in college is commonly of no account to the men in the classes above him, but the tall figure of Chauncey Depew showed a countenance curiously old and manly in all the aspects denoting sense and character, and yet just as curiously young and tender in all those denoting feeling and fineness of nature; so that he commanded respect and won the warm regard of his seniors in standing, as well as of his associates and class companions. He was already a speaker of uncommon originality and force, at once entertaining and persuasive, and was a figure in the college world as one of its most effective popular orators. But more even than this, Depew stood conspicuous above all the men of his time in college for the remarkable union of two sets of qualities: a purity of feeling and conduct, a cleanness of soul and speech, and a largeness and firmness of integrity and honor which are rarely seen, united with a breadth of sympathy, a kindliness of heart and a generosity of good fellowship which drew the best men to him, while even the worst were not repelled by the iron-clad abstinence through which they felt unbounded kindliness of heart expressed in ways that a father confessor of souls could not have improved upon. He never bent, never swerved, never showed any stain to the purest eye; yet he was the best fellow to all sorts of men, the quickest sympathizer and kindliest helper that any man could reveal himself to without reser-

412   *LIFE OF JAY GOULD.*

vation. The grave, good-humored kindliness of his
strong, tender, homely face was prophetic of a life
equal to any position the world could give. He
was, as he is now, one of those men who can win
many sorts of men without letting down his own
ideals or in any way lowering himself. He is not
separated by circumstances, such as great wealth
and great place, from the humble and hard handed
toilers about him."

Mr. Depew was at first, like his father, a Democrat in politics, but at New Haven he fell among
Abolitionist influences and soon became an ardent
member of the Republican party, which was formed
at about the time he left college. He was graduated
at Yale in 1856. The Fremont campaign was then
at its height, and he made no secret of his earnest
adherence to the cause represented by that leader.
A few days after his graduation he went home to
Peekskill and attended a political meeting held by
the Fremont clubs of that vicinity. Mr. George
William Curtis was to be the principal orator, but
was detained from putting in an appearance. There
was danger, therefore, that the meeting would be a
failure. Somebody, however, noticed young Depew
in the audience, and having heard of his prowess as
a speaker at college, called upon him to speak,
knowing well the effect a Republican speech
would have coming from the lips of a member of
the leading Democratic family of that neighborhood. Young Depew took the platform, and,

CHAUNCEY M. DEPEW. 413

with some signs of natural embarrassment at speaking before his old comrades and townspeople for the first time, began to give in forcible language the story of his conversion from Democracy to Republicanism, and the reasons that had led him to that change of faith. He was attentively listened to, and gained courage as he spoke. Taking up the congenial topic of human freedom, he spoke for more than an hour and a half, and roused the enthusiasm of the audience to such a pitch that the meeting was remembered for years as one of the most impressive political demonstrations ever known in Westchester County. Of course, Isaac Depew could not help being proud of his son's success as a speaker, but he was considerably mortified and angered at his political apostacy, as he considered it; so when his neighbors congratulated him on his son's success, he said: " What, do you call that Republican stuff brilliant? Why, I sent Chauncey to college a sensible fellow, but he has come back a fool." Others did not, however, agree with this latter estimate. Within a few days Chauncey was urgently invited by the State and National Committees of the Republican party to take the stump as a speaker for the rest of the campaign. This he was reluctant to do, but finally yielded, and traveled all over the country making stirring speeches in behalf of General Fremont. One of his companions on these tours was James W. Husted, since conspicuous in New York

414   *LIFE OF JAY GOULD.*

politics.   Husted generally presided at the meetings and introduced his companion in a short speech, Mr. Depew making the principal address. Mr. Depew's first vote was cast for General Fremont in the fall of 1856.

For two years after graduation Mr. Depew was an earnest student of law, and in 1858 was admitted to the bar, and began the practice of that profession.   At this time it was his custom to rise at six o'clock in the morning, and then make his brother's life miserable because the latter had not been up an hour already and got the office swept out before sunrise. In later life, as the wealthy president of one of the most important railroad systems of the world, Mr. Depew rises not later than seven o'clock, and makes a frugal breakfast at seven-thirty off a couple of boiled eggs, a bit of toast, and a glass of milk.   His devotion to law did not altogether wean him from politics.   In 1861 he was elected to the State Legislature as Assemblyman from the Third District of Westchester County.   The next year he was re-elected, being in 1863 candidate for Speaker.   A Democrat, Mr. T. C. Callicott, was, however, elected to that position, and Mr. Depew became Chairman of the Ways and Means Committee and leader of the Republican side of the House.   In November, 1863, he was elected Secretary of the State for New York State on the Unionist or Republican ticket, defeating his Democratic rival by nearly 30,000 majority.   In this position he served for one year

CHAUNCEY M. DEPEW.

under the administration of Governor Seymour and one year under that of Governor Fenton. A renomination was offered to him, but he declined it and returned to his law office. In 1866 Mr. Depew was still a young lawyer of inconsiderable practice, but he had a wide reputation as a politician and a rising statesman, and was chosen by the President as Minister to Japan. After several weeks of consideration he declined the honor. "I thought," he afterward said, "that if I accepted that place and so got confirmed in my taste for public office, I would become a political pauper." About that time he was also much thought of as a candidate for Collector of the Port of New York. A few years later he was appointed Commissioner of Emigration in New York, but declined that office also. He was made, in April, 1871, a member of the Board of Commissioners for the new State Capitol at Albany, and held that place four years. In 1877 he was made a Regent of the University of the State of New York, a life-office, which he still holds. He was also in that year appointed a Commissioner to locate the boundaries between New York State and New Jersey and Pennsylvania. In 1872 he was a conspicuous member of the Liberal Republican party in its campaign of that year, and was its candidate for office, but was defeated with the rest of the party.

Not long after the inauguration of President Garfield in 1881, a serious quarrel arose between the President and the two Senators from New York

416 *LIFE OF JAY GOULD.*

State, Messrs. Conkling and Platt, on the subject of federal patronage. The Senators bitterly accused the President of bad faith and broken promises, and rather than be parties to what they considered an unwise and dishonorable proceeding resigned their seats. Their friends in New York State urged their immediate re-election, and a prolonged and bitter contest ensued in the Legislature at Albany. Mr. Depew was immediately put forward by the friends of President Garfield as a candidate for one of the vacant chairs, but after several weeks' fruitless balloting he withdrew from the contest. In 1884 he might have had the unanimous and unchallenged nomination and election to the Senatorship without making an effort to that end, but he declined to be considered as a candidate.

A most important part of Mr. Depew's career has been his connection with what is known as the Vanderbilt system of railroads ; this began in 1866. He had attracted the favorable attention of Commodore Vanderbilt and was selected by him as attorney for the Harlem Railroad. Later he was made attorney for the whole New York Central & Hudson River System, which in 1875 had grown almost to its present size, and was also chosen a director of the roads. In these various capacities he was of untold service to the company as its legal adviser, as its legislative agent, and as a negotiator with other corporations. When Mr. W. H. Vanderbilt retired from the Presidency of the roads, Mr. Depew was made Second Vice-President of the re-organized company, and, on the death of Mr. Rutter, became President of the whole system, a position which he still holds. Although thus the representative of vast wealth, Mr. Depew has not felt the antagonism of the laboring classes which so many great employers have suffered. He has always been a firm friend of the employees of the railroads with which he has been connected, and has had an eye to their welfare as well as to the welfare of the stockholders, rightly believing the two to be indissolubly connected. The men therefore trust him. They have never had occasion to resort to strikes, but, on the contrary, have stood a united army to guard the Vanderbilt roads from implication in the labor troubles of other corporations. There is perhaps no man in the country more popular among the thousands of workingmen with whom he has come into contact, and with whom he stands in the relation of employer than Mr. Depew. On the other hand, he has been a popular and welcome figure in the most aristocratic society of New York and of the whole nation, and a courted and admired figure in the European capitals whenever he has visited them. He has become a member and officer of several of the most conspicuous social and political clubs of New York and President of the famous Union League Club.

He has been called upon to deliver orations at many of the most important public gatherings for

418

LIFE OF JAY GOULD.

years past, and is in constant demand at club dinners, receptions, college commencements, and similar occasions. At one time he was called upon to address a gathering of the Brotherhood of Locomotive Engineers, when he made an eloquent and convincing plea for harmony between labor and capital. He was the orator at the dedication of the monument to deceased newspaper men at Cypress Hills Cemetery. "The soldier," he said, "is inspired with the hope of promotion, the dream of glory, and he becomes a hero in the maddening passion of the battle. But the reporter, with no incentive but duty, shares the warrior's dangers and exposures, notes in the thickest of the fray the fortunes of the fight, and while the camp is asleep rides weary through a hostile country to send to his paper the first account of the carnage and the victory, in a message which electrifies the nation but bears no signature." On another occasion, before a famous Free-Thought club, he made a powerful argument against certain phases of so-called liberalism. "I confess," he said, "I do not understand these evangels of free thought. They use a language of strange terms and beautiful generalities which convey no meaning to me. I have listened to them with the most earnest attention, but when they have tumbled down my church and buried my Bible, and destroyed all the foundations of my faith, what do they offer in return? Nothing but phrases, collec-

CHAUNCEY M. DEPEW.

tions of words, and terminologies as mixed as chaos and as vague as space!"

Speaking at a meeting of the Young Men's Christian Association of Yale College, held in a New York theatre, he said: " I regard student life as more than a curriculum. A young man goes from his home with its narrow horizon to the broader world of young intellects, and what he gains or loses, the changes brought about by attrition, make his character through life. One man's influence upon his fellows is often great. I have known one man to ruin a whole class. In one instance three or four brilliant men, leaders yet debauchees, men who are supposed to do great things without work, ruined hundreds of their fellows. This movement of the Young Men's Christian Association is to do away with such things, to rescue true manhood in the schools, and to teach the lesson that his life is best who lives best and gets most out of it."

Another passage of his eloquence, from his Decoration-Day address in 1879, is worthy of all remembrance: "When the war was over in the South, where, under warmer skies and with more poetic temperament, symbols and emblems are better understood than in the practical North, the widows, mothers, and children of the Confederate dead went out and strewed their graves with flowers, and at many places scattered them impartially also over the unknown and unmarked resting places of

LIFE OF JAY GOULD.

the Union soldiers. As the news of this touching tribute was flashed over the North it aroused as nothing else could have done national amity and love and allayed sectional animosity and passion. It thrilled every household where there was a vacant chair by the fireside and an aching void in the heart for a lost hero whose remains had never been found. Old wounds broke out afresh, and in a mingled tempest of grief and joy the family cried, ' Maybe it was our darling !' Thus, out of sorrows common alike to the North and South came this beautiful custom. But Decoration Day no longer belongs to those who mourn. It is the common privilege of us all, and will be celebrated as long as gratitude exists and as long as springtime flowers bloom."

With this established reputation for eloquence on noble themes, it was highly appropriate that Mr. Depew should have been selected as the orator for the Centennial anniversary of the inauguration of President Washington. His address has been universally accepted as a noble and worthy expression of the loyal affection and admiring veneration of the American people of to-day for the first and greatest captain of the Ship of State.

As a humorous after-dinner speaker Mr. Depew cannot well be described. He must be heard to be appreciated. " Who," said a recent writer in *The North American Review*, " having once seen him rise at a friendly banquet, can forget the tall, solemn figure, the face clean shaven, except for its

CHAUNCEY M. DEPEW.

neatly trimmed whiskers, the large bluish gray eyes, the preternaturally demure demeanor, the appearance and deportment of an English barrister without his wig, or an English clergyman without his gown? Who, having once heard him, can forget the cool, calm, tireless voice that gives a new force to fun and a new depth to eloquence? Unlike all other American humorists, Mr. Depew coins no comic phrases, makes no puns, indulges in no tricks of words or manner. Unlike all other American orators, he seeks to inflame no passions, to excite no prejudice. He says nothing and does nothing to arouse his hearers. Like Antony, he 'only speaks right on,' expressing plain common sense in simple language. If this common sense exposes shams, makes pretenses ridiculous and affectations absurd, the room rocks with laughter; if it inspires patriotism, stimulates sentiment, impresses great thoughts upon the audience, the hall rings with cheers. He is as fluent as Gladstone; but while Gladstone's sentences are verbose, Depew's are terse and clear. His eloquence is like the ocean that tosses up waves of wit and crests them with the foam of poetry, and beneath the sparkling surface is the deep, steadfast and mighty. When his audiences roar, he seems unconscious of the fun. When they hurrah, there is no answering flash in his steady eyes. He means what he says. He has thought it all out carefully, as his logical arrangement and felicitous phrases prove. He says it because it is his

LIFE OF JAY GOULD.

duty to speak ; and he is unconcerned whether those who hear him laugh or cheer, so long as they allow him to convince them of the correctness of his views, be they serious or satirical."

In 1888 Mr. Depew was one of the foremost candidates for President of the United States. He had the solid and enthusiastic support of the entire delegation from New York State to the National Republican Convention. But his generosity and patriotism exceeded his ambition. Finding that it was not expedient for his candidacy to be maintained and pressed longer, he withdrew his name and contributed largely to the nomination and subsequent election of General Harrison. He therefore re-remains President of the great railroads for whose prosperity he has done so much. Every day he is found during office hours hard at work at the Grand Central depot in New York. There he is overrun with visitors, but they are all courteously received and generously attended to, be they millionaires or statesmen, or the brakemen and firemen of the railroad trains. Generally he eats his lunch at his desk, but is fond, whenever possible, of slipping out and going home for it. He always dines at home, and his dinner is what he calls the family circle. He does not dress especially for it; that would be too formal. The household gathers not for a stately banquet, and indeed not merely to eat, but to enjoy an intellectual and social romp. At the head of his own table Mr. Depew tries, as he

ENTRANCE TO LYNDHURST.

CHAUNCEY M. DEPEW. 425

never does at public banquets or on the platform; to
be just as entertaining, amusing, vivacious, and genial as lies within the compass of his utmost power.
Then and there it is that he tells his newest and
best stories, and mimics with an actor's skill the odd
characters who have called on him at the office and
the odd things they have said. The cares and details of business are rigidly excluded, and the dinner
hour is for him, his wife, and children a season of
unalloyed enjoyment and pleasure. His home is a
handsome but unpretentious one, in a house on
Forty-fifth Street, not far from the great railroad
station where he has his office. It is above all else
a home, and his life there is emphatically and distinctively a home life. To make it comfortable and
attractive and lovable to his wife and children, seems
to be the crowning ambition of the great man's life,
and he would rather take one of his boys to the
circus than attend a Union League Club dinner.

Among his old neighbors in Westchester County
Mr. Depew has always been, as he is to-day, incomparably the greatest man in the world. Go among
the thrifty farmers of that region and talk of the
President of the United States, the General of the
armies, the foremost preacher, editor, or other popular idol of the day; talk of Gladstone, Bismarck, or
the Pope, and they will concede their greatness.
But if you would rouse their enthusiasm, make their
eyes flash more brightly, and their hearts beat
quicker, and call the speech of the highest admiration and warmest love to their lips, mention the

name of Chauncey Depew. To them he is not only the greatest personage in the world's contemporary history, not only the manager of untold millions, the leader of public thought, and the admired figure of the most brilliant society, but he is, as they affectionately term him, "Our Chauncey;" he is still the simple-hearted, earnest, wholesome lad who spun queer stories in the village store and tramped about their farms and along their highways. At the height of his greatness he has never been too great to associate with them on terms of perfect equality and good fellowship, to attend their humble social gatherings, to speak at their rural fairs and school exhibitions, to show himself "a judge of prize fat oxen and of sheep," and to keep himself constantly in touch with popular feeling and his great heart beating in unison with the hearts of all his old neighbors and early comrades.

His personal appearance is known to thousands who have seen and heard him. He is not, perhaps, as homely as Abraham Lincoln, but there is an air about him such as though he had been meant for a handsome man but was sorely spoiled in the making. His face expresses too much goodness to be beautiful. It has all the earnestness and seriousness of Mr. Lincoln, without his melancholy. It has a depth of thought and sense, and a dignity of expression that well command a place in the gallery of the world's greatest men, and a kindliness and familiarity that would win the instant confidence and unquestioning love of a child.

ANDREW CARNEGIE

ANDREW CARNEGIE.

ANDREW CARNEGIE was born at Dunfermline, in Scotland, on the 25th of November, 1835. When he was twelve years of age he emigrated to America and settled at Pittsburg with his parents and a younger brother. He was then almost penniless. To-day he is supposed to be worth at least fifteen millions, and he wields an influence in the industrial world as great, possibly, as that of any living man. It may be said that Mr. Carnegie was exceptionally equipped for success both mentally and morally; numbering among his mental qualities shrewdness, persistence, a good memory and an intuitive insight into character, and among his moral qualities integrity, gratitude and geniality. But his phenomenal rise in life must be attributed largely to his following certain clear principles and methods. Some of these he has defined in an admirable address to the students of a commercial college at Pittsburg. These are his maxims summarized:

"Avoid drink; avoid speculation; avoid endorsements. Aim high. For the question, 'What *must* I do for my employer?' substitute 'What *can* I do?' Begin to save early—'capitalists trust the saving young man.' Concentrate your energy, thought and capital; fight it out on one line." (The lack

430　　　*LIFE OF JAY GOULD.*

of concentration he considers *the* failing of American business men.)

To these injunctions he might well have added another, suggested by his own career : "Never think your education ended." Prompt as he is to grasp new ideas and to test every new theory connected with his industrial enterprises, he has never ceased expanding his thoughts and widening his sympathies by varied studies. The extent to which he has "read, marked, learned and inwardly digested" good literature may be inferred from the many apt and unhackneyed quotations with which he fortifies his own views in most of his writings.

One characteristic business maxim of Mr. Carnegie, though invaluable to men endowed with judgment equal to his own, is not without danger to employés who happen to be more aspiring than shrewd. "Break orders to save owners," he advises, reversing an old conservative rule ; "there never was a great character who did not sometimes smash the routine regulations and make new ones for himself. Do not hesitate to do it whenever you are sure the interests of your employer will be thereby promoted, and when you are so sure of the result that you are willing to take the responsibility. Boss your boss just as soon as you can ; try it on early. Our young partners in Carnegie Brothers have won their spurs by showing that we did not know half as well what was wanted as they did. Some of them have acted upon occasion with me as

ANDREW CARNEGIE. 431

if they owned the firm and I was but some airy New Yorker presuming to advise upon what I knew very little about."

Two years after his family had settled at Pittsburg, Andrew was engaged as a messenger in the Atlantic and Ohio Telegraph Company. He asked and was given leave to practice telegraphing in his spare moments, and, having learned to read messages by sound, was soon promoted to be an operator. About this time his father died, and Andrew became the sole support of his mother and brother. In a couple of years he had devised a scheme which enabled the Pennsylvania Railroad to improve the regulation of its traffic by means of the telegraph and to materially increase its carrying power. He now entered the service of this great railroad corporation, and before he was of age had risen to be Superintendent of the Pittsburg division. Prior to this he had judiciously invested most of his earnings in a company formed to manufacture the Woodruff sleeping car. After some other successful investments Mr. Carnegie became one of an association which gave $40,000 for the Storey farm, on Oil Creek where they struck oil and netted over $1,000,000 in one year. His most important venture was the establishment of the Edgar Thompson Steel Works, named after an early benefactor. In addition to this the Carnegie companies comprise, or lately comprised, the Pittsburg Bessemer Steel Works, the Lucy Furnaces, the Union Iron Mills,

432 *LIFE OF JAY GOULD.*

the Union Mill, the Keystone Bridge Works, the Hartman Steel Works, the Scotia Ore Mines and the Frick Coal Company. The capital of the companies named—which is mostly owned by Carnegie himself—amounted, a year ago, to twenty million dollars, and the average yearly output of finished products from the factories considerably exceeds half a million tons. It is to be noticed that the investments which made Mr. Carnegie a very rich man were confined to industrial enterprises whose nature and prospects he was specially qualified to understand.

To his vivid sense of the beneficent effect of education his bounteous gifts to libraries are mainly due. He rightly views a good library as a cheap university for persistent and ambitious talent. In 1880 he gave $40,000 to establish a free library at Dunfermline. In 1885 he founded another free library at Pittsburg at a cost of $500,000, and in the following year he presented Edinburgh with $250,000 for a free library and Allegheny City with an equal sum for a music hall and library combined. He has also established several smaller libraries in other places. A seeming eccentricity of Mr. Carnegie—his purchasing the control of eighteen radical newspapers in Great Britain—was really the result of his democratic zeal combined with his recognition of the educating power of the press.

During his mother's life Andrew Carnegie proved himself a tender and true son. Perhaps the keenest

ANDREW CARNEGIE. 433

enjoyment which his wealth has afforded him has been found in its enabling him to anticipate her wants and wishes. He made a resolution, and kept it, not to marry while she lived. His generosity has embraced several benevolent institutions and several unsuccessful friends. Nor does he try to forget his poor days any more than his humble acquaintances. "It does not hurt the new comer to sweep out the office if necessary," he told the students of the Curry Commercial College. "I was one of those sweepers myself, and who do you suppose were my fellow-sweepers? David McCargo, now Superintendent of the Allegheny Valley Railroad, Robert Pitcairn, Superintendent of the Pennsylvania Railroad, and Mr. Moreland, City Attorney. We all took turns, two each morning did the sweeping, and now I remember Davie was so proud of his clean white shirt-bosom that he used to spread over it an old silk bandana handkerchief which he kept for the purpose, and we other boys thought he was putting on airs. So he was. None of us had a silk handkerchief."

Mr. Carnegie is a genial companion. He can sing a good song, make a good occasional speech, and tell a good story. Nor does he either monopolize the conversation or else sulk, as too many celebrities are prone to do. His skill in driving four-in-hands is well known. In person he is rather short, but strongly made and active. His eyes, which are blue, are large and sympathetic. Altogether, he is a man to inspire children with confidence.

434 *LIFE OF JAY GOULD.*

Besides a few pamphlets and many magazine articles, Mr. Carnegie is the author of "An American Four-in-Hand in Britain" (New York, 1883); "Round the World" (1884), and "Triumphant Democracy; or, Fifty Years' March of the Republic" (1887). The general tendency of "Triumphant Democracy," his most important work, is to laud American methods, industrial, social and political; to decry the vaunted British Constitution, but at the same time to inspire Britons and Americans with mutual esteem and admiration. Mr. Carnegie is for humanity first, and secondly for the great race to which he is proud to belong. With him democracy is the evangel of humanity. It promises every man a fair field and no favor. Mr. Carnegie is revolted at the mere name of a "subject." In his enthusiasm for democratic government he is led into a few paradoxes, which, however, he defends with great ingenuity. "Triumphant Democracy" teems with valuable condensed statistics as well as with characteristic anecdotes. The style is never heavy. Sometimes it is even brilliant, as in the contrast between Lincoln and Bismarck—terse, epigrammatic, true. Amid the author's prolonged pæans upon American triumphs, a critic found his admissions quite refreshing that "no civilized people ever cooked so badly" and that the best roads in the world are not to be found in the United States. Mr. Carnegie has his grand aspirations for a friendly union or alliance of the English-speaking powers—

ANDREW CARNEGIE. 435

America, Britain, and *independent* Australasia—dominating the world and dictating peace to the too heavily armed nations. And he has not the shadow of a doubt that the world-language is destined to be English, and not Volapük.

THE ROTHSCHILDS

THE ROTHSCHILDS.

THERE is, or until recently was, standing in the crowded Juden-Gasse quarter of Frankfort-on-the-Main, an ancient house bearing the symbol of a red shield. Within its walls, in the year 1743, was born Meyer Anselm, the son of well-to-do and steady-going Jewish parents. In boyhood he was destined to become a rabbi, but showed such strong disinclination therefor that he was placed as a clerk in a bank at Hanover. This was much to his liking, and he quickly distinguished himself as a financier. A few years later he returned to Frankfort-on-the-Main, and, in the old house with the red shield, began business on his own account as a banker. Integrity and industry characterized his work. His judgment was far-seeing and almost infallible. Accordingly he prospered. When Bonaparte entered Germany, and began confiscating property right and left, William, Landgrave of Hesse, intrusted to the Frankfort banker all his wealth for safe-keeping. Meyer Anselm assumed the name of Rothschild (red shield), from the insignia on his house, and when he died in 1812 this name was famous throughout Europe as that of one of the foremost money-kings of the day.

This founder of the Rothschild money dynasty left his name and fortune to five sons—Anselm, Solomon,

440   *LIFE OF JAY GOULD.*

Nathan, Charles and James, who established themselves as bankers respectively in Frankfort, Vienna, London, Naples and Paris. They worked in harmony with each other, and established the rule that marriages should be confined within the family circle, in order to keep the family fortune intact. This rule was rigidly observed until very recently. On the death of Charles Rothschild the Naples house was discontinued, but all the others have been maintained, with constantly increasing wealth and influence. The Rothschilds have become the brokers and bankers for nearly all the governments of the world, and have long been masters of the money markets of all European capitals.

Nathan Rothschild, the third son of Meyer Anselm, was born in 1777, and settled in London in 1800, acting there as agent for his father. He was the agent selected to pay the $60,000,000 due, under the treaty of Toplitz, from Great Britain to her German allies. Private agents sent him word of the result of the battle of Waterloo a few hours before it was known by the government, and he was thus enabled to make bargains which netted him $1,000,000 profits. In 1822 the Emperor of Austria made him a baron, but he did not care to be called by that title. He died in 1836, and was succeeded by his eldest son, Lionel de Rothschild, who was born in 1808 and was educated at Göttingen. In 1847 he was elected a member of the House of Commons by a London constituency. But he was

DINING SALOON ON THE ATALANTA.

THE ROTHSCHILDS. 443

unable to take the qualifying oath "On the true faith of a Christian," and proudly refused to abjure his Hebrew faith. So he did not take his seat. He was several times elected, with the same result; but at last for very shame the government passed a law removing the political disabilities of the Jews, and in 1858 he took his seat, the first Jewish member of Parliament. When Lord Beaconsfield in 1876 conceived and accomplished his magnificent project of purchasing for England the Egyptian government's shares in the Suez Canal, it was Lionel de Rothschild who advanced the $20,000,000 needed for the purpose. Lionel de Rothschild received the honor of knighthood, and died in 1879.

The eldest son of Sir Lionel was named Nathaniel Meyer de Rothschild. He was born in 1840, and in 1885 was made a peer, with the title of Lord Rothschild. He was the first Jew to take a seat in the House of Lords, for Lord Beaconsfield, though of purely Jewish origin, had embraced the Christian religion previous to his entering British political life. The eldest son and heir of Lord Rothschild is the Hon. Lionel W. de Rothschild, born in 1868. Lionel de Rothschild left two younger sons, Alfred and Leopold. Mr. Alfred de Rothschild is still unmarried, and is one of the best known and most popular members of aristocratic society in London. Mr. Leopold de Rothschild is one of the few members of the family who have married outsiders. He was married on January 19, 1881, to Mlle. Marie

444   *LIFE OF JAY GOULD.*

Perugia, a wealthy young lady of Trieste. The ceremony occurred in the great Central Synagogue in London, the foundation stone of which had been laid by Lionel de Rothschild in 1870. The service was an imposing one, and was attended by many members of the family and of the English nobility. One of the witnesses who signed the marriage contract was the Prince of Wales, who then attended a Jewish service for the first time. The Prince, Lord Beaconsfield, Lord Houghton and other eminent personages were also present at the wedding breakfast.

The first Rothschild to marry outside of the Jewish faith was Miss Hannah de Rothschild, the only daughter of the late Baron Meyer de Rothschild. She was married on March 20, 1878, to Archibald Philip Primrose, Earl of Rosebery, who has since become an eminent English statesman. The Countess of Rosebery was the first avowedly Jewish lady to wear a British coronet, and she has ever since remained true to the faith of her fathers. On December 8, 1878, however, a Rothschild abjured that faith. This was Mlle. Marguerite Alexandria de Rothschild, daughter of Baron Charles de Rothschild, head of the Frankfort house. She was married on that date to the Duke de Guiche, of France, who, a couple of years later, on the death of his father, became the Duke de Grammont ; and she became a communicant of the Roman Catholic Church. The same course was followed in September, 1882, by

THE ROTHSCHILDS. 445

her younger sister, Mlle. Berthe Marie, on her marriage with Prince Alexander de Wagram, grandson of Bonaparte's famous Marshal, Berthier. It is told, by the way, that shortly before Lord Rosebery and Miss Rothschild were married, some one congratulated the bridegroom's stepfather, the Duke of Cleveland, on the approaching event, and highly praised the amiability and other accomplishments of the young lady. "Yes," said the old lord of Barnard castle, "a very good girl, I believe, a very good girl, and I am given to understand quite rich. Yes, I am told, quite rich." The Duke of Cleveland spoke in good faith. He was so wholly wrapped up in his aristocratic prejudices that the deeds of noblemen of recent creation or the wealth of financial kings were seldom alluded to in his presence. He hardly knew who the Rothschilds were.

The first—indeed the only one—of the earlier Rothschilds to marry outside of the family was Nathan, the founder of the London branch; and it was he who established the system which has so largely restrained the others from doing the same. When he had been only a few years in England, so large were his transactions that one of the Jewish grandees of London, Levi Cohen, selected him as an eligible candidate for the hand of one of his daughters. After the union, the apparently desperate speculations of the young man greatly alarmed the old banker. He believed that Nathan would soon be ruined, and that his daughter would find

446   *LIFE OF JAY GOULD.*

herself in distress.   The father's apprehensions were calmed, however, by the young Rothschild saying : "You have given me but one of your daughters ; it would have been an excellent stroke of business to have given me them all.   Then they would all have died a great deal richer than they will now." Nathan was perhaps the greatest miser of the family.   He so far hated to see a penny of his fortune go out of the family, that he conceived the idea of perpetuating the power of the house by means of consanguineous alliances.   With this view, in 1836 he called a family congress together at Frankfort to consider the proposition.   They all favored it, and as a pledge of this policy his son Lionel was married to Charlotte, the daughter of Charles, then the head of the Naples house. Nathan was overjoyed at the adoption of his matrimonial system, but fell sick on the day of the wedding and died in six weeks.

Evelina, second daughter of Lionel de Rothschild, of London, and Ferdinand, second son of Baron Anselm de Rothschild, of Vienna, were in 1865 married in London at the splendid mansion of the bride's father in Piccadilly.   The bride was attended by fourteen bridesmaids, the foremost of them being Lady Diana Beauclerc, the daughter of the Duchess of St. Albans.   The Duke of Cambridge opened the ball that followed the ceremony. Benjamin Disraeli, who had already been Chancellor of the Exchequer, proposed the health of the happy

THE ROTHSCHILDS. **447**

pair, and the Lord Chief-Justice of England led off and timed the cheers. "So the common humanity of Shylock," a writer remarked at the time, "and of the haughtiest aristocracy of the world is established. So Isaac of York is avenged."

The head of the Paris house is Baron Alphonse de Rothschild, who is married to the eldest daughter of Lionel de Rothschild. At their wedding their health was proposed by the Duke de Persigny, then French Ambassador to England. They took up their home in Paris, in the house once occupied by Emile de Girardin. It was No. 13 Rue St. George, and Baron Alphonse was superstitious. He offered to give $5,000 to the poor if the authorities would let him change the number. They consented, and the house has since been known as No. 11 *bis*. The Baron and Baroness are childless, but otherwise their life has been almost ideally happy. They have been conspicuous in every philanthropic work, limiting their vast and unostentatious benevolence to no race or creed. Their mansion has long been a favorite resort of the best authors, artists and musicians of Paris, of whom the Baron is a munificent patron. A characteristic gathering there was described a few years ago by a correspondent of *The London Telegraph* as follows : " Baroness de Rothschild invited her friends to an 'at home' this afternoon, and, although no mention was made of music, it was not to be wondered at that all the most distinguished people in Paris had made a point of

448   *LIFE OF JAY GOULD.*

being present, for the fame of the splendid new gallery just completed, and rivalling in the magnificence of its collections the most famous museums of France, had spread far and wide, and many celebrities hastened to the house punctually at the hour named, in order to feast their eyes on the treasures of which they had heard so much. The briefest catalogue of the works of art would take up columns of your paper, nor would any description of their arrangement convey so good an idea of the harmonious effect produced by them, as an observation made to me by M. Alexandre Dumas. Looking at this wonderful scene from a playwright's point of view, he said: 'I cannot help thinking at what little cost the effect might be reproduced, of course in imitation works of art. Nothing about the place looks new. The things look as though they had grown in the places they occupy.' Such an assemblage of notabilities is seldom to be found, even in the cosmopolitan society of Paris. For instance, on a sofa together were the Queen of Spain and Don Carlos. In one corner were Lord Lytton and Lord Houghton. Opposite to them were M. Meissonier and M. Ludovic Halevy; while the Duc de Nemours was chatting with the numerous adherents of the Orleans regime. The large *salon* was filled with ladies, whose bright spring toilettes were relieved by the masses of flowers in the room itself, and by the clumps of foliage in the broad garden outside, divided only by trees from the

THE ROTHSCHILDS. 449

Parc Monceu beyond. Here the picturesquely disposed audience remained for nearly two hours, listening to two gifted vocalists, who exerted themselves to such good purpose that however much they sang their hearers called for more. The singers were Mlle. Van Zandt and M. Faure, and never has either appeared to more advantage."

Another less admirable Parisian Rothschild was Alphonse's father, Baron James, whom Balzac caricatured in "Pére Goriot" as the Baron de Nucengen. He it was, also, who moved Heine to say that he (Heine) had become a Christian and abjured Judaism because he did not like to belong to the same faith as Baron James Rothschild without being as rich as he; that he could not be as rich without being as stupid, and that, no other man could possibly be. Baron James died long ago. His wife, who survived him, and died in September, 1886, led an exemplary life, devoted chiefly to deeds of charity. She was the first Jewess ever received at the Court of France. She was admitted to that charmed circle, and made much of, by Marie Amélie, Queen of Louis Philippe. By no means the least notable of the living Rothschilds is Helen, daughter and heiress of Baron Solomon de Rothschild. She inherited a fortune of $70,000,000, and insisted, in spite of strenuous opposition on the part of her family, in marrying the man of her choice, a penniless officer in the Belgian army.

THE ASTORS

THE ASTORS.

HUMAN nature is, after all, pretty much the same in all times and places, and human society, in whatever country and under whatever laws, drifts into certain well-defined and conventional channels. In the American republic, founded upon a Constitution radically different from those of the monarchies of the Old World and upon a social code as far removed from that of Europe as is its political, the tendency towards European thoughts, manners and customs has been marked and unmistakable. The absence of an hereditary peerage has not prevented the formation of great families endowed with hereditary wealth, and the absence of laws of entail and primogeniture has not prevented the transmission of immense landed estates from generation to generation.

Foremost among the great families of America, whose wealth and family influence have been almost invariably for good, are the Astors. Their origin was in the quiet village of Waldorf, in the Grand Duchy of Baden, Germany. Not long after the peace of Hubertsburg, in 1763, George Astor left that village for London. There he was married, and became established as a maker of musical instruments. He became a partner with Broadwood, the famous piano-manufacturer, and more than a hundred years ago the pianofortes of Broadwood &

454 *LIFE OF JAY GOULD.*

Astor were world renowned. A few of them, imported to this country before the Revolutionary war, are still to be found as treasured heirlooms of ancient families. The firm of Broadwood & Co. still exists in England and maintains its former high repute, ranking with the foremost houses in the piano-trade of the world. George Astor was the eldest of several brothers. Another of them, Henry, followed him to England, and entered the cattle trade. After accumulating a small fortune, he took advantage of the outbreak of the Revolutionary war and came to America, where he engaged in the same business, furnishing supplies of beef-cattle to the armies. The seat of his business was in New York city. He became very rich, for that time, but died without a family.

The youngest of the three brothers was John Jacob Astor, who was born on July 17, 1763, at Waldorf. He was educated at home under a French Protestant tutor named Valentin Le Jeune. At the age of seventeen he determined to leave Waldorf and follow his brothers to England. He was almost penniless, his father being unwilling to advance him any money for the purpose of leaving the family home, but the village pastor was interested in his welfare and assisted him in his preparations for the journey, saying, "I have no fear of Jacob. He will go straight through the world; he has a clear head and is all right behind the ears." Mr. Astor in after years used to relate that he had only two

THE ASTORS. 455

dollars in his pocket when he set out. He made his way afoot to the Rhine, and on the bank of that river, sitting beneath a tree to rest, he made a covenant with himself always to be honest, to be industrious, and never to gamble. On the Rhine he took passage on a raft bound from the Black Forest to Holland, and reaching the sea he secured passage for London. There he entered his brother's service, studied the English language, and out of his meagre wages contrived to save a little.

He was a trifle more than twenty years old when, in November, 1783, peace having been declared between England and America, he borrowed $300 of his brother, took some violins and other musical instruments, and set out for Baltimore. After a long and stormy voyage he reached that city at the end of January, 1784. On the voyage he made the acquaintance of a German dealer in furs, who gave him some valuable account of the New World and the prospects of business there. This man advised him not to stop in Baltimore, but to make his way to New York, which was bound to become, he said, the foremost city of the western continent. This advice young Astor followed, and on reaching New York soon found out his rich brother Henry, who introduced him to Mr. Robert Bowne, a Quaker furdealer, the foremost member of that trade in America at that time. Mr. Bowne became interested in the adventurous and earnest young German, and sent him to Montreal in quest of furs. This journey

456   *LIFE OF JAY GOULD.*

and its profitable results determined the future course of Mr. Astor's life. He became a fur-trader. On returning from Montreal he went to Ohio, which at that time was a country more remote from New York and more difficult of access than the other side of the world is at present. Both his journeys were successful ; that to Ohio so much so that he went back to London, laid his plans before his brother George, obtained from him a larger loan, and, in 1786, returned to New York to establish himself for life. Although devoted chiefly to the fur-business, he brought back with him a large consignment of musical instruments, for which he found a profitable sale. For a time he boarded at the house of Mrs. Todd, at 91 Pearl street, the house now known as No. 362 Pearl street. For some time that was his headquarters. He sold there his brother's musical instruments, and from thence set out on fur-trading journeys to the North and the far West.

It was not long after he became established at Mrs. Todd's that he fell in love with his landlady's second daughter, Sarah. They were soon married, and Mrs. Astor contributed largely by her sound sense and unerring judgment to the building up of his fortunes. Her elder sister, Margaret, married Captain William Whitten, who was mate of the American vessel in which Astor originally came to this country, and through whom the latter was introduced into the family of Mrs. Todd. Captain Whitten was chiefly engaged in the China trade, and soon attracted young

THE ASTORS.

Astor's attention to the great opportunities for acquiring wealth which it offered. Mr. Astor applied to his brother Henry for capital to enable him to enter that business also, and on that basis he sent cargoes of American furs to China in exchange for silks and teas, which he sold in this country at cent per cent. profit. At that time there were in existence so-called Carolus dollars, a depreciated coin, the legitimate predecessors of that modern abomination, the Trade Dollar. These also Mr. Astor sent to China in payment for goods.

By the beginning of the present century Mr. Astor was worth probably a quarter of a million dollars. His fur-trading enterprises had been extended to all parts of the North American continent. The city of Astoria on the North Pacific coast is a landmark of his enterprise. About that time he built himself a house at No. 223 Broadway, and there for more than a quarter of a century he continued to reside. The famous Astor House hotel now occupies that site and a number of adjoining lots. Not long after he began purchasing real estate on Manhattan Island, some in what was then the heart of the city and is now the extreme downtown region, but a great deal more in what was then the open country, improved and unimproved farm-lands. Property that he then bought for a few dollars an acre is now worth many thousands of dollars per city lot. It is in this way that the Astor fortune has been chiefly developed. The rule of

458　　*LIFE OF JAY GOULD.*

the family from the outset has been to buy land but never to sell, and to keep all houses and other buildings on their estate in the best possible condition. The Astors are and have ever been the model landlords of New York. In his various enterprises Mr. Astor was frequently associated with other men, but never had a partner. He acted on the principle of limited liability, and was very careful and usually successful in his choice of agents to conduct his business for him. To the very end of his long life he retained a lively interest in the pursuits of his youth; he was an excellent judge of musical instruments, of silks and teas, and, above all, of furs. It is related that, in 1833, while visiting Paris, he went to a famous art-gallery, and noticed a painting of rabbits and other game, which commanded his admiration. " The man who painted that," he said, "understood his business. Those rabbits have their winter fur on."

Mr. Astor died in 1848, leaving a fortune estimated at more than twenty millions. He left several children ; Magdalen, the eldest, was married to Governor Bentzon, of Santa Cruz, a Danish officer of rank ; after his death she was married to Mr. John Bristed, of Bristol, Rhode Island. His second child was William B. Astor, born in 1793, who was married to Miss Margaret Armstrong, a daughter of General John Armstrong, and his wife, Miss Alida Livingston. The third, Dorothy Astor, was married to Mr. Walter Langdon, of New Hampshire.

STERN OF THE ATALANTA.

THE ASTORS. 461

One of her children married Mr. Delancey Kane, father of the Delancey Kane who has done much to cultivate in America a taste for the English amusement of driving stage-coaches. Another child, Eliza Astor, was married to a Swiss nobleman, Count Vincent Rumpff; she died childless. The youngest of the family was John Jacob Astor, Jr. He was weak-minded, and to the end of his days was under the care of a guardian.

The bulk of the Astor fortune of course went to Mr. William B. Astor. He was carefully educated at the University of Göttingen, and spent several years in European travel as the companion and pupil of the illustrious Chevalier Bunsen. He devoted himself after his father's death chiefly to the improvement and extension of the landed estates of the family. He distinguished himself also by various gifts for religious and benevolent purposes—such as the great Astor Library in New York, for which he gave about half a million dollars, to which benefaction his successors have very largely added. He was a member and officer of the famous Trinity Church in New York, and on his death a magnificent marble reredos was erected in its chancel to his memory at a cost of about $80,000. He left three sons, John Jacob Astor the third, William Astor, and Henry Astor. He had also four daughters: Emily, who was married to Mr. Samuel Ward, of New York; Margaret, who married Mr. Winthrop Chanler; Alida, who married Mr. John Carey;

462   *LIFE OF JAY GOULD.*

and Laura, who married Mr. Franklin Delano.
Margaret Astor and her husband, Mr. Winthrop
Chanler, were the progenitors of the Mr. Chanler
who married Miss Emilie Rives, the novelist. The
Astor fortune was left by Mr. William B. Astor
ostensibly to his sons John Jacob and William, but
the bulk of it was really to be held by them in trust
for their children.

The bulk of the estate was left to Mr. William Waldorf Astor, who may now be properly looked upon
as the head of the family. He is the son of Mr.
John Jacob Astor the third, and his wife, formerly
Miss Augusta Gibbes. He was born in 1848, and
after a thorough collegiate training was sent to Rome,
where he studied sculpture and painting. On returning to this country he studied law, and was admitted to the bar. Before he was thirty years old he
was elected to the Assembly of New York State
from a New York city district, and there made for
himself a brilliant and honorable record as a careful
and painstaking public servant. He was married on
June 6, 1878, to Miss Mary Paul, of Philadelphia.
He has since been United States Minister to Italy,
and while residing at Rome and Florence, wrote
"Valentino," a mediæval Italian romance, dealing
with the times of Lucrezia Borgia. It is a work of
decided literary and artistic merit, and has done
much to correct the false impressions that have ever
been widely prevalent concerning the character of
the much maligned Lucrezia.

THE ASTORS. 463

It is related of Mr. William Waldorf Astor that when he was a boy of ten or twelve years, his father was desirous that he should not contract the habit of smoking tobacco, at any rate not until he became a man ; so one day he said to him, " My son, you're now getting to an age when foolish boys are apt to begin smoking. Now, if you will promise not to smoke until you come of age, and will keep your promise, I will give you a thousand dollars." " All right, father," said the boy, " I'll do it." Seven or eight years afterward the father said to him again, " Well,.William, you remember your promise not to smoke. Have you kept it ? " " Yes, sir," was the reply. " Good," returned the father ; " now you stick it out to the end, and on your twenty-first birthday I will give you five thousand dollars instead of the one thousand I promised." The young man kept his promise and the father kept his, and when the twenty-first anniversary was reached the eldest Astor said to his son : " My boy, you've done well. Here is your five thousand dollars. Now if you want to smoke, go ahead and do it. Here is a box of cigars for you to begin on." So saying, he handed him a box of the strongest Havanas the market contained. Had the young man smoked one of them he would probably have been sick for a month, but he was too shrewd to be caught that way. He took the cigars to his room and locked them up, and next day went off into a secluded place in Central Park and prac- tised on some very weak cigarettes.

464   *LIFE OF JAY GOULD.*

The Astors are now by far the largest landlords in New York city, occupying a position in a measure comparable to that of the Duke of Portland or the Duke of Westminster in London. They own vast blocks of property in all parts of the city, covered with buildings of all kinds ; banks and stores, warehouses along the water-front, and rows of the finest private mansions on the fashionable uptown avenues. They still purchase whenever favorable opportunities are offered, but seldom or never sell. They are noted for the excellent repair in which all their buildings are kept, and for the pains they take for the welfare, comfort and convenience of their tenants ; at the same time they expect and exact of their tenants certain obligations in return, to take good care of the property and to repair all damages occurring from the tenants' carelessness or neglect.

They continue to pay much attention to charitable and other philanthropic causes. To the church they are generous givers. The interests of the Indians, especially Indian schools, have found in them valuable patrons. To the Metropolitan Museum of Art, in New York, they have made gifts of almost inestimable value. The Astor Library is a large brick building on Lafayette Place. It has in recent years, by living members of the family, been greatly enlarged, and richly endowed, until it is now probably the foremost institution of the kind in America. It has always, under the

THE ASTORS. 465

terms of the gift, been entirely free to all comers. Its alcoves are accessible to students desiring to pursue special courses of study, or to search out special topics in literature, science or art, and it has thus become an important educational centre. The Astors have long been the unchallenged leaders of the highest society of New York city. They have lived in large and richly furnished, but externally plain and unpretentious mansions on Fifth avenue. They are the largest taxpayers in New York city; probably the largest private taxpayers in America. Their actual wealth it is almost impossible to estimate with any degree of accuracy. Probably the total value of their real-estate holdings in New York city is in the neighborhood of $225,000,000.

JOHN W. MACKAY

JOHN W. MACKAY.

"BONANZA" has come to be a synonym for wealth, or for any business enterprise or investment that is a source of great profits. A fitting use of the term that is, too ; for the Bonanza mines, from which it sprang, were the producers of wealth at a fabulous rate, wealth almost beyond the power of man to comprehend, wealth that almost in the twinkling of an eye transformed poor miners into millionaires. Their history is a potent rival to the romance of Monte Cristo, and in that history the foremost actor is the subject of this sketch.

John William Mackay was born at Dublin, Ireland, on November 28, 1831. He came from a line of hardy Scotchmen, planted in the north of Ireland by Cromwell ; the sort of men who defended Londonderry in its famous siege. The Scotch-Irish stock is a notable one in America. It has produced a host of leaders in law, statesmanship, warfare, literature, science, theology, journalism. These men combine happily the hardheadedness of Scotland with the warmheartedness of Ireland ; they are shrewd, far-seeing, cool, acquisitive, resolute, but at the same time generous and cabable of ardent enthusiasms. They possess, also, a peculiarly pure and robust moral fibre, and have pre-eminently

470 LIFE OF JAY GOULD.

sound minds in sound bodies. Such a man young Mackay grew up to be. He was nine years old when his parents, poor but industrious folk, brought him to New York. Soon after his father died, but the widow was able to keep the lad at school a few years, until he had a good common-school education, and then he was apprenticed to a shipbuilder. Many a ship in those days was built to make the voyage "around the Horn" to California. Young Mackay worked on some of these. There was much talk among his comrades in the ship-yard about the fortunes that were being made in the land of gold. He listened to them, caught the fever, and went out with the Forty-Niners.

"The many fail, the few succeed," was true of those Argonauts. Some amassed fortunes; more a competence; but the great majority fell into the ranks as common miners and never got promoted. The spirit of speculation and of gaming was rife, and many a man who had "made his pile" soon gambled it away. Mr. Mackay did not make a great strike at first. He wielded the pickaxe and shovel for years, sometimes as a day laborer for others, sometimes on his own account. His luck was not above the common run. Now and then he made great gains, and then again he lost them. At thirty years old he had been rich and was poor again. But he had acquired a thorough knowledge of every detail of the mining business. Moreover, he was conspicuously temperate and steady in his habits. The wild carousings that constituted the chief social feature of those pioneer days had no attractions for him. Sometimes his comrades chaffed him and sneered at him as a "Puritan," but they respected him and soon began to acknowledge his leadership.

Mr. Mackay left California for Nevada in 1860. There he made a paying investment at Gold Hill, and carefully looked over the whole of the famous Comstock lode. He satisfied himself that here was one of the richest mineral deposits in the world, and he attempted, at Union Ground, in the northern part of the Comstock, to sink a shaft. Lack of means, however, baffled him, and he looked about him for assistance. Two other young men had also come out to the Pacific coast in 1849, and started a grocery and liquor-shop at San Francisco. Their names were James C. Flood and William S. O'Brien. They were gradually drawn into speculating in mining stocks, and on the whole prospered. They made handsome profits out of the Kentuck stock, on which Mackay had lost heavily. They got control of the Crown Point and Belcher mines, and much of the Comstock lode. But they had not much practical knowledge of mining, and did not appreciate the potentialities of wealth that lay within their grasp. It has been said that the discovery of the great Bonanza wealth was a lucky accident. It was no such thing. It was all due to the rare knowledge and persevering searches of Mr. Mackay.

472   LIFE OF JAY GOULD.

The only luck there was about it was the coming
together of Mr. Mackay and Messrs. Flood and
O'Brien. That was an incident full of good fortune to
them all. The fourth partner in the original firm
was J. M. Walker, brother of a former Governor of
Virginia. He, like Mr. Mackay, was a skilled practical miner. This combination of forces was effected
in 1864, and work was immediately begun on the
lines indicated by Mr. Mackay.

They began with the Hale and Norcross mine.
Ore was taken out in vast quantities, and the price
of stock went up to a fabulous figure. In the three
years, 1865, 1866 and 1867, the net profits were
more than a million dollars. This was almost unprecedented, but it was merely the first rain-drop of
the deluge. In 1868 Mr. Walker withdrew from
the firm, and James G. Fair, superintendent of the
Hale and Norcross mine, was taken into partnership
in his place. He, too, was a practical miner, who
had worked his way up from the bottom. Immediately the firm began to enlarge its operations, always relying upon Mr. Mackay's judgment in the
purchase of property. The California and Sides,
the Central, the Kenney, and the White and Murphy
mines were bought for a small price; all on the
Comstock lode, which Mr. Mackay had prospected
years before. These were all united under the name
of Consolidated Virginia. But for a time the outlook was gloomy. There was much work and great
expense with no returns. Shaft after shaft was sunk

JOHN W MACKAY.

473

in vain. The public regarded the whole enterprise as a hopeless failure. Even the partners began to feel anxious. But Mr. Mackay never lost faith. The ridicule and scorn which the rest of the mining world poured upon him he did not deign to notice. "Boys," said he to his partners, "the ore is there, if we only get down to it." "But we've gone 600 feet already," said they. "Six hundred? Make it six thousand, then!" was his reply; and they kept on digging. They got down 1,160 feet, and then began to tunnel on the level. A great fire burned out all their machinery; but this only delayed it, not discouraged them. More than half a million dollars had already been spent. And then they "struck it rich."

From 1874 on, visitors to Nevada used to tell of seeing from afar vast piles of glittering silver, heaped up like bricks or stone, at the mouths of the Bonanza mines. There was no exaggeration in this. The output of the mines was such as never had been dreamed of in the world before. In four years the mines paid $75,000,000 in dividends on their stock. The four partners regularly drew $750,000 each per month as their shares. In six years the Comstock mines yielded something more than $300,000,000 in gold and silver ore, chiefly silver. This changed the financial history of the world. The silver markets everywhere had to be reorgan_ ized in the face of such a glut, and a new chapter had to be written in political economy. In this vast

474   *LIFE OF JAY GOULD.*

wealth Mr. Mackay had a two-fifths interest, twice that of each of the other three "Bonanza Kings." In 1879 the mines began to show symptoms of exhaustion, although they are at the present time still profitably productive. That year Mr. O'Brien died. The other partners stuck togther and sought new enterprises. The Bank of California was founded, with $10,000,000 capital, all paid up. Then Mr. Fair, who had become a United States Senator, withdrew from the firm. Mackay and Flood held together through various enterprises until the death of the latter in February, 1889. Mr. Flood's death was doubtless hastened by the famous "wheat corner" of 1887. Mackay and Flood had founded and were practically the proprietors of the Bank of Nevada, of which George Branders was president. The bank, chiefly, it is said, through Brander's speculations, was involved in the great wheat deal. That deal collapsed disastrously. Flood was ill, and telegraphed to Mackay, who was in Europe, to come home at once. Mr. Mackay did so. He went to the bank and looked over the books. The bank was liable for between twenty-two and twenty-three million dollars! That was enough to stagger any man, but Mr. Mackay only smiled as he looked up and said to Flood: "Well, old man, it looks as though we might have to go to work again!" The actual loss sustained by the bank was $11,000,000.

Mr. Mackay in 1884 formed a partnership with Mr. James Gordon Bennett, of the *New York Her-*

JOHN W. MACKAY.

ald, and laid two cables across the Atlantic Ocean. These are under a management known as the Commercial Cable Company, but are really the personal property of Mr. Mackay and Mr. Bennett. In 1885 he was offered the position of United Senator for Nevada, but declined it, preferring to devote his attention exclusively to private affairs. For some years past he has resided chiefly in Europe, where he has been a munificent patron of fine arts and where his wife has been a conspicuous leader of the best society in London and Paris ; he has devoted much of his wealth to charity, in an unostentatious manner, giving freely to the Roman Catholic Church, of which he is a member. He has also founded and endowed a fine orphan asylum at Nevada City. Mr. Mackay has few living relatives. His only sister became a nun, and died some years ago in her convent. Mrs. Mackay was a Miss Hungerford, and is on one side of the family of French descent. Her mother is still living and draws freely on the Bonanza millions for purposes of charity.

Mr. and Mrs. Mackay have no children of their own. They, however, adopted the orphan daughter of a close friend, Miss Eva Bryant, who was ever afterward known as Miss Mackay. She was much sought in marriage, as much for her own graces and beauty, it is easy to believe, as for her wealth. The ex-Queen of Spain, Isabella, asked her hand for her favorite nephew, the Marquis de Val Carlos, and

476   *LIFE OF JAY GOULD.*

Prince Philippe de Berben-y-Braganza also made a proposal of marriage, both of which offers were rejected. At last, however, a genuine love-match was made, and she was married on February 11, 1885, to Don Ferdinand Colonna, Prince de Galatro, a scion of the illustrious Roman house of Colonna. "Mrs. Mackay told me," says her old-time friend, Mrs. Emily Crawford, "that her husband is so intensely American that she was at first afraid he would not approve of Miss Eva's matrimonial project. But if there is one American institution that he likes better than another it is personal freedom. He hates aristocratic pride and prejudices, and has not a high idea of aristocratic virtue. But when he saw Prince Colonna he was favorably impressed by him and at once determined to wish Miss Eva joy upon the conquest she had made. The formal proposal was made to the parents of the young lady by two old bachelor uncles of the young gentleman, who had adopted him when his father died, and not only settled on him the reversion of a very handsome fortune and patrimonial residences, but an important annuity in their lifetimes. They asked for no dowry." Mrs. Mackay's sister, Miss Ada Hungerford, who is a very accomplished lady, is married to Count Telfner, of Rome.

The Mackays, at their mansions in Paris and London, have entertained many notable personages, including the Comte de Paris and the Prince and Princess of Wales. Their entertainments have

MRS. GEORGE GOULD AND MISS ANNA GOULD.

JOHN W. MACKAY.

always been characterized by refined taste rather than by ostentatious display. Their home has been a centre of artistic and intellectual life, and also of charitable work and wide benevolence. A charming and truthful picture of Mrs. Mackay in her Paris home is given by Mrs. Crawford, as she saw her a few days before her daughter was married to Prince Colonna. "Mrs. Mackay," she says, was dressed in a black cashmere dress, very neatly made and sparingly trimmed with jet. She has a pretty little figure and just the right amount of *embonpoint*. Her voice, like that of Annie Laurie, is low and sweet. There is no accent in the speech, but, the distinct and deliberate American enunciation. She must have a musical ear. The intonations of her voice reveal one, and the upper floor of her house, where her living rooms are, is a perfect aviary. There are cages of song birds everywhere, and in a vestibule a big parrot talks to himself in solitary grandeur in French, Spanish and English. The grand stairs are horse-shoe-shaped and very fine. Some groups of statuary ornament them, the hall and the glazed over-court. But there is no ostentatious display of great wealth anywhere. As I went up and down by a lift and was first taken to the top floor and then to Mrs. Mackay's boudoir or *petit salon* on the first floor, I saw a good deal of the house. Corridors, of which there are many, are richly carpeted, but have rather an air of snugness than of wealth. The little drawing room is in blue

480 LIFE OF JAY GOULD.

and old gold satins and brocades and what Whistler might term a harmony of colors and broken and soft outlines. It also gives the idea of being furnished for use and convenience and to please an impressionable eye. The most prominent objects in it are three portraits, nearly full length, two of which are by Cabanel. I should say the third is by Bonnat. It represents Mr. Mackay and hangs high. The expression of the face is one produced by a life of mental tension and concentrated and intelligent purpose. In seeing his portrait one understands why its original is Big Bonanza and has not come to grief in any financial crash. I should say that his mental powers are as firmly fixed upon the problem how to put his money out to profitable interest as they were upon the task of making a fortune. The domestic establishment shows liberal expenditure, good stewardship and a complete absence of vulgar ostentation.''

TERENCE V. POWDERLY

TERENCE V. POWDERLY.

WHILE Terence V. Powderly's name does not properly belong in a list of capitalists and men of great fortunes made through commercial enterprise, he has been more or less associated with them as the Grand Master Workman of the Knights of Labor. Anticipating the desire on the part of the reader to know something of the life of Mr. Powderly after reading his correspondence with Mr. Gould over the Missouri Pacific Strike, the following facts are appended:

The history of labor organizations is the history of the development of two ideas. The elder is that of the association of men of like employment. Common tradition has it that thus the order of Freemasons was founded; thus, certainly, were founded the great European guilds of the Middle Ages, and the trades-unions of later date. The guilds became almost omnipotent in Germany; the trades-unions in England became one of the foremost factors of industrial economy. In the United States, also, trades-unionism has greatly flourished. The other and younger idea is that of a union of all workingmen, without regard to calling. This principle is the growth of the past fifty years. It was first promulgated in France, early in the reign of Louis Philippe. In 1864 the "International Association

484   *LIFE OF JAY GOULD.*

of Workingmen," commonly called the "International," was organized in Europe, where it was generally regarded as a revolutionary body. Indeed, it so allied itself with Communism and Anarchy in Paris, in 1871, as practically to kill itself. It never gained much footing in America. The next important effort in this direction was made in the foundation and development of the order of Knights of Labor, a purely American organization. With that order the name of the subject of this sketch is inseparably associated, though he was not one of its founders.

The order of Knights of Labor was founded at Philadelphia, Pennsylvania, on Thanksgiving Day, 1869, by Uriah S. Stephens and six comrades, all garment-cutters by trade. Stephens was a New Jerseyman, of colonial ancestry, of mingled Quaker and Baptist stock, and an enthusiastic Freemason. He was a man of fine education and wide travels. At his house, then at 2347 Coral street, on November 25, 1869, he unfolded his plans for what he called "The Noble and Holy Order of the Knights of Labor;" a secret, oath-bound society, modelled as to ritual, etc., largely upon Freemasonry, and intended to include men of all trades. His associates were James L. Wright, Robert C. Macauley, Joseph S. Kennedy, William Cook, Robert W. Keen, and James M. Hilsee. On December 28 following they all signed the obligations and oaths, and called their body simply "Knights of Labor." Meetings were

TERENCE V. POWDERLY.

held weekly; on January 13, 1870, officers were chosen; a year later the membership had increased to sixty-nine; early in 1873 the first "Local Assembly" was formed, and in that year no less than twenty-seven such Assemblies or lodges, in as many different trades, were formed in Philadelphia alone. By January, 1875, the number of Assemblies in the whole country was more than 300. These Local Assemblies associated themselves in District Assemblies, and on January 1, 1878, delegates from these District Assemblies met at Reading, Pennsylvania, and organized the first General Assembly. In this body seven States were represented and fifteen vocations. The delegate from District Assembly No. 16, of Scranton, Pennsylvania, was Terence V. Powderly.

This remarkable man was born on January 22, 1849, at Carbondale, Luzerne county, Pennsylvania. His parents were hard-working Irish people, and he was one of their nine children. From seven to thirteen years of age he attended school, and was then put to work as a switchtender in the employ of the Delaware and Hudson Canal Company. Four years later he was taken into that company's machine-shop, where he learned the trade of a machinist. He was temperate, intelligent, industrious, and faithful, and was highly esteemed by his employers. At the age of nineteen he went to Scranton, and entered the machine-shop of the Delaware, Lackawanna and Western Railroad Company. He also

486   *LIFE OF JAY GOULD.*

at this time joined the Machinists' and Blacksmiths' Trade-Union, and was for several years President of the Union at Scranton. During the troubles of 1873 he was suspended from the employment of the company because of his membership in the trade-union, whereupon he left Scranton for Galion, Ohio. There he secured work, but as soon as he was found to be a trade-unionist was dismissed. Next he went to Oil City, Pennsylvania, where he remained for some time. He was conspicuous in the Machinists' and Blacksmiths' Union there, and at its International Convention, at Louisville, Kentucky, in 1874. He became a deputy-president of the Industrial Brotherhood, and organized several Assemblies of it around Pittsburg.

Mr. Powderly returned to Scranton in 1875 and was employed by the Lackawanna Coal and Iron Company in putting up their steel-works. He at once joined the Knights of Labor there, and was soon made Secretary of the District Assembly to which the Scranton Local Assembly belonged. After the steel-works were completed he was engaged by the Dickson Locomotive Works as foreman of a department. At this time he became interested in politics, organized the Greenback-Labor party in Luzerne county, and worked so hard during the campaign as permanently to injure his health. Ever since then he has been compelled to wear eye-glasses to aid his impaired sight. But his services were recognized by the public. In 1877 he was elected

Mayor of the city of Scranton by a handsome majority, and in 1878 was re-elected. In that year he declined a nomination for Lieutenant-Governor of Pennsylvania, on the Greenback-Labor ticket, and in 1879 declined, for reasons to be explained presently, a nomination to a third term as Mayor, although he would certainly have been elected. During his mayoralty he studied law, and, though not admitted to the bar, became an excellent lawyer.

The first General Assembly of the Knights of Labor was held, as stated, on January 1, 1878. The membership of the order now numbered many thousands, and it was an intensely secret organization This fact caused trouble. The oaths of secrecy, and the use of the Bible in taking them and in the ritual, brought it into conflict with the Roman Catholic Church, to which, of course, many of its members belonged. Many Local and some District Assemblies were disbanded on this account. Matters got so bad that a special General Assembly was called at Philadelphia, in June, 1878. This gathering adopted resolutions removing largely the ban of secrecy and expunging all Biblical quotations from the ritual, and submitted them for ratification to the Local Assemblies. They were ratified, and thereafter the friction between the order and the church gradually disappeared. Mr. Stephens, the founder of the order, was its head as Grand Master Workman, from the outset up to the third regular annual General Assembly, in September, 1879, at Chicago.

488   *LIFE OF JAY GOULD.*

At that time he tendered and urged his resignation, which was accepted, and Terence V. Powderly was elected as his successor. The reason for this change, briefly stated, was this : Mr. Stephens was an immovable believer in the secret system and the use of the Bible ; Mr. Powderly, a devout Roman Catholic, favored the modification of both those features ; and the order had decided in favor of the views held by Mr. Powderly. Mr. Stephens accordingly retired, honored and almost venerated by the order, and Mr. Powderly, as the foremost exponent of the new system, took his place.

It was his elevation to this office and the labor it imposed upon him that constrained Mr. Powderly to decline a third term as Mayor of Scranton. Thenceforward he devoted all his energies to the interests of the order. Again and again he was re-elected to its head, and indeed has been kept there by almost unanimous choice down to the present year. Under his administration the order has grown enormously, and been almost transformed in character. At the fourth General Assembly, at Pittsburg, in 1880, rules were adopted prohibiting and denouncing strikes, except in extreme cases. At the fifth, in 1881, much business of the highest importance was transacted. It was decreed that the name and objects of the order should be made public, that the constitution and ritual should be radically revised, that women should be admitted to membership on perfect equality with men, and a benefit-insurance

TERENCE V. POWDERLY.

489

system and co-operative system were established. These changes were chiefly put forward and urged by Mr. Powderly. At the next General Assembly the "strike element" was in the majority, and resolutions favoring strikes were adopted, but Mr. Powderly remained at the head and exerted a strong conservative influence. In 1883, at his suggestion, the title of his office was changed from "Grand" to "General" Master Workman. There were now 52,000 members. A year later 71,000 were reported, and rules against strikes and boycotting were adopted. In 1885 there were 111,000 members, and still stronger action was taken against strikes and boycotting. At this time there arose some conflict between the order and the trades-unions. In 1886 the membership reached half a million, and, by the beginning of 1887, probably exceeded a million. It has decreased rather than increased since that time, and has suffered much from being drawn into strikes and violence, though always against the will of Mr. Powderly, who has steadfastly opposed strikes as an evil and all violence as a degradation of labor. For the first four years of Mr. Powderly's official work with the Knights, his salary was $400 a year, out of which meagre sum he paid all his expenses as General Master Workman, devoting what was left to the building up of the order. In 1883 his salary was increased to $800, in 1884 to $1,500, and in 1886 to $5,000 per annum. At the last session of the General Assembly the salary was again

490   *LIFE OF JAY GOULD.*

fixed at $5,000, but Mr. Powderly informed the con-
vention that he would draw but $3,000 for the year,
and if at the next session the members considered
that he had earned the other $2,000 they could dis-
pose of it there.

The objects of this order are " to make industrial
moral worth, not wealth, the true standard of individual and national greatness, and to secure to the
workers the full enjoyment of the wealth they
create, sufficient leisure in which to develop their
intellectual, moral and social faculties, all of the
benefits, recreation, and pleasures of association ; in
a word, to enable them to share in the gains and
honors of advancing civilization." To this end it
calls for much State legislation for the protection
and encouragement of laboring-men. It calls for
equal pay for equal work, regardless of the sex of
the worker ; for a co-operative system ; and for
arbitration. No distinctions of race, color, sex or
creed are recognized. Intemperance is denounced,
and no one is admitted as a member who makes or
sells, or is in any way connected with the making or
selling of intoxicating drinks. For other prudential
reasons lawyers, bankers, stock-speculators, and
gamblers are excluded. The motto of the order is :
" That is the most perfect government in which an
injury to one is the concern of all." Of late years
various portions of the order have won discredit by
violating its principles.

Why Businessmen Need a Philosophy of Capitalism

By Adam Starchild

Capitalism has built the modern world. Although there are some who would dispute that claim, it is clear, at least for those who examine the facts without bias or political intent, that economies based on capitalism are stronger and expand at a faster rate than other economic systems. This fact has been well established throughout history.

At its simplest and purest, capitalism is an economic system in which private individuals and companies produce and exchange goods and services through free markets. Ideally, capitalism is not hindered by governmental controls; in reality, however, there are many shades and nuances of capitalism that result in economic systems that are often described as a *mixed economy*. In some lands, capitalism is restrained by laws and governmental regulations; the degree determined by political and social objectives. Many political leaders hope to influence their people via the economy, they may attempt to protect domestic business from foreign competition, or they may try to increase revenue with tariffs or export duties. That these types of objectives usually only hinder economic activity over the long term is frequently ignored, lost in the rhetoric about social considerations and goals.

494   *LIFE OF JAY GOULD*

Of the many factors that can affect how the capitalist spirit develops in a country, one which is often overlooked is that of entrepreneurship. In lands where capitalism is unfettered by unnecessary regulation and where entrepreneurship is dynamic, impressive economic gains and advancements can be expected. Entrepreneurship is perhaps one of the greatest driving forces of capitalism. Indeed, the two are inseparable.

Capitalism is an economic system in which the means of production and distribution are privately owned and operated, and an entrepreneur is an individual who undertakes to start and conduct a business. Entrepreneurs propel capitalism forward. The bottom line here is quite clear: if a person is restricted in his ownership of a business through governmental regulations or social constraints, why should he or she risk starting any economic enterprise? Conversely, if an individual perceives that his or her efforts will be the overall deciding factor in economic gain or loss, he or she is more likely to risk investment in a business venture.

The world has seen many different economic systems throughout history. With its origins deep in the mists of ancient societies, barter was one of the first economies in which individuals and groups exchanged goods and services, paying for one commodity with another. Rudimentary forms of capitalism were not far behind and their origins are likewise obscure. Capitalism is generally thought to have arisen in various places around the world, gained prominence in old Europe centuries ago where it developed slowly and gradually

AFTERWORD 495

spread through most of the world, reaching its zenith during the 19th century and remaining dominant until World War I. For a time during the 20th century, communism, a system in which the state plays a major role in economic ownership, regulation, and intervention, challenged capitalism's dominance, particularly in the Eastern Hemisphere, but as the century ended, capitalism, in one form of another, has re-emerged as the world's premier economic system.

The effect of capitalism extends far beyond economics, however, for capitalism is a major factor in the evolution of nations. Virtually every great nation through history has been a potent economic power as well. An excellent example of this in the 20th century is the ascendance of the Soviet Union as a world power after World War II. For a time the Soviet Union, founded on communism, seemed ready to challenge the United States for world military, cultural, and economic supremacy, but their threat was short-lived. While some observers of the world scene argue that it was American President Ronald Reagan's hard-line military stance against the Soviet Union that led to the eventual breakup and dissolution of that communist state, it was American economic power, based on capitalism, that provided Reagan with the foundation on which he could make his stand. Communism could not keep pace with America's economic strength. Reagan's policies also have led to the People's Republic of China slowly but steadily turning to capitalism to enhance their economy. Mainland China's appreciation of capitalism is well illustrated with the reversion of Hong Kong – one of the world's

496   *LIFE OF JAY GOULD*

greatest free-market success stories – to Mainland control and the pledge of the Chinese government not to tamper with Hong Kong's economy, a promise the Chinese have honored.

The resurgence of capitalism at the end of the 20th century has been driven by a powerful tide of entrepreneurship in the technology sector, most apparent in the explosive growth of the Internet, and has led to spectacular economic gains. E-commerce (electronic commerce) is without question changing the way the world does business, and it can easily be termed E-capitalism.

We are in a period in which economic opportunity has seldom been greater. As technology and the Internet continue to advance, every business or enterprise that can benefit from them has the opportunity to advance as well. Ten years ago, few of the top Internet companies had even been imagined. Ten years ago, we were only on the verge of the new capitalist economy that, while built on the old principles of capitalism, is immeasurably enhanced by technological know-how. Ten years ago, traditional businesses were still the norm. And now, new ideas are giving rise to new companies every day. The businesses, services, and companies that may dominate the economic landscape ten years from now are still in the formulation stages of their creators. The opportunities for entrepreneurs are perhaps greater than ever.

Certainly we are witnessing the coming of a new economic age in which those individuals and companies that produce the goods and services that satisfy the needs of a

AFTERWORD

modern, fast-paced world will be the most successful. Technology permits customers to buy the items or services they desire with a mere click of a mouse. Individuals who embrace the spirit of the entrepreneur and who are able to ascertain the needs of potential customers stand to benefit handsomely.

After all, entrepreneurs have been creating and running businesses since primitive times. Going back to the earliest societies, farmers, fisherman, and merchants traded their goods and services. Every business that exists today at one time was the dream and ambition of an entrepreneur. The entrepreneur is the visionary, the man or woman with the better idea, the innovator, the doer. It is the entrepreneur who creates the original product, acquires the facilities and materials, obtains the capital, assembles the workforce, and brings the finished product to market. It is also the entrepreneur who reaps the profits of a successful venture. In the case of failure, the entrepreneur stands to take the major loss.

Capitalism and entrepreneurship are closely linked. Capitalism is the economic system most conducive to entrepreneurship, and entrepreneurship provides the innovation and energy of capitalism. Each sustains and gains strength from the other, together forming a solid bedrock for economic activity.

While opportunity for entrepreneurs is present in the most advanced economies, clearly developing economies offer the greatest opportunities because of their nature, which usually

498   *LIFE OF JAY GOULD*

includes a rapidly growing middle class with a strong desire for consumer products. As companies attempt to meet the needs of these new consumers, entrepreneurs are likely to find countless opportunities. In advanced nations new products and services are typically brought to market by major corporations that maintain huge staffs, whose primary purpose is the design and creation of new products. In smaller, developing nations, however, niche markets and special needs present an environment that is ripe for innovation. In many of these nations, governments may actively support entrepreneurs through a variety of special programs, including tax incentives, special trade status, and an assortment of grants, to encourage investment and economic activity. The leaders of such governments are aware that entrepreneurs energize capitalism, which in turn leads to economic growth.

As the global economy continues to expand, world trade will undoubtedly increase. At the same time, because of the growing role of technology, boundaries between nations and markets will shrink, providing entrepreneurs will marvelous opportunities, limited only by their own imaginations. The world is entering a rare and wonderful environment for the entrepreneur.

AFTERWORD

About the Author:

Over the past 25 years, Adam Starchild has been the author of over two dozen books, and hundreds of magazine articles, primarily on business and finance. His articles have appeared in a wide range of publications around the world -- including Business Credit, Euromoney, Finance, The Financial Planner, International Living, Offshore Financial Review, Reason, Tax Planning International, The Bull & Bear, Trust & Estates, and many more.

Now semi-retired, he was the president of an international consulting group specializing in banking, finance and the development of new businesses, and director of a trust company.

Although this formidable testimony to expertise in his field, plus his current preoccupation with other books-in-progress, would not seem to leave time for a well-rounded existence, Starchild has won two Presidential Sports Awards and written several cookbooks, and is currently involved in a number of personal charitable projects.

His personal website is at http://www.adamstarchild.com/

CPSIA information can be obtained
at www.ICGtesting.com
Printed in the USA
FSHW010540270519
58490FS